AS MOSCOW SEES US

AS MOSCOW SEES US

American Politics and Society in the Soviet Mindset

RICHARD M. MILLS

New York   Oxford
OXFORD UNIVERSITY PRESS   1990

Oxford University Press

Oxford   New York   Toronto
Delhi   Bombay   Calcutta   Madras   Karachi
Petaling Jaya   Singapore   Hong Kong   Tokyo
Nairobi   Dar es Salaam   Cape Town
Melbourne   Auckland

and associated companies in
Berlin   Ibadan

Library of Congress Cataloging-in-Publication Data
Mills, Richard M.
As Moscow sees us: American politics and society
in the Soviet mindset/ Richard M. Mills.
p.   cm.
Includes bibliographical references.
ISBN 0-19-506260-4
1. United States—Foreign public opinion, Soviet.
2. Public opinion—Soviet Union—History—20th century.   I. Title.
E183.8S65M55   1990
973—dc20   89-25559   CIP

9 8 7 6 5 4 3 2 1

Printed in the United States of America
on acid-free paper

To my parents for their nurturing
To my family for their unflagging support
To my teachers for their example

PREFACE

The aim of this book is to present a broad range of Americans with a comprehensive and comprehensible picture of how their politics and society are viewed from the perspective of a radically different culture. Knowing how the Soviets interpret the American experience should help identify areas where better communication could facilitate improvements in Soviet–American relations.

The focus is on identifying and analyzing continuities and changes in Soviet interpretations—a combination of continued criticism of American political and social institutions and processes together with a growing appreciation of them that has led to selective Soviet borrowing of ideas and methods. The progress the Soviets have made is balanced against the substantial roadblocks to further advancement.

The introduction explores how the Soviet mindset has affected Soviet perceptions of the United States and how it is being modified. Part I analyzes the traditional Soviet framework of concepts for discussing American politics, and Part II does the same for American society. Part III considers why and on which points traditional Soviet approaches have been modified and also shows how change, creativity, and adaptation have been accomplished. Part IV critically examines the larger and deeper intellectual issues raised by the discussion.

It is my pleasure to acknowledge the many people who have helped make this book possible.

My wife, Judith, participated in the work at every stage, and her contributions have been invaluable. Rebecca, my daughter, also assisted in the enterprise. The intellectual stimulation and encouragement of colleagues in Fordham University's Political Science Department—especially Stephen David, John Entelis, Paul Kantor, and Rev. Richard Regan, S.J.—were vital. Encouragement for my project came at an early stage from Frederick Barghoorn and Dean Harry J. Sievers, S.J., midway from Robert C. Tucker, and in the final stages from Ivo Banac, David Mayhew, and Dean Mary Powers. The following graduate research assistants unearthed helpful materials: Joshua Berkowitz, Kathleen Conolly, Aleksandr Dvorkin, Mark Meirowitz, Charles Nagy, Patricia O'Leary, and Philip C. Wagner.

I am grateful to Fordham University for its institutional support in the form of faculty fellowships and Fordham University Research Council grants. Without the cheerful and efficient assistance of librarians at Fordham, Columbia, Harvard, and Yale universities and the Library of Congress this book could not have been written.

My warmest appreciation goes to my editors Valerie Aubry, Ellen Fuchs, Marion Osmun, Niko Pfund, and Carole Schwager for their ease and grace throughout the entire process.

Finally, two quintessentially American institutions deserve recognition: the little girl next door, Stella Kaplow, who helped organize the original working bibliography, and the carpool (Rudolph Ellenbogen's), whose spirited members gave a rousing start to many a research morning at Columbia University's indispensable library.

New York   R.M.M.
October 1989

CONTENTS

Part IV   Interpretation

AS MOSCOW SEES US

INTRODUCTION

> When I'm taking books to an American exhibit I don't take
> books Americans wouldn't like. In our books, we look at
> American politics the way we look at it, but we have never
> taken these books to the United States.
>
> *Tankred Golenpolsky, manager of the*
> *Sixth Moscow International Book Fair, 1987*

Truth be told, Tankred Golenpolsky's remarks are overly critical.[1]
Too many Soviet books on American politics do substantiate his
forebodings, but some are not as offensive as he thinks. Yet even
the better books would be alien to American sensibilities insofar
as they reflect the typical Soviet mindset at work trying to fathom
the internal political dynamics of the Western superpower.

This book is partly based on the volumes that Mr. Golenpolsky
would keep from the American public. Beyond that, it explores a
variety of Soviet writings to answer a question that continues to
pique our curiosity: how successful have the Soviets been in their
efforts to improve their understanding of America's social and
political systems?

Especially at summit time, we become immersed in speculation
about just how much the Soviets know about us and how well they
understand the operation of our systems. It is time to take a discriminating look at the many Soviet publications that can begin to
sate our curiosity.

Mainstream Soviets have long viewed the United States with
decidedly mixed emotions. Some have been positive, but most
were negative, and powerfully so. Even now they clearly admire
the United States for its technical innovations and practical know-
how in industry, transportation, agriculture, and the service sector.
However, they remain highly critical of the overall operation of
the American economic, social, and political systems.

These attitudes, especially the critical ones, have been expressed
in a flood of publications about American art and literature, film,

3

industrial management, science, philosophy, the media, the economy, the society, politics, and many other facets of American domestic life, not to mention foreign policy. There is no complete bibliography, but a partial list of Soviet books on these topics published between 1960 and 1976 contains some 700 titles (Raskin 1976). A comprehensive list of Soviet books and articles published between 1945 and 1970 on American history alone contains 3,669 items (Okinshevich 1976).[2]

The primary focus of this book is politics in the United States as interpreted by Soviet analysts over the decades. Aspects of Soviet domestic life that have affected these interpretations are a secondary concern.

In the West, politics is defined in many ways. Philosophically, it is the study of how to achieve the common good or ensure that the public interest is served. Functionally, it deals with how conflict among parts of the community can be managed successfully, how the state is organized and operates, or how a community makes binding policy decisions about the allocation of its resources. But the Soviets define politics in the United States as the activities that keep the nation firmly in the hands of the ruling class.

Soviets have traditionally seen American politics as a struggle among the social classes that is generated by the way people relate to each other in their economic activities. The Soviets develop their analyses of American politics directly from their views of American society. It is for good reason that they call their own framework for interpreting politics not only Marxism–Leninism but also "the class approach" or "class analysis."

In the mid-1980s the class approach lost its prominence when the Soviet leaders abandoned it as the basis of Soviet foreign policy, adopting what they called "new thinking" about foreign affairs. Rather than seeing world politics as a struggle between capitalism and communism, the stress would now be on overcoming threats common to all humans (whether capitalists or communists) such as nuclear war and ecological disaster. It seemed that a new mainstream was being created as the leaders diminished the ideological component in foreign policy. In Soviet domestic politics a new mainstream was being created through the practice of openness (*glasnost*) and democratization.

No such substantial changes have yet taken place in the way the

Soviets view American domestic politics and society. The dramatic changes wrought in the way the Soviets now perceive and practice politics at home and abroad bring into sharper relief the comparatively minimal changes made so far during the Gorbachev era in Soviet interpretations of American domestic politics and American society.

Mainstream Soviet attitudes are the time-hallowed ways in which Soviet politicians, academic experts, and even a good portion of the Soviet populace have thought about and discussed American politics and society in their public statements and writings. The Soviet study of American politics is still based on the assumption that economics at least shapes, or more likely determines, the contours of a society and the politics that take place within it. For that reason Soviet writings on purely economic issues are not directly applicable here, whereas those that probe the relationship of economics to society and politics are highly relevant.

A major objective in exploring Soviet views of U.S. politics is to establish how much of this general Soviet interpretive framework and the worldview behind it has been modified or, equally important, has not been modified when the United States is the object of analysis. In cases where their study of American politics and society has little or no impact on the Soviets' outlook—when it seemingly should—we are confronted with problems of intercultural perception. This serious issue in Soviet–American relations has been approached in various ways in both scholarly and general writing in the West.[3] Seweryn Bialer stated the problem neatly: "We should remember that it is as difficult, if not more so, for the Soviets to understand our beliefs, values, goals, and social-political organization as it is for us to understand theirs" (1985, 272).

The true depth and extent of these intercultural problems became fully evident only in the 1970s when American intellectuals tried to communicate with recent Soviet émigrés. As Edward Keenan, a close and incisive observer of these interactions, comments, "Their understanding of American legal and social institutions, and their tolerance for the complexity of pluralism, seem to their American counterparts distressingly limited" (1979, 277). Since the dissident émigrés were generally presumed to be the very Soviets who should be most in tune with American values and beliefs, many Americans found that realization especially disturbing.

Intercultural misperceptions create problems in political analysis that are not confined to Americans and Soviets. Even well-informed leaders of America's Western allies, who more closely share a political culture than the Soviets, have difficulty understanding significant aspects of American politics. Suzanne Garment notes that after almost forty years of uniquely close involvement with the American political system, Israeli politicians still do not understand how some fundamental elements of the legal and judicial system operate (1987).

The risks in studying intercultural perceptions were signaled by Helmut Sonnenfeldt and William G. Hyland, whose experience in dealing with the Soviets would be difficult to match: "Any attempt by foreigners to comprehend and represent the conceptions of other nations and their leaders is always beset by pitfalls; these dangers are almost certainly more pronounced when dealing with the USSR" (1986, 220). This warning prefaced their informative study of Soviet perceptions of national security.

If we are to help erode East–West perceptual and political barriers in the hope of improving relations, we must know the extent, depth, strength, and persistence of the barriers to be overcome. Because they are more complex than ever suggested in previous Western studies, there is good reason to pursue this book's primary topic—establishing and evaluating continuities and changes in the substance of what the Soviets have published about American politics and society.

The secondary focus is on the political and intellectual forces in the Soviet Union that produce these continuities and changes in the Soviet analytical framework and therefore in Soviet perspectives on American politics and society. Six factors are basic: the shifts that occur in the overall political climate in the Soviet Union; the continuities and changes in how the Soviets understand their own official ideology; the dynamics of Soviet intellectual and academic life; Soviet responses to their discovery of American political science; cultural exchange with the United States; and aspects of American reality that either challenge or confirm Soviet images of American politics and society.

Each factor warrants investigation in an individual volume. I address them mainly in Chapter 5 but also as subthemes at relevant points, and there are many, throughout the book. The last factor is so controversial in both the United States and the Soviet Union that very little of a nonpolemical nature has been written about it in either country. Among Sovietologists, Alexander Dallin's measured statement remains a rare exception, even though written a decade ago: there are distortions in the Soviet image of the United States, but some of them do have a basis in negative aspects of American life (1980).

My aim is to deepen Americans' understanding of how mainstream Soviets think about, discuss, and explain American politics and society to themselves in their publications. In this era of rapidly increasing contacts between Americans and Soviets at every level, with spacebridges and "CongressBridges," it is important that not only policymakers and Sovietologists be aware of the various ways in which the Soviets can and do view American politics and society.

Yet it is not enough for Americans simply to know that there is variety, within limits, in Soviet views. They ought to know the significance of the views they confront in their reading or conversations. The materials presented in the first four chapters approximate the ways that most top Soviet leaders are likely to view American politics and society given their social origins, the training they receive as potential party leaders, and their political experience as regional party leaders before assuming top positions in Moscow. This background encourages them to think and perceive in terms of the Soviet conventional wisdom.[4] Recent books by Politburo member Aleksandr Yakovlev (1985) and former member Andrei Gromyko (1985), which have been translated into English, are good examples.[5] As Soviet historian Roy Medvedev remarked during Mikhail Gorbachev's first summit visit to the United States: "The Soviet leader is tied to a doctrine, to a certain ideology. He can't jump outside its limits. In the West people don't understand these limits. They're not brought up on them."[6]

These mainstream attitudes, what I call the Soviet mindset, are illustrated in Chapters 1 through 4. In contrast, the materials in Chapter 6 most nearly reflect the better informed views of many, though not all, Soviet academic specialists and experts on American politics—these comprise a subset of the mindset. Americans are by now familiar with participation by Soviet academics and diplomats in American television discussions of current domestic and international events. This book goes behind these performances to examine the typical intellectual commitments that Soviets make when they discuss American politics in published form at home among themselves—the acid test of openness in the Soviet Union.

Mainstream thinking is characterized by a high degree of fit with current official Soviet perspectives. Mainstream attitudes are of two basic kinds—elite and mass. The elite's hallmarks are dedication to the fundamentals of the Marxist–Leninist world outlook and acceptance of the Communist party's particular interpretation of those fundamentals at any given time.[7] The mass attitude is shaped by the educational system's programs up to the secondary school level, by the media, and by the frame of mind and expectations that the rigors of everyday living in the Soviet Union create. The elite mindset receives greatest attention in this book, but since elite and mass attitudes overlap considerably they can together be called the Soviet mindset.

Subsets are created when, for instance, a person refuses to change a particular, short-term mainstream stance or changes it only partially. During the Khrushchev and Brezhnev eras Soviet citizens could either retain positive feelings toward Stalin or look at him with a measure of disfavor and find that party officialdom was tolerant of each attitude. A person could be moderately liberal or conservative about many issues and experience the same tolerance. Characteristically, in these subsets a degree of fit with current official modes of thinking and perception remains. In the past this brought about limited variety within a larger unity.

Gorbachev and his closest associates are a unique subset. Some of their views are radically at odds with tradition, and under Gorbachev the elite and mass attitudes have been modified significantly in some respects so that a much greater variety of opinion is possible—but still within a now broader unity. That these modifications still do not encompass American politics and society is authoritatively illustrated in a new book to which two of Gorbachev's closest advisers, Aleksandr Yakovlev and Georgii Shakhnazarov, contributed (Yakovlev, ed. 1988).

This exception is attributable to Gorbachev's continued adherence to the class approach when thinking about the difference between capitalist and socialist societies. Specifically, Gorbachev has an exalted vision of what socialism ought to be as opposed to what it actually had been in the Soviet Union prior to his incumbency. He maintains that the Soviet people declared themselves in favor of that vision in the 1989 elections, which were unique in providing for a choice of candidates: "Yes, the Soviet people have unequivocally spoken in favor of socialism, but in its renewed and humane form, and in favor of a socialism that really serves the interests of the people and ennobles man" (*Pravda*, April 27, 1989).

It was this vision that Anatolii Dobrynin, another of Gorbachev's closest advisers, had in mind when he said: "There is an alternative to capitalism—and that alternative is socialism" (*Pravda*, April 13, 1988). Gorbachev has spoken very negatively about capitalism and its social and political systems in ways typical of the Soviet mindset, as he did in his major speech following his return home from the Reykjavik summit (*Pravda*, October 15, 1986). Consequently, when he unexpectedly began adopting Western political terminology and applying it to Soviet political life he also *adapted* those terms by prefacing them with the word "socialist" as in "socialist pluralism," a term he has used often, or in the less often used "our own socialist system of checks and balances" (*Pravda*, November 29, 1988). Clearly, these concepts will be applied in a refined, purified, or corrected version consonant with Gorbachev's vision of socialism, and not as practiced in the capitalist countries in ways that are discussed in Chapter 2.

Soviet specialists on the United States have thus far not radically changed the way they write about our country in contrast to other Soviet writers who have applied new thinking to world politics or *glasnost* to Soviet domestic politics. In particular, only a few articles that break radically new ground have appeared in the Soviet monthly magazine devoted exclusively to the study of the United States and Canada. They will be discussed in Chapter 5.

Soviet specialists on the United States are a subset of the elite mindset. Within this subset, as in all of them, there are subdivisions that can be identified on the basis of traits specific to each. The administrators and staff of the Institute of United States and Canadian Studies are a subdivision simply because of their abnormally easy access to the American print media. Some of them also travel to the United States frequently, a privilege that distinguishes them from most other members of the subset.

Soviet participants in academic exchanges sponsored by the International Research and Exchanges Board comprise another subdivision. Under these auspices many Americanists have spent varying periods up to a year at American universities. Top leaders like Aleksandr Yakovlev and Yevgeny Primakov, nonvoting Politburo member and president of the upper chamber of the Soviet legislature, were participants years ago.

Alexandra Costa (1986), now a resident of the United States, had lived and worked in Washington while a Soviet citizen and knew Soviet embassy personnel well. Soviets who have the opportunity to live in the United States are a subdivision of the larger subset of specialists on America who know the United States only or primarily from the print media. The embassy staff told her how difficult it would be for her, as it was for them, to communicate with other Soviets (the mindset) about their own experiences in America and what they, the subdivision, had learned from those experiences—the folks back home just couldn't understand.[8] The embassy personnel remained loyal Soviet citizens, but their unusual experience had added some noticeably different perspectives that they could not communicate to even their closest friends and relatives.

A similar subdivision is composed of Soviet journalists stationed in New York or Washington who afterward wrote books on American politics (Beglov 1971) or society (Gerasimov 1984).

Curiously, recent Western studies of Soviet perspectives on American politics and society exhibit a Western mindset, giving far more attention to Soviet perceptions of American foreign policy than to Soviet views on the domestic political system that produces the foreign policy.

Foreign policy has been considered in detail by Stephen Gibert (1976), Morton Schwartz (1978), John Lenczowski (1982), Franklyn Griffiths (1984), and Robert Huber (1988). It is also the topic of a forthcoming book by Robert Legvold, *The Soviet Union and the Other Superpower.*

In these previous studies Soviet views on American domestic politics are but a small, sketchy component of the larger analysis that focuses on American foreign policy. Three of the authors try to show how the Soviets perceive the links between American domestic politics and foreign policy: the title of Lenczowski's chapter on domestic politics is "Domestic Determinants of U.S. Foreign Policy," Griffiths's article is entitled "The Sources of American Conduct: Soviet Perspectives and Their Policy Implications," and Huber has a chapter called "Soviet Perspectives on the Process of Congressional Involvement in U.S. Foreign Policy." Gibert and Schwartz in their respective chapters on American domestic politics do not attempt to forge such links. Of all these authors, Schwartz alone discusses Soviet views on American society, but in fewer than a dozen pages which treat only social movements and give no attention to Soviet discussions of American social structure.

The Western analyses that touch on Soviet views of American domestic politics in these ways have not captured the larger and deeper senses that the Soviets have of the structure and exercise of power in the United States, and neither has the one book that deals exclusively with Soviet views on American domestic politics. In it, British author Neil Malcom treats Soviet analyses of the dominant role played by the top of the American power structure, and on that basis alone he then discusses Soviet perceptions of political conflict in America (1984).[9]

Soviet writings also reveal the much more complex understanding of the relationship of the social structure to politics, covered here primarily in Chapters 3 and 4. As far as the Soviets are concerned, it is not only the people at the top who are important politically. As Gorbachev commented: "In any country the people have the decisive voice, and that includes the American people" (*Pravda*, October 14, 1986). This book therefore in contrast to earlier Western works conveys a very different sense of how the Soviets understand American political dynamics. It considers a much wider sample of Soviet scholarly writing, the differing Western appraisals of those writings, and the effects of Gorbachev's openness policy on the study of American politics and society.

To foster a fuller awareness of the road the Soviets have traveled in their understanding of the American sociopolitical setting, there is more history here than in any of the previous studies.

This effort entails reevaluating the role of the Institute of United States and Canadian Studies (IUSAC). Some previous Western analysts have used the publications of IUSAC as prime data sources to demonstrate that the Soviets borrowed ideas and insights from American political science and that their understanding of American politics consequently improved (Schwartz 1978; Malcom 1984).

That coin has another side. Consulting a broader range of Soviet information sources makes it apparent that the continuities in Soviet views on American politics and society are no less important than the changes, and, further, that IUSAC has not been the most important vehicle for changing the Soviets' analytical framework and concepts. The point is not to underrate, much less denigrate, the institute, but to define its role in influencing the mindset within a more meaningful, balanced, and comprehensive context. A part of the fifth chapter is devoted to this endeavor.

In the Gorbachev years a new factor entered the picture when two specialists on the United States joined the Soviet top leadership. Anatolii Dobrynin, the Soviet ambassador in Washington for a quarter of a century, and Aleksandr N. Yakovlev (Iakovlev), author of several books on the United States and Soviet ambassador to Canada for almost a decade, were appointed secretaries of the party's Central Committee in March 1986. In a meteoric rise, Yakovlev then became a candidate member of the Politburo itself in January 1987 and quickly a full member in June 1987. He thus joined Andrei Gromyko, who had until then been the Politburo's diplomatic expert on the United States, just as Iurii Andropov had been the Politburo's intelligence specialist on America. Each represents a different subdivision of the mindset capable of influencing it at or near the very top.[10]

Soviet scholarly writings on American politics and society are a very special example of the mindset in operation. Soviet scholars draw their information from a wide array of American sources: public documents, the publications of political scientists, liberal and radical critiques, the findings of investigative reporters—to give a very partial list. They then interpret these data in works normally printed in editions of 2,000 to 10,000 copies if they are books or 50,000 if they are articles in journals. These contain the most balanced information, and the least ideologically colored data, about American politics that can be found in print in the Soviet Union. As we shall see, the studies are not intended to be dispassionate, nor are their authors striving for objectivity. Nevertheless, they are at the opposite end of the spectrum from the negative and outright propagandistic books, printed in editions of 50,000 to 100,000 copies.

Though confidential governmental or party studies are not published, something about them can be surmised from conversations and negotiations with the Soviets who are privy to these materials. Even particular Soviet actions reveal previously unsuspected expertise; for example, the shrewd purchases of American grain in 1972 showed that Soviet foreign trade experts were intimately familiar with the operation of the American grain market despite an ideological distaste for it.

This study is based on Soviet scholarly publications because they function much like an information-processing or an information-patterning system of the type that Karl Deutsch (1966, 80) described as "a *self-modifying communications network* or 'learning net'":

> As long as it has autonomy, the net wills what it is. It wills the behavior patterns (the "personality") that it has acquired in the past and that it is changing and remaking with each decision in the present. Thanks to what it has learned in the past, it is not wholly subject to the present. Thanks to what it still can learn, it is not wholly subject to the past. Its internal rearrangements in response to new challenges are made by the interplay between its present and its past. In this interplay we might see one kind of "inner freedom." (108)

In a sense, this book is a study of what influences Soviet publishing policy, of the control system that encourages or discourages the publication of information of various sorts (and not just negative) on the United States. Its aim is to determine the degree and extent to which the Soviet system is able to exercise the inner freedom to change that Deutsch had in mind. Central authorities have long controlled and directed writers and publishers in the Soviet Union, but there was also the more subtle operation of a system similar to a hidden hand of self-control that produced results. There was also the irresistible drive to advance, to publish the previously forbidden. This tendency was strengthened markedly under *glasnost,* but it has had limited impact on the themes treated here.

How the Soviets communicate with each other in their published works about the United States and who in the Soviet Union has how much access to those materials are very significant matters addressed throughout, but especially in Chapter 6. Diffusion of this information is a critical issue because it has characteristically been disseminated on a need to know basis—*who* needs to know and *what* do they need to know? Undoubtedly, future changes for the better will occur: not only will *glasnost* and new thinking ultimately have a favorable impact on how information on the United States is treated, but the contested elections that are at last being held in the Soviet Union have already created a large new "market" for more information on American politics. In 1989 Fedor Burlatskii, a major innovator in Soviet analyses of American politics, won seats in both of the new Soviet national legislatures. Other specialists in American politics also ran, and others served as advisers to various candidates. As important, Burlatskii is a personal friend of the Gorbachevs (Walker 1987). Georgii Shakhnazarov, another innovator in Soviet studies of American politics, became a personal adviser to Gorbachev in 1988. They are respectively the vice president and president of the Soviet Political Science Association.

A very important new channel for learning about American politics was opened in 1989 when Soviet legislators, whose decisionmaking role was now considerably enhanced, began visiting the United States to study American political practices firsthand. This book should help the Americans involved in these interactions to identify, better understand, and overcome the difficulties involved in assimilating such learning.

Nevertheless, the pervasive compartmentalization of information that had long characterized Soviet life remains highly significant. For example, it was only in 1984 that the first one-volume analysis of American politics that provided a coherent overview of the establishment, development, and current operation of the political system's institutions and processes was published. However, it was not written by a Soviet author but was, predictably (as I'll explain in Chapters 5 and 6), a translation of an American text, Thomas R. Dye and L. Harmon Zeigler's *The Irony of Democracy: An Uncommon Introduction to American Politics* (1970–1986).[11] Also predictable was its small printing of 4,210 copies, a sure sign that it was intended for limited distribution.[12] Granted that textbooks are not everybody's idea of "must" reading, even a much larger press run would have sold out instantly given the widespread insatiable Soviet curiosity about the United States. This is an especially revealing example of how "the net wills what it is" as it exercises its "inner freedom." Inner freedom has been exercised in many different ways.

All these considerations influence the structure of my analysis and the methods used to pursue it.

Parts I and II are an extended answer to two questions: How have the Soviets characteristically explained American politics and society when they interpreted them in the most orthodox Marxist–Leninist fashion? What restrained criticisms have Soviet writers themselves made about the adequacy of their mode of interpretation while working within the parameters of the mode itself? Three approaches to the United States have been typical at various times. Chapter 1 treats the first, which portrayed America as virtually under the totalitarian domination of big business. In this version of orthodoxy, in vogue during the 1950s and early 1960s, some Soviets believed that they had discovered *the* hidden mechanism by which the American political system was controlled. This approach is seldom used now, yet in modified form it has left an indelible imprint on the Soviet mindset.

Chapter 2 considers the second approach, which is still very much used and fundamental to understanding the mindset. It centers on the manipulation of the political institutions, processes, and symbols of liberal democracy essential to retaining control over the political system. The focus is on the processes of control rather than on a specific mechanism. The American political system is portrayed as permitting considerable give and take rather than as an outright dictatorship.

The third approach is based on the Marxian concept of the class struggle. This controlling perception of what American politics is about is so important and so complicated that in order to present a comprehensible analysis of that dynamic in Chapter 4 I found it necessary to clarify in Chapter 3 how the Soviets perceive America's social structure, something about which too little has been written in the West.

Chapters 1 through 4 are typically Soviet in their language, focus, argumentation, and spirit because they are an evocation of the Soviet mindset and they present what Raymond Garthoff has called the "general understanding" the Soviets have of the United States (1985, 1119). I have attempted to recreate for American readers the typical style of Soviet analysis with all its characteristic terminology and themes, insights and oversights, self-congratulation and self-criticism, immobility and development, orthodoxies and diversity. Too much would have been lost had I written a conventional Western exposition and criticism of the Soviet intellectual disposition, stressing my disagreements with it and the conclusions it produces. Readers would have been unable to experience that crucial sense of, or "feel" for, the way in which the Soviets typically discuss the topics of this book among themselves.

If I deliberately use Soviet vocabulary to give American readers an experience in the Soviet mindset at work interpreting American politics, I periodically revert to Western terminology to break the monotony and to recall the intellectual context within which I live and do my analysis. Among the Western studies of Soviet perspectives on American politics and society the approach of this volume is unique.

Parts I and II are a political sociology of the United States that emerges from Soviet perspectives. Once readers have experienced the mindset at work trying in its own terms to understand American politics and society, Part III prompts them to consider the fluid mix of continuity and change in Soviet perspectives. Chapter 5 functions as a transitional device linking the four chapters on the mindset with Chapter 6, which discusses how the mindset has adapted to American reality as it assesses political institutions and processes. It begins with an explanation of why the Soviets have interpreted American politics and society in terms of the mindset and why they continue to explain them in those ways, but to a lesser degree as time has gone by. The last part of the chapter initiates a discussion of how and why the Soviets began to change some of their perceptions. Several case studies illustrate how some Soviets began to incorporate perspectives from American political science into their analyses. On that basis Chapter 6 presents a more detailed and concrete picture of where changes have and, equally important, have not been made in the Soviets' views. In its approach to the study of American politics, this chapter, together with Chapter 7, is the least characteristically Soviet and the most recognizably American.

Chapter 7 is an exercise in what the Soviets would call "bourgeois objectivism" because it contains my critical evaluation of the various Soviet approaches and explanations. I compare the class approach with the two major alternative theories, pluralism and elitism, that attempt to map the distribution of political power in the United States. No Western author has yet examined the Soviet version of the class approach in light of the debate among American political scientists and sociologists over power distribution. It is time to do so because of the growing Soviet interest in, and familiarity with, American political science. If the Soviets are to accelerate development of their perspectives on American politics, sooner or later they must confront the intellectual issues addressed in Chapter 7.

The book's structure is closely connected with my methods of presentation. Had I followed a more usual practice I would have placed Chapter 5 at the book's beginning. Indeed, some readers may wish to read it first. But since the mindset is the most important cultural factor at work, consideration of it had to have primacy of place. In keeping with the learning net concept, and also my focus on publication policy, I am more concerned than previous Western authors with the "information load" or informational function of particular books and articles. While I do identify the liberal or orthodox thrust in the writings of individual Soviet authors, I tend to differentiate writings more than writers. That has a strong impact on the arrangement of the materials in the sixth chapter and others as well.

The question of how to present the materials is complicated by the fact that this study bridges two academic disciplines—American studies and Soviet studies. In addition, because of the way politics is studied in the Soviet Union (combining politics, economics, and sociology) I must use broader social science approaches rather than focusing narrowly on political science alone. In terms of political science my approach is unusual in that I treat American politics from a comparative perspective.

I use the author–date notation system within the text. In Chapter 6 I modify it to include page numbers in Soviet sources to show how scattered the Soviet information on American political institutions and processes is and how much attention Soviet authors have given to particular topics. The scattering results when the

Soviet Marxist–Leninist mindset fits information about American politics into the analytical framework illustrated in Chapters 1 through 4. It also appears to result from a desire to avoid clearly describing aspects of American politics that do not fit the interpretive framework or that contradict it.

That would not be a significant problem for Soviet readers if general, overarching studies of the American political system were widely available to provide a context that would make the dispersed data more understandable. Soviet specialists on American politics do not have this problem since they are immersed in the relevant Soviet and American writing. But mainstream Soviets not in that subset lack this advantage, as does the general Soviet reading public.

The absence of integrating studies forces me to synthesize the Soviet materials in order to analyze them systematically and comprehensively.

PART I

American Politics and the Soviet Mindset

1 WHO RULES? ECONOMIC POWER AND POLITICAL POWER

Americans normally believe that their politics are unique. Soviet analysts have found very little unique about them. In the Marxist view politics derive ultimately from the economic system and directly from the struggle of social classes to keep or obtain power. So, for the Soviets, the politics of Great Britain, France, the Federal Republic of Germany, Japan, and the United States are similar less because these countries call themselves democracies than because each has a highly developed capitalist economic and social system.

The Soviets consider today's capitalist economic system to be two stages removed from the capitalism Karl Marx described in the mid-nineteenth century. In his day free competition among a large number of small manufacturers was a basic feature of the capitalist system. But Marx predicted that this very competition would eliminate most competitors and that production would be concentrated in the hands of fewer and more powerful owners.

In the late nineteenth century Marxist analysts described this process as the transition from free competition capitalism to monopoly capitalism. In this second stage big business predominated in the form of giant corporations and powerful banks. Taken together, these were called the monopolies. "The monopolies" soon became, and remained, a constantly repeated key term in Soviet writing on American politics. This term rather than the more familiar "big business" will be used throughout the book along with many other typically Soviet terms to communicate a sense of the Soviet mindset at work analyzing American politics.

As capitalism developed further in the early twentieth century Marxist writers identified growing governmental intervention in economic affairs as its most prominent new characteristic. Like most Marxists at the time, Lenin originally called this "state capitalism," but to describe the situation more precisely he coined another key concept: "state–monopoly capitalism" (Lenin 1958–1965, vol. 31, 433). State–monopoly capitalism (SMC) will be used in the description that follows as a shorthand designation for the analytical model developed by Soviet writers to interpret politics in capitalist countries.

Three processes are fundamental in the SMC model. First, the monopolies coalesce with the state. The major manufacturing companies and the largest banks develop such numerous and close ties with the government that they and the state are virtually one. Second, state intervention in the economy expands dramatically in order to shore up the faltering capitalist system that is dominated by the monopolies. Third, an ineffective last-ditch attempt is made to preserve capitalism by violating the consummately capitalistic principle of keeping private enterprise free from governmental interference. Lenin interpreted these processes as comprising "a complete *material* preparation for socialism, the threshold of socialism, a rung on the ladder of history between which rung and the rung called socialism *there are no intermediary rungs*" (Lenin 1958–1965, vol. 34, 193).

As a strategy, SMC is an attempt to use politics to save capitalism from economic self-destruction. But this particular combination of politics and economics has only served to deepen what Soviet analysts call the general crisis of capitalism.[1] When spelled out, this concept of crisis provides a comprehensive description of why and how the Soviets feel that capitalism has faltered and declined in the twentieth century.

The first omens of the general crisis were apparent before World War I, but it was the war that gave birth to the crisis. Competition among the monopolies on a world scale had led to war among the major capitalist nations. As a direct result of that war the world's first socialist state, the Soviet Union, came into being as a highly visible competitor and alternative to capitalism. The capitalist system itself grew weaker as a consequence of its internal problems manifested in the world depression of the 1920s and 1930s. The monopolies tried to bring this aspect of the general crisis under control through increased governmental intervention in the economy, so contributing to SMC's further development. These events of the twentieth century's first four decades comprised the first stage of the general crisis.

The second stage began with World War II, which was caused, like World War I, by rivalry among the imperialist powers. Just as World War I had led to the appearance of the Soviet Union, World War II resulted in the creation of a number of socialist nations in Europe and Asia.

The third stage began in the 1950s with the emergence of the Third World nations, an anti-imperialist force in the Soviet view. Also characteristic of this stage was the growing strength of the Soviet Union and the worsening of economic problems both within the capitalist countries (notably inflation) and among them (the struggle for world markets). This stage differed from the other two because it started during peacetime and reflected new conditions. Specifically, socialism was replacing capitalism as the decisive factor in world development; the new nations rejected the different forms of capitalist exploitation that had replaced outright colonialism; and finally, the 1970s witnessed increased instability and accelerated decay within the capitalist countries as evidenced by growing unemployment and inflation, shortages of raw materials, energy, and food, and the inability of governmental regulatory activity to cope with economic problems (Sorko 1975; Inozemtsev and others, eds. 1976).

The typical response to these signs of crisis had been to increase governmental regulation of almost every aspect of life in capitalist countries, especially the economy. That strengthened the tendencies characteristic of SMC for a while.

However, the general crisis took on new forms with the appearance of the "multinational monopolies," whose activities and interests were often at odds with the national interests of the capitalist countries. Nevertheless, capitalist governments have supported the multinationals by eliminating some governmental regulatory activity and by acting to ensure high profits for the military–industrial firms even at the cost of slowing the rate of growth in the economy as a whole. This last factor signifies to the Soviets that a very serious structural crisis has now been built into the economy that deepens the cyclical recessionary crises long normal for the economy and contributes to the budget deficit (Men'shikov 1981; Men'shikov 1986; Pletnev 1986; Iaz'kov, ed. 1988; Yakovlev, ed. 1988).

After the most advanced capitalist countries had weathered the depression and World War II without experiencing either a major economic crisis or a revolutionary social upheaval, Soviet analysts had to develop some sort of explanation for capitalism's survival despite its having entered the third stage of its general crisis. The interpretation they devised served to systematize and expand the concept of SMC. In the 1950s and 1960s an extensive elementary model was developed in two major versions.

The Model: Basic Concepts, Features, and Versions

State–monopoly capitalism was born when the monopolies merged with the state. The monopolies were simply the big corporations and big banks. The concept of the state was more complex.

The Soviets start with a distinction found in the writings of Marx and Engels (Draper 1978), first considering the state's basic, or essential, function and then its several subsidiary functions. At the basic level of analysis Fedor Burlatskii captured the essence of the issue in classic form: "The political power of the economically dominant class—this is the essence of the state and the nature of its relation to society" (1970, 125). At this analytical level Soviet writers deny that the state can stand as a neutral force above and beyond social classes and act as an arbiter between them. In principle, in its very nature and essence, the state is an instrument that the economically dominant class uses to suppress all other parts of society. Vladimir Guliev, who has written extensively on the issue, expressed this consensus tersely, calling the capitalist state "a weapon of systematic, constant, organized force and compulsion" (1970, 166 [quotation]; 1965).

This was the state the Soviets saw merging with the monopolies to form SMC in their earliest analyses. Following a series of mergers of big banks with big industries in the late nineteenth century, the new industrial and banking monopolies then merged with the state in the early twentieth century. The early mergers produced a small number of extremely wealthy and powerful people, who together comprised the financial oligarchy. According to Lenin in his *Imperialism: The Highest Stage of Capitalism* (and quite tellingly in Part II: The Banks and Their New Role) the mergers of private businesses took place through a "personal union," his term for interlocking directorates. Similarly, Lenin continued, even before World War I a personal union began forming in Europe between the monopolists and various governments. Not only did the monopolists (major industrialists and bankers) or their agents hold key positions in their respective governments, but officeholding politicians sat on the boards of large banks and industrial concerns. Here was the origin of the link between the new form of economic power (monopoly) and the government (Lenin 1958–1965).

In the United States the personal union between monopolists and government was established during World War I. It was strengthened in the depression years and during World War II and developed very rapidly in the postwar period when as a matter of course corporation executives and members of large financial firms became prominent in government, especially as members of the cabinet.[2]

Accompanying the process of state–monopoly merger was the growth of state intervention in the capitalist economy, another major component of the model. Even in capitalism's free competition stage the state had intervened in the American economy through imposing taxes and in many other ways (Efimov 1934, 1969). But state intervention intensified sharply and assumed new forms after the monopolies appeared, and it accelerated during the state-monopoly stage.

In the Soviet view the growth of state intervention is inevitable for several reasons. First, during wartime under twentieth century conditions the governments of capitalist nations had no choice but to coordinate and control economic activity (Dalin 1961). Second, economic crises, especially the depression starting in the 1920s, necessitated heightened intervention (Dalin 1936). Third, the new need to face the competition of the socialist system arose. According to Soviet analyses typical of the 1960s, since World War II the capitalist world had been experiencing immense economic, political, and social traumas, while the socialist countries were moving from achievement to achievement. These deteriorating domestic and international circumstances were forcing the capitalist governments to increase intervention to improve the operation of their system (Cheprakov 1964; Dalin 1961). Finally, governmental action was required to raise sagging profit levels, ensure production expansion, bail out some unprofitable older industries (coal, shipbuilding, railroads), and create an internal market by awarding large military contracts, thereby expanding the otherwise limited purchasing power of the population (Cheprakov 1964).

Heightened governmental intervention eventually turned into governmental regulation in a process called *ogosudarstvlenie,* increasing governmental control of economic activity and its eventual bureaucratization. It began in 1913 when the Federal Reserve System was established, expanded during World War I, and accelerated markedly in the New Deal and World War II periods. It reached new heights in the war's aftermath with a dramatic increase in the size of the federal, state, and local bureaucracies that regulated all the important sectors of the economy to one or another degree (Bobrakov and Fedorovich, eds. 1976; Yakovlev, ed. 1988).

Paradoxically many of the activities connected with government's growing role in the economy noted by the Soviets have also long been cited by American conservatives as examples of creeping socialism. Soviet analysts would agree with this conservative proposition, but only to the extent that they view these processes as examples of the highest degree of nationalizing the control of productive property that is possible under capitalism. Ideologically, that level is reached just before capitalism must inevitably disappear and be replaced by socialism. Moreover, the Soviets emphasize that the intention motivating the American initiators of the processes is not to lay the groundwork for socialism but to try to save capitalism from its general crisis. However, like the conservatives, the Soviets insist that the regulatory activities have failed to solve the country's economic problems (Bobrakov and Fedorovich, eds. 1976; Evenko, ed. 1985; Men'shikov 1981). Indeed, one writer said flatly that Reaganomics was really "an official admission" that governmental regulation in the SMC mode had failed (Bobrakov 1981, 47).

The dilemma basic to the model is the relationship between the state and the monopolies: the state is supposedly controlled by the monopolies, yet in its economic regulatory role it controls the monopolies. That raises the problem of politics.

Political Features

For the first two decades following Lenin's death in 1924 Soviet analysts concentrated less on the political aspects of SMC than on the economic. They focused on the tendency in western, central, and eastern European countries for the private sector of the economy to coalesce or merge with the state sector, Germany being taken as the classic example.[3] Politically, this process was associated with the rise of fascist dictatorships.

Following World War II much more attention was given to the political side of the model. Because of its new position as strongest of the capitalist powers the United States became the classic example of advanced SMC, the chief source of data for the model, and the country against which the model would be tested.

However, in the immediate postwar years there was yet another, and temporarily more important, source for developing the model than American data—direct orders given by Stalin himself. In his last published work, *Economic Problems of Socialism*, Stalin took brief but compelling issue with the way that unnamed Soviet analysts were interpreting the relationship of the monopolies to the state. They had expressed it in the traditional way as "the coalescence of the monopolies with the state machine." Stalin demanded that this formula be replaced by "subjugation of the state machine to the monopolies."[4] In obeying these instructions, Soviet writers created a version of the model in which the monopolies totally dominate the state.

Two Classic Versions
COMPLETE DOMINATION BY BIG BUSINESS

For Soviet analysts it was and remains axiomatic that the ruling class controls the state. Stalin's formula forced them to maintain that only one part of the ruling class, and not the entire class, exercised that control. This issue is not a quibble over words: it is at the heart of the Soviet perception of how democracy works in capitalist countries.

It is fundamental Marxism that in a developed capitalist society the state is controlled by the capitalist class—or, in the language favored by the Soviet mindset, the bourgeoisie. Yet the bourgeoisie is not of a piece. As Marx had done in the nineteenth century, Soviet analysis continued to divide the bourgeoisie into the big bourgeoisie, the middle bourgeoisie, and the petty bourgeoisie. But as the monopolies began to figure more prominently in Soviet analyses, Soviet writers varied the language, replacing the term big bourgeoisie with monopoly bourgeoisie. The term middle bourgeoisie was sometimes dropped in favor of nonmonopoly bourgeoisie. In this context Stalin's formula meant that the state was subordinated to only the monopoly bourgeoisie, and that component used the state to pursue its interests against those of all other elements of society: the nonmonopoly bourgeoisie, the petty bourgeoisie, and the proletariat (Kuz'minov 1955; Shneerson 1956).

This version of the SMC model, which one Soviet writer aptly called "the system of the dictatorship of the monopolies" (Levin, ed. 1964a, 44) and which I call the primitive SMC model, remained attractive to some Soviet authors well after Stalin died, in part because it was reiterated forcefully in the Soviet Communist Party's Program adopted in 1961. That Program was superseded only in 1986. Part IV of the 1961 Program, "The Crisis of World Capitalism," is replete with statements like "The state has become the committee for managing the affairs of the monopoly bourgeoisie" (XXII S''ezd KPSS, vol. 3, 246). A number of writers continued supporting the primitive model into the late 1960s.[5]

Adherents of this version often quoted Lenin's statement that as the capitalist economy develops, in politics there is a "change *from* democracy *to* political reaction. Democracy corresponds to free competition. Political reaction corresponds to monopoly. 'Finance capital strives for domination, not freedom,' Rudolf Hilferding rightly remarks in his *Finance Capital*" (Lenin 1958–1965, vol. 30, 93).

"Reaction" is another major Soviet analytical term. It signifies "resistance to social progress; a political regime established to maintain and strengthen an outmoded social order. Reaction usually manifests itself in the struggle against the revolutionary movement, in the suppression of democratic rights and liberties, in the persecution of progressive political, public, and cultural figures, in mass terror and violence, in racial and national discrimination, and in an aggressive foreign policy" (*Great Soviet Encyclopedia*, vol. 21, 517). Political reaction in the United States was particularly severe in the 1940s and 1950s, though not necessarily in all its forms noted in the preceding definition. Examples the Soviets cite from that period include concentrating power in the hands of the president at the expense of Congress, transferring power from the states to the federal government, adopting antilabor legislation, requiring loyalty oaths, denying passports to citizens, and taking actions against the Communist party.

The Soviets saw these events in postwar America as a repetition of the fascistization that was characteristic of capitalism's development in some European countries before the war. During the 1950s and 1960s the Soviets identified the National Association of Manufacturers and the Chamber of Commerce, "the general headquarters of the monopolies," as the source of this process (Shakhnazarov 1955, 116; Bel'son 1960; Guliev and Kuz'min 1969). But in 1969 a detailed Soviet study comparing these with similar organizations in other advanced capitalist countries concluded that the NAM and the Chamber did not play as large a role as their analogues in the other countries, and little more has been said about this matter.[6]

While the complete monopoly domination version of the model may have been ideologically or emotionally satisfying to some Soviet analysts, it was subjected to criticism on various grounds by others. In so doing, they produced a partial monopoly domination variant.

PARTIAL DOMINATION BY BIG BUSINESS

Critics of the complete domination version cited Lenin to show that repression was indeed a major tactic employed by the ruling class. But along with this, granting concessions was used to undercut pressures coming from the workers, and this second tactic was no less important than the first (Levin and Tumanov, eds. 1974). If only the monopolies were able to affect government policy, the political forces opposed to the monopolies would have few prospects for achieving their progressive goals (Kulikov 1969). In Soviet analyses of capitalist societies the class conflict is often described as a struggle between the forces of progress and those of reaction. Soviet scholars and politicians uniformly have been optimistic that the progressive forces will triumph over the reactionaries. Contrary to that expectation, the complete domination version of SMC, so attractive to some Soviets for other reasons, disturbingly intimates that the struggle for progress is in vain, at least in the short run.

Thus in the heyday of the complete domination version, when almost all writers were still predicting a worsening of reaction in the United States, Georgii Shakhnazarov was able to argue that the course of events was moving in a direction favoring democracy since the democratic forces were proving strong enough to prevent the monopolies from subordinating the state to themselves (1955). This position later prevailed among Soviet analysts, as did Shakhnazarov himself.

Some writers rejected the complete domination version for an ideological reason. Because the essential functions of the state remained unaltered (politically suppressing the exploited class as well as defending both private property and the continuing economic exploitation of labor) they felt that the state must defend the interests of the entire bourgeoisie and not just those of the monopoly faction of that class (Shakhnazarov 1955; Guliev 1973). The distinguished Soviet economist Evgenii Varga concluded that the state could reflect the interests of either the monopolies or the whole bourgeoisie, depending on concrete circumstances (1968).

Another criticism, this one based on a consideration of the state's subsidiary functions, was that the complete domination version ignored a factor that some Soviet scholars eventually discovered to be an important element in Marx's analysis of politics—the relative autonomy of the state (Guliev 1970). Taking this concept into account, one critic remarked, avoids the complete domination version's oversimplification wherein the state becomes for all practical purposes a structural extension, or even a component, of the monopolies (Tumanov, ed. 1967).

The concept of relative state autonomy asserts that the state has a partial or relative (but not absolute) autonomy from society as a whole and even from the dominating class.[7] This is a significant qualification of the older Soviet position that the ruling class completely dominates the state. Yet the fact was that Marx and Engels did say that there were times when the state had acted against part of the ruling class and even, on rare occasions, the entire class (Guliev 1965, 1973).

Guliev and an associate explained relative autonomy as necessary to enable the state to regulate and mitigate disputes arising among the monopolies while they divided the national income among themselves; to mitigate conflicts between the interests of individual monopolies and the general interests of the monopolies as a whole; to reflect the interests of the middle bourgeoisie and any other political forces interested in maintaining the capitalist system; and to reflect the interests of the entire people as in the case of wars against fascism (Guliev and Kuz'min 1969).

In addition to these system maintenance activities, some factors of scale and process were offered to explain the state's relative autonomy from the ruling class. The large bureaucracy that is part of the state comprises millions of people who are difficult to control, the extremely complex process of policy formation and decisionmaking inhibits control even by the powerful monopolies, and the expansion of the state's economic functions creates similar complications in exercising control as does the pressure on the state from social forces that are opposed to the monopolies (Burlatskii 1970). Finally, in very Marxian fashion, an economic basis for the state's relative autonomy has been found in the huge governmental budgets and in the capital funds accumulated by the state (Guliev and Kuz'min 1969; Marinin 1967a). These authors were making the fundamentally important point that big business does not totally control the government, nor does it own the government.

The relative autonomy of the state plays two major roles in the partial monopoly version of the SMC model. It provides a sovereign arbiter among the competing monopolies, so endowing the system with a kind of balance wheel, and it explains why the government has the freedom to act in defense of "the whole political and social structure in its entirety" (Burlatskii 1970, 260). That is, sometimes the state must subordinate the narrow interests of some monopolies to the general interests of the bourgeoisie as a whole or to the interests of the system. President Kennedy's treatment of the U.S. Steel Corporation is an outstanding case in point.

Relative autonomy provides an explanation for the unity of society, of the entire bourgeoisie as a class, and of the monopolies themselves. The SMC model's partial monopoly domination version is, after all, perhaps the most conflict-ridden model in all social science, and some explanation is needed of why the United States simply hasn't collapsed.

The complete monopoly domination variant focused so strongly on the classic conflict between the ruling class and the oppressed class that it not only ignored or underplayed a host of other conflicts considered important in the model's partial domination version, but it also minimized the level of conflict among the components of the ruling class. Instead, it concentrated on the monopolies and "the constant cooperation [among them] which only in rare cases is interrupted by insignificant differences."[8] In the partial monopoly domination version the monopolies are in conflict with each other as well as with the class enemy, and the intramural conflicts are serious: in vying for economic advantage the monopolies are torn by "profound internal contradictions, rivalry, and competition" (Tumanov, ed. 1967, 54).

Some analysts have gone so far as to picture the state using its relative autonomy to support "ordinary" monopolies and small and medium-sized businesses against "supermonopolies" and "oligopolies" to preserve a plural economic system in the sense of one not entirely dominated by a few enormous economic entities. If this degree of economic concentration were to be achieved, it would mean that the class composition of society had become so nearly polarized that the end of the capitalist system was at hand. To prevent that outcome, and to preserve the class domination of the entire bourgeoisie, government policy must sometimes be directed against precisely the largest and most powerful monopolies (Nikiforov, ed. 1972). In the complete domination version these very monopolies are portrayed as always succeeding in dictating their will to the state. The relative autonomy of the state represents the striving, expressed through governmental actions, to limit the monopolies by maintaining to some degree the traditional nineteenth-century capitalist values of private initiative, freedom of competition, and the free market (Guliev 1973).

Varga pointed out that the relationship between the monopolies and the less powerful parts of the bourgeoisie is not entirely one of conflict. Insofar as both have coinciding interests in safeguarding the entire capitalist social system and in exploiting labor as a major source of income, the monopolies are supported by large landowners, rich farmers, the nonmonopoly bourgeoisie, managers, the higher civil servants, the higher labor union officials, and even the most highly paid strata of the workers themselves. However, insofar as the monopolies seek to use the state to redistribute the national income in their own favor, their interests conflict with all, or nearly all, the groups just mentioned—and that creates the possibility of forging an "antimonopoly coalition" composed of the nonmonopoly bourgeoisie and all the exploited groups in society (1968, 57).

But the causes tending to unify all parts of the bourgeoisie are many and strong. What unites them is the struggle to prevent a proletarian revolution, the struggle to maintain private ownership of productive property, the defense of the credit system, and the fact that many middle-sized businesses are subcontractors to the monopolies and are therefore beholden to them. Yet the fierce competition between the monopolies and small and middle-sized businesses still leads to disunity. So, in order to sustain the ties that bind, the financial oligarchy frequently finds it necessary to make concessions to both the middle and petty bourgeoisie. The sharper the divisive competition becomes among the various sections of the bourgeoisie, the larger the concessions are likely to be. In this way the state remains the servant of the entire capitalist class and not just of the financial oligarchy (Dalin 1961).

Adherents of the partial monopoly domination version also regularly cited Lenin to legitimize their position: "Nowhere in the world has monopoly capitalism existed, nor will it ever exist, without free competition in a number of branches" (Lenin 1958–1965, vol. 38, 154). And from his *Imperialism, the Highest Stage of Capitalism*: "The monopolies, having grown out of free competition, do not replace it, but exist above it and alongside it and thereby give birth to a series of particularly sharp and intense contradictions, clashes, and conflicts" (Lenin 1958–1965, vol. 27, 386).

It follows that the monopolies alone cannot totally control the state since they are not the exclusive economic power in the country (Dalin 1961). This position was sharply attacked in 1969 by Melaniia Kovaleva, a relatively unknown writer, in an outburst that seems to have been the last major restatement of the complete domination version.[9]

Elements of the older version have an irresistible ideological attraction for Marxist–Leninists, and one part of Kovaleva's argument derives from an ideological tenet that was long sacrosanct in the Soviet Union: "The state fulfills the demands of monopoly capital, i.e., the superstructure is determined by the economic base and serves it" (1969, 231). Besides, some aspects of the partial domination variant could lead to conclusions that were logical but dangerous. Vladimir Guliev, for example, quoted approvingly A. G. Mileikovskii's statement that carried the concept of the state's relative autonomy to its logical ideological conclusion. However, for his own safety he interpolated defensive qualifications: " 'In SMC there is ever more distinctly apparent a certain independence (a relative one—V.G.) and autonomy (limited, in the final analysis—V.G.) of the superstructure' " (1970, 128). Nonetheless, the scholarly consensus that emerged in the late 1960s favored the partial domination variant.

The partial domination version is actually a return to the earlier Soviet position that the monopolies coalesce or merge with the state through personal union. But it identifies newer elements contributing to the merger such as lobbying activity, the exchange of useful information between business and government, and the development within the monopolies' organizational structure of special offices and departments for dealing with the government (Chetverikov 1974). Even though the monopolies remain the dominant political force in society, in the interest of maintaining the system's stability they must take into account not only the interests and needs of the other parts of the bourgeoisie but even those of the proletariat (Iakovlev, ed. 1969). The state must pursue a policy of granting concessions, particularly to the workers, in order to prevent discontent from reaching a level that could ultimately create a revolutionary movement. These concessions are called "conquests of the working class," victories in the class struggle between the haves and the have nots. They are usually, but not always, taken by Soviet authors as a sign of the very reluctant ultimate responsiveness of the system controlled by the bourgeoisie to some of the demands long made by the workers and not satisfied until it simply becomes impossible to continue saying no.

The point is that starting in the 1930s the monopolies have retained their control only through yielding to pressures to establish a minimum wage, social security, unemployment benefits, and the like. These and similar measures ultimately lead to further socialization of production and so further limit the scope of unfettered private enterprise—yet another illustration that SMC, in its attempt to save capitalism, is undercutting it (Nikitin 1971).

The two versions of the SMC model both differ and intersect at various points. And while proponents of each argued hotly, Burlatskii attempted a partial reconciliation through dialectically linking elements of the two positions (1970). It is true, he noted, that the power of the monopolies had been growing, but so too had the political activity of the working class and the other social strata opposed to the monopolies. When reaction grows stronger, it seems that resistance to it in the form of a widespread popular striving to broaden democracy increases as well. Finally, as the absolute subordination of the state to the bourgeoisie grows, so does its relative autonomy from both society as a whole and the ruling classes for the sake of better defending the totality of their interests.

Whether these ingenious formulas clarify, further obfuscate, or simply leave the problem where it already stood is debatable. But because the monopolies play the major political role in either version of the model it is important to consider them in greater detail with particular attention to the cleavages among them.

The Model in Operation: Big Business and Politics

In the Soviet lexicon monopoly is an umbrella term for a phenomenon that has taken many forms such as trusts, cartels, concerns, syndicates, and multinational corporations. The preferred concept used to analyze the network of control in industry and finance is "financial groups." These groups are the critically important behind-the-scenes political players according the Soviet analysis of American politics.

Financial Groups: How Big Business Is Organized

Financial groups are complexes of banking and industrial monopolies formed mainly through alliances of several wealthy families often located in a specific geographical area (Men'shikov 1969). For these reasons financial groups are identified in Soviet writing either by a dominant family (for example, the Rockefeller group, the Mellon group) or by geographical location (the Boston group or the Cleveland group, for instance). Within each geographical group there are usually several family groups.

The geographical division of financial groups has been important in the analysis of politics. As used by the Soviets, the term Wall Street is shorthand for all the financial groups located between Delaware and Massachusetts and as far as Pennsylvania's western border (Beglov 1971). Wall Street was long viewed by the Soviets as dominant in both economics and politics. But it was challenged now and then by the "new" midwestern financial groups (the Chicago and Cleveland groups), the Giannini group (the Bank of America), and others in California. Much attention has been given to the challenges posed by southwestern oil wealth (Tsagolov 1968) and to the southwestern and California components of the military–industrial complex supporting Ronald Reagan (Tsagolov 1985; Mel'nikov 1987). Just how serious these challenges have been to Wall Street and what their cumulative effects have been became the subject of a debate among Soviet specialists on the United States.

In the 1950s it almost became standard practice for the Soviets to view the domination of the "old" Wall Street financial groups as being effectively challenged by the "new" groups. Wall Street naturally fought back, trying to recover its former unchallenged position and bring the western upstarts under control. But it did not quite succeed. The result was portrayed as something of a standoff, with Wall Street still dominant but not to the degree and not in the same ways as before (Rubinshtein and others, eds. 1958; Zorin 1964).

This interpretation was contested by the late Ivan Beglov, an international affairs specialist who had spent ten years in New York as head of the TASS bureau (1971). He argued that by comparison with eastern finance and industry the role of the Texas and California magnates was modest. Even though there was much big industry and a good deal of money in the West, little of it was owned by the local or regional capitalists. Wall Street retained its preeminence.

This disagreement has important consequences in the analysis of politics to the extent that the Soviets believe that independent economic power is coterminous with independent political power. If Beglov is correct, there is far less diffusion of power among the monopoly bourgeoisie than suggested by certain Soviet analyses that had posited a greater pluralism within the ruling class. Obviously, they should update the argument in view of whatever shifts in economic and political power from the North to the South may have transpired in the 1970s and 1980s and the rise of the multinationals. But no major Soviet studies have appeared yet except for a book on the creation of conglomerates that does not address the political consequences (Cheprakov 1984). Studies on the military–industrial complex do, however, locate the centers of power in the West and Southwest.

On the other hand, all Soviet analysts joined in a consensus that, however the monopolies rule, they rule in their own interest—even when granting concessions to the workers. Yet these analysts sometimes admit that even the interests of the Wall Street financial groups are not all the same. The interests of the Rockefeller, Morgan, and Lehman Brothers groups, all of New York, do not coincide except when their shared dominating position is threatened. Outside that there is fierce competition characteristic of the financial oligarchy's inner life.

As noted, the partial domination version gradually gained ascendance as the 1960s wore on. More Soviet analysts who had either lived and studied in the United States under exchange programs or who had traveled there began to write about American politics. Moreover, as Soviet scholars developed a greater familiarity with Western social science, additional modifications of SMC theory were made. Some of its excesses were corrected and gradually new analytical terminology and ideas that were earlier deemed unacceptable were introduced. There was a gradual shift from discussing the SMC model's versions as such toward a relatively more empirical consideration of American politics.

In the heyday of SMC analysis in the 1950s and 1960s no Soviet studies appeared that integrated comprehensively the essentials of the model with the actual operation of American political institutions and processes. Only one analyst made a partial, limited attempt at such integration (Boichenko 1970). But her book, published just as SMC analysis was losing favor in the Soviet Union, was largely ignored by the Soviet scholarly community. It was only in the 1980s, during a resurgence of SMC-based studies which created yet another version of the model, that a book was published containing an integrated treatment (Peregudov, ed. 1984).

Political Dynamics: How Big Business Controls Politics

As the natural culmination of this chapter it is useful to sketch the essentials of how the partial domination version has been applied to the study of American politics.

In the Soviet view the very reason for the monopolies' existence and actions is economic. They are the result of the concentration of production and wealth, and they direct their activity toward expanding control over a greater share of the economy. But there were obstacles. Foremost was the economic competition among the giant monopolies themselves. Monopoly fought monopoly for the sake of advantage or even elimination. Dog eat dog. . . .

Another obstacle was political. Antitrust legislation was, the Soviets maintain, an early but ineffectual reaction to the appearance of monopolies in the nineteenth century. These laws were an example of the continuing conflict between the two basic factions of the bourgeoisie, the monopolistic and the nonmonopolistic, with the latter strongly backing antitrust policies, although to little avail (Kozlova 1966). But because the monopolies need allies in defending the private enterprise system, they do not press to the full their heavy economic advantages over the nonmonopoly bourgeoisie so as not to eliminate much-needed supporters.

The final major obstacle, a sociopolitical one, was the classic opposition of the working class to the concentration of power by the monopolies. In this case, the monopolies had to be careful not to use their formidable power to ride so roughshod over the class enemy as to produce a revolution.

Although their economic power is overwhelming, the monopolies realize that they must observe some political self-restrictions, and so they relate to politics in roughly the same way they relate to the economic system: no one monopoly is able to attain complete control over either. Together, the monopolies dominate politics and the economy, but in so doing they engage in that almost universal competition characteristic of SMC. They compete with one another in a fierce political struggle, and they are forced to take into account, and make concessions to, the nonmonopoly bourgeoisie and, more rarely, the workers as well. The position of the monopolies is preponderant, but eternal concession-making is the price of preponderance.

The central point in the analysis of SMC politics is the personal union between the monopolies and the state. Since that is essentially a question of how monopoly interests are represented in government, SMC analysts were concerned with the staffing of governmental decision-making bodies, especially executive and legislative ones—and in that order. In answering the questions of who gets into these positions and how much influence the people in them have, primary attention was given to the role of presidential elections and the executive branch appointments made in their wake.

Through generous campaign financing of congressional and presidential campaigns the monopolies use the electoral process to place sympathetic candidates in office or to sway unsympathetic ones. During the 1950s and 1960s, in contrast to past and future practice, Soviet writers were far more interested in the executive branch appointments made by presidents following their election, and there were excellent reasons for that grounded in the theory of SMC. If in the nineteenth and early twentieth centuries the legislature was clearly predominant in capitalist political systems, a shift toward executive predominance began during the second decade of the twentieth century. And following World War II the executive branch amassed enormous power in the United States. The tendency has been toward greater centralization around the president and toward creating a unitary state at the expense of federalism.[10]

Discussion of the monopolies' political activity since World War II therefore revolved around presidential elections in the first instance, the selection of cabinet members and other highly placed appointees, and then the performance record of all the appointees in making decisions favoring specific monopolies.

Prior to the presidential nominating conventions the conflicting monopolies would begin to identify persons from among the candidates who would most faithfully reflect the views and interests of, or be most susceptible to pressures from, financial groups sharing current or long-range interests. Prenomination campaigns were searches by the monopolies for candidates who are the most amenable to them and, no less important, attract large voter followings. The selection of the final two presidential candidates was the outcome of a contest among the representatives of the monopoly groups at the conventions. In the days before presidential primaries became so important Soviet authors took American smoke-filled rooms very seriously indeed, not so much because of which politicians were in them as which monopolies were behind the politicians. In the partial domination version the presidential campaigns themselves became contests between contending factions of the monopoly bourgeoisie. Historically, each monopoly tended to identify with one or the other party in the nomination process, but for compelling reasons in specific elections support was switched to the other party. The average voter therefore had no real choice: whichever candidate won, the monopoly groups behind that person were the real victors.

Because the winning presidential candidate was indebted to them for their financial support, specific monopoly groups were now able to control the staffing of the most influential positions in the executive branch with candidates at least favorable to those groups' interests, if not persons who were practically granted leave of absence from their executive jobs in private industry to serve in the government. They would merely continue to serve, in a different capacity, the interests of the monopolies whose candidate won the election. The remainder of the monopolists had to content themselves with taking whatever was forthcoming from the opposing monopolies, biding their time until they could take control of the critical presidential office in a future election.

A close analysis of the executive appointment patterns produced, SMC analysts felt, a good index of the relative strength of the various monopoly groups. Through this exercise in what I would call monopolyology, which is in some striking ways reminiscent of Kremlinology, the predominating groups could be identified, as could the lesser components that were awarded positions on the basis of their relative economic and political weight. Soviet writers found that on occasion even the monopolies that supported the losing candidate managed to have a representative or two in the cabinet owing to their objective economic power.

Utilizing these methods, the monopolies controlled the executive and legislative branches of government. But what of the judiciary? Soviet analyses of the Supreme Court were rare until the 1980s, and the one systematic effort to show how the monopolies control the court stressed that justices are chosen who are graduates of elite universities, who are substantial owners of real estate or stocks, or who had strong connections with big business in one way or another (Zhidkov 1985).

Even though they control the politics of the nation the monopolies must face the fact that they are not the only politically significant force in American society. Since, as the Soviets so often put it, there is only "a handful" of monopolists (an overwhelming minority of the population one might say) there are limits to their control, and their power is not boundless. The handful of monopolists employ large numbers of top executives who are a source of political support. Yet even if the term monopolists is extended to include them, that larger group is still very small compared to the totality or workers, farmers, service personnel, small businessmen, office workers, lower-level managerial personnel, and so forth, who make up the bulk of the voters and whose opposition to the rule of the monopolies always must be taken into account by the financial oligarchy.

To retain their control over politics the monopolies were periodically forced to compromise with the demands raised by either the nonmonopoly bourgeoisie or even the masses, the exploited class, the proletariat, the working class—as the Soviet terminology variously put it. Since the compromises are all the greater during times of particular stress, as in the depression of the 1930s, there are obvious advantages to the monopolies in not pressing the population too hard, which would lead only to the need to make more painful compromises in order to pull the monopolistic chestnuts out of the revolutionary fire.

The important conclusion is that the monopolies have not exercised all the power they possess, and they have granted concessions, in the interest of their self-preservation. Scattered throughout primitive SMC analyses are hair-raising expressions like "the total domination of finance capital," "the dictatorship of the monopolies," and "monopoly control of political life in the United States." If these ideologically irresistible descriptions were literally true, there would have been little reason for Soviet authors to write, as they often did, about the continual struggle of the proletariat against the monopolies, not to mention the victories by the underdogs in that struggle.

It is important to note a sharp decline in Soviet analyses of American politics in the SMC mode in the 1970s. One reason for that was the turmoil in American political life in the 1960s, which prompted the Soviets to switch their focus from monopoly control to another aspect of the ideology that was more appropriate for analyzing mass protest movements. They then concentrated on the class struggle in which the rulers were portrayed as under severe attack. The other reason was the slow incorporation of Western analytical approaches from political science into Soviet academic writing.

Yet, as so often happens, the earlier approach reappeared in two forms. In the 1980s a group of writers used SMC-type analysis to show that the military–industrial complex has become the dominant force in both domestic and foreign policy (Yakovlev 1985; Tsagolov 1985, 1986; Kornilov and Shishkin 1986; Bogdanov 1986). The importance of these writings is underlined by repeated evidence that Mikhail Gorbachev favors this interpretation of American politics.[11]

The revival of an approach reminiscent of the total monopoly domination version was accompanied by the reappearance of a partial domination version stressing the coalescence of big business with the government. The focus here is on the policies followed by the multinational corporations in working together with the state to create a flexible, differentiated, facilitative relationship calculated to adapt the system of control to new political, economic, and technological challenges at home and abroad (Nazarevskii, ed. 1984; Peregudov, ed. 1984; Evenko, ed. 1985; Yakovlev, ed. 1988; Iaz'kov, ed. 1988). Even IUSAC picked up the theme in its monthly, a sign that a new analytical wave had arrived (see Timofeev 1986).

The monopolies, it seems, continue to rule—whether partially or almost totally. But if Soviet analyses of American politics simply posited monopoly rule with no conflict among the monopolies and no opportunity for meaningful political activity by the remainder of the population, there would be little reason to write this book. Since the opposite is the case, there is every reason to enter into the complexities of Soviet perceptions of American politics.

2 HOW DO THEY RULE? LIBERAL DEMOCRACY IN AMERICA

In the Soviet view, the interaction of various segments of a society attempting to defend or advance differing interests produces politics (Guliev 1973; Boichenko 1970). Economic interests are paramount, and the clash of class interests, particularly those of the exploiting and the exploited classes, plays the determining role (Burlatskii 1970).

In the past some ruling classes periodically attempted to mask the fact that they were in control by claiming that everybody ruled. In classical Greece and feudal Europe, for instance, those classes established political systems that were called democracies but really were not since the majority of the population was excluded from participation (Guliev 1970). The Soviets maintain that the same is largely true of the political system characteristic of capitalist nations.

They call this masking process bourgeois democracy, their designation for liberal democracy. All versions of the SMC model incorporate this older socialist idea and postulate that the ruling monopolies must purposefully claim that everybody rules.

The Origin of Liberal Democracy

Bourgeois democracy originated in Europe in the eighteenth and nineteenth centuries during the struggle for supremacy between the fledgling capitalists and the dying aristocracy while the aristocracy still held political power. As an essential element of their mindset, Soviet writers repeat Marx's description of that struggle's dynamics. The bourgeoisie needed allies to overcome the aristocracy. To attract the support of the newly forming working class, they proclaimed democracy as the basic principle of a restructured political life and organization (Guliev 1973). Beyond the political rationale, there were also economic motives for advocating democracy. The capitalists' need for laborers required a promise of at least minimal personal freedom for individuals; in particular, it meant releasing the serfs from their feudal bonds and the handicraftsmen from the ties binding them to their shops so that they could work in the factories (Shakhnazarov 1955).

Soviet Americanists have long recognized that this classical Marxist interpretation does not fit some of the conditions in eighteenth- and nineteenth-century America.[1] At that time freedom had a very specific meaning for colonial American frontiersmen. It was freedom from the mercantilist system of governmental monopolies and freedom to use extensive free lands. It was widely believed that these liberties would lead to prosperity, happiness, and equality of opportunity for all. In America governmental noninterference in business affairs, laissez-faire, was an ideal not only of manipulative entrepreneurs but also of many genuinely committed to democracy (Nikitin 1971).

Despite these important differences between Europe and America, Soviet analysts contend that the basic characteristics of early bourgeois democracy were the same on both sides of the Atlantic. Some people were more free and more equal than others because the rights and freedoms, that were the precepts of bourgeois democracy and formally guaranteed to all citizens were not put into practice. For instance, the formal equality of citizens before the law was the equality of persons in the abstract and did not take into account the varying concrete social positions of individuals. It was the unequal equality of the exploiter and the exploited, of the well fed and the hungry, of the owner and nonowner of property. Similarly, in the theory of liberal democracy individuals had the right to participate in managing government through voting and were also guaranteed the inviolability of their person and residence. But in the nineteenth century those rights were exercised primarily by the bourgeoisie since the franchise was limited to property owners, and because few people in fact owned property. The rights of freedom of speech, the press, conscience, and meeting were mere formalities for individuals who lacked the material means for exercising those rights fully (Shakhnazarov 1955).

Finally, in addition to these features of bourgeois democracy, which were innovations that the bourgeoisie developed, that class also adopted as its own some older political institutions and processes such as local self-government, elections, and the judicial system, changing their nature and form to suit its own needs. The Soviets therefore insist that bourgeois democracy, in its origins and development, was limited, incomplete, democracy. And since the advocates of liberal democracy constantly claimed that it was democracy for all, the Soviet contention is that bourgeois democracy was, and has remained, hypocritical.

On the other hand, the early bourgeois demand that due process replace the arbitrariness characteristic of absolute monarchy served eventually to put some limits on the exercise of power by the bourgeoisie itself. Its own power was limited by emphasizing elective representative institutions and political parties, and particularly the multiparty system (Levin, ed. 1964a; Guliev 1970).

The Soviets offer the Constitution adopted at the Philadelphia Convention as a splendid example of the processes at work in the early phase of bourgeois democracy. After the radical democratic language of the Declaration of Independence had promised so much, the Convention adopted a constitution that said not a word about such elementary bourgeois democratic rights as freedom of speech, the press, and conscience (Iakovlev, ed. 1976). The Bill of Rights was added only because of the pressure exerted by a strong popular movement. Although this was a major democratic gain by the people, the disadvantaged position of women, blacks, and Indians did not change (Iakovlev, ed. 1969). Popular sovereignty was a sham and remained so even in the twentieth century (Guliev and Kuz'min 1969).

These events are cited by the Soviets as examples of the basic patterns of bourgeois democracy that operate to this very day: broadly appealing promises are made but are drastically limited when finally incorporated into laws or other political decisions. It then becomes incumbent upon the vast majority of the people, disadvantaged by this outcome, to mount a struggle against the limitations placed upon governmental decisions by the economically and politically powerful ruling class, which essentially amounts to an oligarchy.

How Liberal Democracy Developed

Soviet analysts maintain that the fate of bourgeois democracy was naturally contingent upon the development of capitalism and the class structure peculiar to it. In particular, in the late nineteenth century, the bourgeoisie differentiated into the monopoly and non-monopoly divisions with the monopoly faction—big business and big banks—exercising overwhelming political power. And as the twentieth century progressed the once independent small busi-nessmen became increasingly dependent not only upon the faceless power of the financial oligarchy and large corporations but also upon the enormous federal bureaucracy, which coalesced with the monopolies. In these circumstances, to continue the nineteenth-century laissez-faire policy could only mean giving a free hand to big business and the large banks (Nikitin 1971).

Any attempt to obtain that free hand was inevitably subject to limitations since the nonmonopoly bourgeoisie avidly defended its interests against the monopolies. The working class also resisted. The more farsighted monopolists exercised self-denial in using their power, sensing that too great a concentration of economic power (and the too severe exploitation of the workers that results) might create an unstable situation that the ruling class could not control (Nikitin 1971).

According to Lenin, the net result of this combination of bour-geois power and caution was that two very different basic policies were applied by the ruling class: force and concessions. The one, the other, or both could be used (Lenin 1958–1965). Lenin iden-tified two possible consequences of the interplay of these factors—either a turn away from democracy toward complete domination or a sharpening of the struggle between the democratic aspirations of the masses and the antidemocratic tendency of the monopolies. With reference to the second Lenin noted: "Imperialism does not stop the development of capitalism and the growth of democratic tendencies in the mass of the population, but it *sharpens* the an-tagonisms between these democratic strivings and the antidemocratic tendency of the trusts" (1958–1965, vol. 30, 102). In the first case liberal democracy is restricted; in the second it is extended.

Most Soviets writing in the 1940s and 1950s agreed that bourgeois democracy was being restricted, and in the 1960s and early 1970s there was a near consensus that it was being expanded. In line with the old tradition of dialectical analysis (recognizing that opposites coexist and interact) of Marx and the Marxists, it was not unusual in each of these periods to find the same Soviet author at least considering both possibilities or even actually managing to take both sides at the same time. In the interest of greatest clarity, here I shall consider each tendency separately and then discuss current Soviet perspectives.

Restricting Liberal Democracy

A powerful economic interest motivates restricting democracy. "For the monopolies political domination (dictatorship) is a necessary condition for the unfettered extraction of maximum profit" (Shakhnazarov 1955, 38). The dominating class works to eliminate obstacles to economic exploitation and political suppression of the proletariat by turning from bourgeois democracy toward reaction (Guliev 1973). Consequently, if the financial oligarchy could have its own way, it would prefer an autocratic or aristocratic form of rule to bourgeois democracy (Guliev and Kuz'min 1969). Once monopolies and imperialism appeared, the Soviet argument ran, the small group of very powerful reactionary monopoly capitalists attempted to turn the clock back beyond the nineteenth century to eliminate even the imperfectly operating and limited institutions and processes of bourgeois democracy.

In the United States reaction took the form of strengthening the executive branch (particularly the bureaucracy) because it was directly dependent upon the monopolies and was less subject to pressure from the masses than Congress. Reaction also meant heightening the activity of the Supreme Court against labor and limiting the court's role in curtailing racial discrimination until the early 1950s. Likewise, the role of Congress increased at the expense of the states. In these ways the country was being transformed from a federal state into a unitary one.[2]

In the premonopoly period of capitalism, prior to the last quarter of the nineteenth century, the precepts of bourgeois democracy were violated by the bourgeoisie only episodically, primarily when the workers attempted to use the limited rights and freedoms they possessed against the bourgeoisie. But, some Soviets argued, in the twentieth century the violations became so systematic that the situation could be described as a complete flouting of bourgeois legality (Levin, ed. 1964a) or even as a form of totalitarianism (Burlatskii 1970).

This state of affairs is symptomatic of what was finally called the dictatorship of the bourgeoisie. In it, the financial oligarchy sub-ordinates the state to itself by populating the state apparatus's top positions either with its own members or with "henchmen" like Lyndon Johnson and Richard Nixon taken from the petty bourgeoisie. Characteristically, the oligarchy prefers to rule obliquely through its henchmen rather than directly through its members' holding political office. In this way it rules even more securely because the system of indirect rule creates two illusions: that the politicians are independent and that anybody and every-body can be a politician. These illusions captivate both the poli-ticians and the population at large—and the financial oligarchy continues to rule most effectively (Beglov 1971; Burlatskii 1970).

In this bourgeois dictatorship political control is increasingly exercised through institutions not mentioned in the Constitution and not responsible to elective bodies, the voters, or public opin-ion; the National Security Council and the House Un-American Activities Committee are two examples (Guliev 1970).[3] The role of the military, the police, the intelligence and counterintelligence agencies, and the courts expands. The activities of nongovern-mental bodies that exert ideological control such as youth orga-nizations, establishment-oriented trade unions, and scientific and church organizations also increase (Guliev and Kuz'min 1969; Gu-liev 1970; Shakhnazarov 1955; Levin and Tumanov, eds. 1974).

The dictatorship solidified, various governmental bodies pursue two sets of policies favorable to the monopolies. Valentin Zorin, a proponent of the complete domination variant, enumerated the economic policies in a chapter entitled "Policies of the Billionaires and for the Billionaires": large appropriations for arms are made; generous oil depletion allowances are instituted; export of capital is encouraged through favorable tax policies; defense purchases are concentrated in the largest corporations; the small farmer is run off the land; and natural resources are squandered (1964). Another set of policies is directed against the political enemies of the monopolies and against democratic institutions and processes, especially against what the Soviets call bourgeois legality. Examples are the Smith–Connolly Act, the Taft–Hartley Act, loyalty checks, election laws discriminating against the American Communist party, trials of the party's leaders, narrowing voting rights through unreasonable eligibility requirements, and establishing control of the major media by the monopolies (Levin, ed. 1964a; Mishin 1954; Guliev 1970).

The political system sanctions and maintains the exploitation of hired labor, the domination of the minority capitalist class, and the organized, systematic suppression of the proletariat through a mix of legal actions and raw power (Guliev 1970).

That the bourgeois dictatorship, unless it is of the fascist variety, uses legal action as a means to its end suggests that neither is it the worst possible dictatorship nor does it coincide with Lenin's famous definition of the dictatorship of the proletariat: "Dictatorship is power based directly upon force and is not bound by any laws" (1958–1965, vol. 37, 245).

Nevertheless, a few extremists took the concept of bourgeois dictatorship so literally that one concluded that "the American people never ruled their state. The U.S. state not only never carried out the will of the people, but, on the contrary, it always acted against the people" (Gromakov 1958, 5).

Although a few Soviet analysts would agree with most of this statement even today, many have disagreed that the state always acted against the people. In fact, an entire group of analysts argued that in the twentieth century bourgeois democracy has been broadened rather than restricted.

Extending Liberal Democracy

Vladimir Guliev attacked the oversimplified model of capitalist political development which, he said, often appeared in Soviet scholarly literature. In that model the period of free-competition capitalism was a time when the institutions, processes, and rights characteristic of bourgeois democracy flourished. Later, during monopoly rule and imperialism, these rights were cut back until finally reduced essentially to zero. Guliev contended that this model ignored the historical fact that it was precisely in the period of imperialism, of monopoly and state–monopoly capitalism, that the workers in capitalist countries achieved the greatest expansion of their rights (Tumanov, ed. 1967).

This criticism was as fundamental as it was valid—and even obvious. On the other hand, the oversimplified model he was criticizing was a direct product of a unique sequence of events transpiring in the Soviet Union and the United States: Stalin's directive in 1952 that the subordination of the state by the monopolies be stressed by Soviet scholars along with the real problems involving civil rights and due process in the United States during the McCarthy era and then in the struggle against racial discrimination. Because Stalin's death and the ensuing attack on the cult of his person removed his ideological dictatorship, and since the civil liberties cause won some substantial gains and the United States did not turn into a fascist dictatorship, it eventually became possible for Soviet analysts not only to adopt a critical stance toward the oversimplified model but also to offer a version based upon changed circumstances and buttressed by Lenin's observations that antagonism between democratic and antidemocratic tendencies grows as monopoly capitalism develops and that the bourgeoisie uses a mixture of force and concessions in exercising its rule.

The model's alternate version centers on the attainments of the democratic forces in society, particularly on the concessions (i.e., the social reforms) they wrest from the ruling class. Supporters of this approach concluded that "despite the obviously increasingly reactionary character of the ruling class, in general and on the whole the political life of present-day capitalist society is becoming more democratic (especially in comparison with the capitalism of the nineteenth century)" (Guliev and Kuz'min 1969, 154). This outcome was possible because, as Lenin had pointed out, the monopolies cannot eliminate medium and small capitalist production. Consequently, some free competition remains in the economic realm, enabling the petty bourgeoisie to demand greater political freedom and equal rights. Moreover, the workers and their allies not only defend the democratic rights and liberties they won in the past but they also struggle to expand them. Finally, the socialist nations are loud in their defense and support of democratic forces everywhere, and the worldwide peace movement attracts the masses in every country to struggle against the forces of reaction. In other words, public opinion is mobilized on a worldwide scale to influence events within the United States (Guliev 1970; Levin and Tumanov, eds. 1974).

In addition to these pressures, some in the ruling class realized that they could retain power and prevent the outbreak of a proletarian revolution only by reforming (Mal'kov 1973; Gusev 1974). Decades ago some farsighted members of the ruling class understood that it was in the general interest of the class to stabilize capitalism by moderating the class struggle through creating a flexible social policy administered through the state. This realization prompted Theodore Roosevelt's Square Deal, Wilson's New Freedom, Franklin Roosevelt's New Deal, Truman's Fair Deal, and Lyndon Johnson's Great Society (Tumanov, ed. 1967).

The main disagreement among the monopolies had been over the appropriate or tolerable degree of state intervention in implementing these policies (Guliev 1965). By the mid-1970s the American establishment as a whole came to favor accommodation, pragmatic decisions, and compromises expressed in social reforms, granting partial concessions to the workers and their allies, and regulating the economy in ways peculiar to SMC (Fursenko and others 1974).

The tendency to make concessions was reinforced by the need for forecasting and planning, which led the monopolies, some more than others, to seek ways to ensure the uninterrupted functioning of the production process through creating positive psychological links between the workers, their jobs, and their place in capitalist production and even in society as a whole (Anikin, ed. 1972). Moreover, certain minimum needs in housing, education, and health care are a prerequisite of extracting maximum surplus value from the workers (Gusev 1974; Guliev 1965). Some concessions can be profitable.

The policy of granting concessions is called either social maneuvering or bourgeois reformism. The latter term was used by socialist writers starting in the nineteenth century to describe the reforms adopted by governments controlled by urban business interests and large landowners. In the 1930s Soviet writers therefore took umbrage at the sense then current in the United States that the New Deal was a purely American way of reforming capitalism. To them it was simply the state regulation of the economy characteristic of all capitalist countries in periods of major wars or world economic crises (Dalin 1936; Beglov 1971). And the lesson the monopolists learned from the New Deal was that the state could "much better defend their long-term and vitally important interests by infringing a bit upon the transient interests, but not upon the primary ones, of the middle bourgeoisie, and even by partially infringing upon the interests of the big bourgeoisie" (Gantman and Mikoyan 1969, 40).

Yet some analysts recognized that Roosevelt was forced by circumstances to expand his originally limited objectives, and that significant changes had taken place in the extent of state control over the economy when elements of planning on a national scale were introduced (Mal'kov and Nadzhafov 1967).[4] In a strategy typical of social maneuvering, bourgeois politicians portrayed the improvements that materialized from these selfish considerations, or from necessity, as achievements of the American system (N. Iakovlev 1965). These claims strengthened the illusion fostered by the bourgeoisie that the state did not serve the interests of any one class exclusively and that it was solicitous of the needs of all classes (Iakovlev, ed. 1976). As a result, Roosevelt managed to forge a bloc of voters, which was one of the most important factors in maintaining domestic stability during his time (Fursenko and others 1974). While one analyst lamented the New Deal's having raised the prestige of bourgeois reformism for a time, he took comfort in the thought that the reforms created more favorable conditions for labor to press its battle with capital and that the limited nature of the reforms was to some extent ultimately responsible for the massive protests of the 1960s (Iakovlev, ed. 1976).[5]

The Soviets maintain that World War II accelerated the development of SMC but note that concessions on the scale of the New Deal were not made. The immediate postwar period has not been the subject of any major specialized investigations on the policy of concessions. Only rarely have the Soviets discussed the Employment Act of 1946 (for example, Likhacheva 1971). Even more telling is their failure to study the GI Bill of Rights. The mindset is very much in operation here in several ways. Traditionally, the postwar period has been treated as a time of reaction not conducive to even proposing, much less adopting, large-scale social programs. That in itself would discourage research on topics that might undermine the prevailing Soviet attitude. In addition, the fact that the GI Bill produced the greatest surge in upward social mobility in American history ran counter to important ideological imperatives about growing impoverishment.

The usual Soviet conclusion is that whatever was proposed or enacted in the realm of social reform during that period (which encompassed the Fair Deal) amounted to so little that a noticeable gap appeared in the level of social services and social security between the United States and other capitalist as well as socialist countries (Liven', 1975). The social and economic policies of the Eisenhower administration dissatisfied not only the broad masses but even the monopolies, which saw the need for more flexible and adroit initiatives (Zorin 1964; Terekhov 1984). But by then the resolution of social problems had to be considered in the context of the economic growth problem, a question that became a primary political issue for the first time in American history during the Kennedy administration (Men'shikov, ed. 1964).

The Great Society program was a massive change in the direction of social reform and concessions. But it failed for many reasons. The resource drain occasioned by the Vietnam War was a primary constraint. The government simply could not put all the program's elements into effect without massively expanding the bureaucracy. Millions of average Americans were alarmed at the prospect of large tax increases to support the program, and big business was becoming disenchanted with the high cost and low effectiveness of social maneuvering (Shamberg 1968b; Androsov 1971). In the end, the Great Society was "in fact more advertised than financed" (Liven' 1975, 200). Something new appeared during the crisis of the late 1960s when the direct role of the corporations in developing social policy increased, a step favored by President Nixon.[6]

During the Carter administration budgetary constraints and shifts in public opinion away from supporting social programs reduced the latter to the level of "preventive maintenance" (Oleshchuk 1987, 59–79). There was also a growing conservatism among Democrats owing to the ineffectiveness of neoliberal Keynesian policies and the weakening of the labor unions and the civil rights movement. That shift deepened after Ronald Reagan's victory in 1980 and a new liberal–conservative consensus on limiting social programs determined the course during the 1980s (Plekhanov, ed. 1988).

The Reagan administration's cutbacks in social programs were considered a policy of "social revenge" that nevertheless had to be moderated following Republican losses in the 1982 elections—but only somewhat because the Democrats did not have a viable alternative to Reagan's policies (Oleshchuk 1987). The alternatives would be narrow in any case: "It is not by chance that the ruling elite emphasizes poverty assistance. Both the liberals and conservatives agree that it is more advantageous to buy off the poor—the differences in the views of both lie only in the size of the 'price'" (Plekhanov, ed. 1988, 97).

In sum, the Soviet position is that the policy of social maneuvering has succeeded in staving off a revolutionary upheaval, but it has not solved many problems which, along with other factors, may one day contribute toward producing just that.

Evaluations of Liberal Democracy

The Soviets have an ambivalent view of liberal democracy: "From the point of view of Marxism, bourgeois reformism, as a side result of the class struggle, has a dual character. It signifies a limited step toward the better, and at the very same time it pursues the aim of weakening and extinguishing the energy of the masses and of obscuring their consciousness" (Mikhailov, ed. 1970–1971, vol. 1, 526). Soviet writers stress that the concessions the working class and its allies must struggle to win from the bourgeoisie and the state that it controls must be forced upon the rulers because granting concessions is contrary to the exploitative essence and nature of both the bourgeoisie and the state. The concessions are made only to save the system (Guliev 1970; Keremetskii 1970; Geevskii 1973; Gusev 1974).

Concessions are also characteristically partial and are not the comprehensive solutions to social problems that the Soviets prefer (Gusev 1974). Some workers content themselves with partial gains and do not struggle for a radical political transformation (Levin, ed. 1964a; Gusev 1974; Zorin, ed. 1971). The incrementalism typical of enacting social legislation in the United States is seen not merely as the American way of doing things but as generated by fundamental economic causes. Concessions are kept within bounds because it is against the interests of the bourgeoisie to eliminate poverty and unemployment completely since these factors are prerequisites of the ability to exploit labor to the maximum (Moroz 1971). Retaining what Marx called the reserve army of the unemployed is a vital necessity.

There is an objective reason for engaging in social reform: Marx said that in any society the state must maintain a necessary minimum of social welfare without which it is impossible for a civilized society to function (Levin and Tumanov, eds. 1974). On the economic side, the nature of the capitalist economic system requires that the purchasing power of the population be maintained (products must be marketed) and that the potential work force be educated and trained.[7] Sometimes bitter pills can have sugar coatings for the bourgeoisie, as when private firms and contractors amass large fortunes from implementing social programs (Tumanov, ed. 1967).[8]

Finally, there is a consideration that was in vogue among Soviet analysts in the 1950s but was dropped until recently: Congress may enact laws to improve the status of the workers, but it does so in the knowledge that other parts of the government, exercising checks and balances functions, will essentially nullify the laws (Gromyko 1957). A major recent study of the Supreme Court makes the point that, overall, the number of its decisions overturning acts of Congress and the state legislatures to the benefit of the ruling class has increased (Zhidkov 1985).

The Soviets agree in part with American liberal commentators who feel that outbreaks of war were responsible for the incomplete or aborted implementation of the reform programs, even if individual reform measures were implemented. World War II forced the end of the New Deal, the Korean War ended the Fair Deal, and the Vietnam War ended the Great Society program. Though wars did play a role, the real reason the programs fail is that

America is torn by irreconcilable social antagonisms which create political obstacles to adopting and effecting positive social policies (Androsov 1971).

Soviet commentators interpret the concessions and reforms produced by bourgeois democracy as pretexts the monopolists use to demonstrate the democratic nature of the state and society as a whole in order to create illusions among the proletariat. The illusions disorient some workers, who then content themselves with partial gains and do not struggle for a radical political transformation. It is difficult to cement unity within the working class (Levin, ed. 1964a; Gusev 1974; Zorin, ed. 1971).

The situation becomes even less promising when American political analysts and commentators use the concessions and the various forms of state intervention in the economy to create theories that vindicate twentieth-century capitalism. Mainstream Soviets consider them all to be groundless, whether they be people's capitalism, the welfare state, pluralist democracy, industrial and post-industrial society, the great society, the technetronic era, the disappearance of classes, convergence of capitalism and socialism, or the exceptional and unique nature of freedom and democracy in America as contrasted with all other countries (Levin and Tumanov, eds. 1972; Guliev 1965). The social programs of neither government nor private business worked, nor did the gamut of SMC policies—and all contributed to inflation (Lan 1967; Shapiro 1970).[9]

Some analysts tried to strike a balance between the advantages and disadvantages of bourgeois democracy or to correct Soviet excesses in interpreting certain of its features. Perhaps the most concise statement of attempted balance came from Guliev and Kuz'min: "Despite the limited nature of all those measures, their character of having been forced, and the obvious inconsistency in their application, it is impossible not to note their objectively positive significance, since they in some measure ease the condition of the toiling masses" (1969, 33).

One writer attempting to correct dogmatic oversimplifications controverted the assertion that various governmental social programs (housing construction, for example) benefit the capitalists exclusively (Tumanov, ed. 1967). Moreover, as Georgii Arbatov, director of the Institute of U.S. and Canadian Studies, has argued, whatever the shortcomings of bourgeois democracy and the partial concessions characteristic of it, they are better than fascism, and that difference has an enormous significance for the well-being of the working class (1972). The time had come for a change in tune on the part of those Soviet authors who had refused to recognize the benefits of social programs to workers. In order to be effective, the policy of social maneuvering must produce some real material, social, and political gains. Once basic material needs are satisfied, issues such as equality of access to education arise where the bourgeoisie has only limited room for maneuvering (Burlatskii and Galkin 1974).

The very fact that the ruling class is forced to engage in social maneuvering makes it possible for the workers to battle more effectively for social reforms and thus to affect state policy (Liven' 1975). This perception raises some delicate problems for Soviet analysts, particularly regarding the mechanism through which the concessions are secured and what that says about participation in politics by people outside the bourgeoisie. The four versions of the SMC model and the description of American politics provided by the bourgeois democracy approach are based on the proposition that the political system belongs to the bourgeoisie: it is designed to operate, and does operate, to exclude the mass of the population from real or meaningful participation in politics. Nevertheless, the people who are excluded do manage to advance their interests by creating organizations that operate within the system although they are not integrated into it (Burlatskii and Galkin 1985).

The excluded groups also manage to extract concessions from the system's managers. When discussing concessions Soviet analysts use a very standard terminology whose meaning is carefully circumscribed to ensure that the perspectives just described remain as inviolate as possible. Since concessions result from the pressures created by the fierce struggle of the working class to expand democracy and improve its own social and material conditions, concessions are often called gains in a very special sense. The Soviets use the word for conquests (*zavoevaniia*) to denote them. This language of physical combat captures for them the spirit of the class struggle.

Burlatskii was one of the very few writers who remarked that the typical Soviet understanding that concessions result from the struggle of the working class was too general an explanation, and that it was necessary to make explicit the concrete institutions and processes through which they gained those concessions. As examples, he mentioned the trade union movement, the press, the legislative battle, and strikes. Soviet experts should analyze these factors to predict more accurately the extent to which the *structural* changes in the capitalist political systems being demanded by the workers would be adopted. Studies of this kind would aid in conducting the class struggle more effectively (Burlatskii 1970).

As is usual in Soviet writing on the United States, when a startling innovation is made it is done in the name of upholding orthodoxy. No Soviet reader would have been surprised at Burlatskii's mentioning the unions and strikes in this context since they had long been part of the standard analysis. But to suggest that the press and legislative politics were involved was striking and disturbing. The mass media and the Congress were considered to be almost totally dominated by the monopolies.[10]

But discretion ruled Burlatskii in a later major work where he did not expand on his insight and repeated old orthodoxies (Burlatskii and Galkin 1974). The Soviet consensus on this critical issue is therefore best represented by Guliev's contention that concessions "in no way signify any kind of participation of the proletariat in the exercise of state power" (Tumanov, ed. 1967, 80). The fact that concessions are made is not an indication that some of the state's sovereignty is thereby transferred to the workers—power remains exclusively in the hands of the ruling class, and concessions do not change that reality (Guliev 1970).

For any Soviet analyst to pursue Burlatskii's original position would mean rethinking the basic definition of the state as the weapon of class oppression. Rather than run such risks it is safer to maintain that any changes in the bourgeois state since it first appeared in the eighteenth century have not significantly transformed its essence or nature. The changes amount only to modifications better described as accommodations (Tumanov, ed. 1967).

This evaluation of bourgeois democracy creates a number of problems for the Soviets. Some worry that even though the workers are still oppressed, their successes in wresting concessions may create "constitutional illusions," the belief that they will be able to achieve all their aims through the bourgeois version of democracy as enshrined in liberal democratic constitutions (Levin, ed. 1964a). There is also concern that some Soviet analysts may fall into the extreme leftist error of contending that the worse things are for the proletariat, the better they are for the communist cause since the revolution will be hastened as exploitation worsens. The appropriate position to take here is to recognize that the more concessions won, the more limited the scope for arbitrariness by the monopolists and also the more limited the sphere of possible social maneuvering in the future (Levin and Tumanov, eds. 1974).

Guliev and Kuz'min cautioned that although there is much to criticize in bourgeois democracy, such criticism is not intended to assist in replacing it with Bonapartism, a military and police dictatorship, or fascism (1969). Criticism may backfire, but their hope is that it will help extend bourgeois democracy by prompting the elimination of its limitations. The end result would be the full (as opposed to the partial) realization of the freedoms and rights it proclaims. Examples of typical limitations the Soviets associate with liberal democracy are a multiparty system structured to operate so as not to threaten the monopolies' control; legal, though limited, possibilities for organizing and acting against the dictatorship of the monopolies within the bounds of bourgeois legality; the critical role played by manipulated elections in staffing the major governing bodies; the formal (though not really applied) recognition of the separation of powers and of the major role of representative institutions (Levin and Tumanov, eds. 1974).

Taking a global view of all the countries where bourgeois democracy has existed, Burlatskii maintained that no matter how much progress had been made within the framework of bourgeois democracy, that form of government could not satisfy the demands of the population for peace, national independence and sovereignty, agrarian reform for the benefit of the poorer peasantry, guaranteed jobs for the workers, freeing the intellectuals from enslavement to monopoly capital, and equal rights for women. Burlatskii insisted that these goals can be achieved only in a new kind of democracy, socialist democracy, of which the Soviet political system is the best example (1970).

At its very best bourgeois democracy boils down to a perpetual dynamic deadlock in which a period of limited democratic transformation is followed by a period of reactionary counterreforms (Tumanov, ed. 1967). In addition, whatever is accomplished is never enough. During the 1960s the Soviets welcomed the major gains made in extending bourgeois democracy, but in the mid-1970s they began to criticize the system for preserving inequities that violated socioeconomic human rights: unemployment, unequal taxes, women's inequality, an inequitable health care system, racial discrimination, governmental intrusions on privacy, rising crime rates, and inflation (Kuz'min 1977). Much of this commentary was a direct reaction to the Carter administration's criticisms of human rights problems in the Soviet Union. Thus in the early 1980s there was greater concern with the violation of constitutional rights (Vlasikhin and Linnik 1980; Kalenskii 1983) and with what was depicted as a secret war against American dissenters conducted by the FBI, the CIA, and the Pentagon with the periodic assistance of organized crime (Setunskii 1981 is just one of many examples).

On the level of political theory bourgeois democracy is attacked for propounding a set of ideals and goals which never have been realized in practice—and, as far as the Soviets are concerned, never can be in a society dominated by the bourgeoisie. They maintain that most American definitions of, and writing on, democracy are "abstract" and deal with a "pure" concept of democracy having little in common with the concrete realities of political life in the United States, all of which is simply part and parcel of the masking process (Kuz'min 1977, 1970; Kerimov and Keizerov 1972).

Soviet writers have long stressed that liberal democracy in America is experiencing a serious pervasive crisis revealing a contradiction that they think will be fatal to liberal democracy: the ruling class controls the political system, but it cannot resolve the crisis (Slavin 1967; Burlatskii and Galkin 1985). Like the general crisis of capitalism, this one began long ago when the monopolies appeared. Their excessive power overturned the existing system of balances within the ruling class and enabled them to trample on the rights and freedoms of the middle and petty bourgeoisie. The monopolies' expanded political power also seriously aggravated the already existing "despotism of capital over labor" (Guliev 1965, 83).

The basic attributes of the crisis are much the same as the factors considered in the section "Restricting Liberal Democracy," but with some variations.[11] These signs of crisis are highlighted in the public mind by the many political scandals associated with them. Because of that it is now more difficult to use bourgeois democracy to mask the power of the ruling monopolies. Traditionally, the masking involved manipulating both the image and the activities of the legislature to portray it as the primary vehicle of government by the people. Burlatskii and Galkin maintain that this form of manipulation became unworkable and was replaced by a new form, the manipulation of mass political consciousness through control of the information communicated in the electronic media (1985). Since the ultimate purpose of the manipulation is to limit and channel the political role of the citizenry and leave the real governing to the ruling class, the electronic media's entertainment functions, combined with its informational function, became a means of "total manipulation" (Burlatskii and Galkin 1985, 106). But that in turn created an unwanted degree of apathy toward politics, which depressed the level of political participation in elections—another sign of the crisis.

As mainstream Soviet analysts see it, with political power still in the hands of the monopolies, with the masking process having led to a dead end, and with a host of unresolved political, social, and economic problems, the obvious conclusion is that the class struggle continues; the conditions and means are considered in the next two chapters.

PART II

American Society
and the Soviet Mindset

3 WHO ARE THE RULERS AND THE RULED? THE CLASS STRUCTURE

If the Soviets see differing interests as the motive for politics, then the conflict of class interests is the most significant political activity. In Soviet analyses the class struggle that goes on under the conditions of liberal democracy is the underlying dynamic fact of American political life.

Like Marx himself, Soviet writers have devoted considerable attention to the class struggle in capitalist countries but little to systematically studying the class structure.[1] In the Soviet case the neglect was caused mainly by the politics of Stalin's rule, which brought the study of class effectively to a halt. Major Soviet studies on class in general and specifically on American class structure began to appear only in the 1960s.

Soviet analyses of the class struggle, and even of politics itself, are incomprehensible without an understanding of what the Soviets mean by class now that they have further developed their perspectives on class structure in advanced capitalist societies.

Classes and Other Components of Society

Any number of classification systems may be used to distinguish persons according to race, ethnic identity, religion, income, wealth, perquisites, or social status. Each system normally produces a few neat categories, many that overlap, exceptions, and gray areas—not to mention endless disputes among specialists over almost every aspect involved in constructing classification systems.

It is not surprising that, despite the efforts Soviet scholars have expended in studying class since the 1950s, complete clarity has not been achieved.

Like many readers of Marx–Engels's works, Soviet analysts were strongly attracted to the simple, fundamental division of capitalist society into two classes, variously called the bourgeoisie and the proletariat, the capitalist class and the working class, the exploiting class and the exploited class, or the ruling class and the oppressed class. Marx and Engels then subdivided the classes into a few components such as the petty bourgeoisie and the *Lumpenproletariat*. This essentially two-class scheme without nuances remained the orthodox interpretation in the Soviet Union for many years.

Following Stalin's death Soviet studies of class structure began to develop on the basis of intense study of the collected works of Marx–Engels and Lenin. The first result was a differentiation in the Soviet understanding of class when some Soviet analysts quoted Lenin's 1917 statement that "in capitalist and semicapitalist society we know of only three classes: the bourgeoisie, the petty bourgeoisie (the peasantry being its chief example), and the proletariat" (Lenin 1958–1965, vol. 34, 292). A debate ensued over whether there are two classes, as the old orthodoxy required, or three, as Lenin had plainly stated. Most Soviets adopted the policy of clearly delineating two classes and leaving the status of the petty bourgeoisie indefinite. Then a major writer on class insisted that there are only two classes, firmly denying that the petty bourgeoisie was a class (Semenov 1969). During the ensuing debate it was asserted, although on one occasion only, that there are four classes: the bourgeoisie and proletariat constitute the basic classes and the peasantry and urban petty bourgeoisie the nonbasic classes.[2]

The argument revolves around sharply differing perceptions of the petty bourgeoisie's status at various points in the development of capitalist societies. Whether or not a particular Soviet writer views that group as a class, and whether it is correct to speak of simply the ruling class rather than the ruling classes, as some Soviets do, there is a consensus that in the long run the petty bourgeoisie will at least drastically shrink in size, if not disappear completely. Most of its members are expected to be ruined economically in the merciless competitive struggle with the monopolies and thereby be forced to become proletarians. In the meantime, since the petty bourgeoisie remains an especially important factor in forming the psychological outlook of the bourgeoisie as a whole, it plays a significant role in defining the relations between or among the classes (Baichorov 1982; Diligenskii and others 1985).

If the Soviets maintained that American social structure is composed of only two or three classes, it would be a relatively simple matter to determine each person's class status. But since they have identified several additional social components to which individuals may be assigned rather than to classes, determining an individual's social status has been a problem.

Lenin was one source of more categories for differentiating the components of American society. He had subdivided the bourgeoisie into the monopolies and the financial oligarchy. Additionally, some terms that the Soviets use to describe their own social structure have been applied to the United States: "the intelligentsia," a category composed of highly educated people working in academe, science, the arts, and technology, and "employees," comprising office workers and technicians, are among them.

These components are called "strata," "intermediate strata," or "middle strata." Confusion in distinguishing between strata and intermediate strata flows from the very definition of strata, which is ambiguous. Strata can be "intermediate or transitional social groups which do not have all the characteristics of a class," in which case they exist outside the two, or three, classes. But they can also be "parts of a class, parts of its internal structure" (Arzumanian and others, eds. 1963, 31; Semenov 1969; Shneerson 1961). In practice, most Soviet authors use "strata" to designate parts of classes and the terms "intermediate strata" or "middle strata" to designate such nonclass components as the intelligentsia and employees. An example of a stratum that is part of a class would be the "middle bourgeoisie," an ill-defined and amorphous category existing between the big and the petty bourgeoisie.

Finally, further differentiations are made when Soviet writers identify "elements" within the strata and then even smaller "social groups." Within the proletariat, elements would be the skilled, semiskilled, and unskilled workers. White-collar workers ("employees," in Soviet terminology) are divided into social groups consisting of office workers, service employees, teachers, and laboratory technicians.

The typical order in analyzing American social structure is to discuss classes (*klassy*), then strata (*sloi*), intermediate strata (*promezhutochnye sloi*) or middle strata (*srednie sloi*), elements (*prosloiki*), and social groups (*sotsial'nye gruppy*).

As the Soviets published more analyses of class, the analytical terminology grew in complexity and much of it is not yet fixed and fully defined.[3] If in many respects this terminological fluidity is confusing, positively it means that they are developing a more sophisticated understanding of the complex dynamics of social differentiation in contemporary capitalist societies. The simple traditional image of single combat between proletariat and bourgeoisie has been modified to take into account the various components found in these societies, whether they exist within the classes or outside them.

The most comprehensive Soviet study of class structure in the United States is still Anatolii Mel'nikov's book published in 1974, whose title translated into English is *The Contemporary Class Structure of the U.S.A.* It embodies best the more highly nuanced approach toward social structure resulting from both the more sophisticated social science analyses that became possible in the Soviet political and intellectual climates since Stalin's death and also shifts in Soviet perceptions of the growing complexity of American society itself that have been engendered by rapidly changing modern technology. Even so, Mel'nikov and all other Soviet analysts, whatever social changes and differentiation they may highlight, still envisage an ultimate polarization of society produced by the operation of what the veteran Americanist Sergei Dalin called the Marxian "law of social development which leads to the unification of all persons who work as hired laborers, i.e., of the absolute majority of the population, in the struggle against the domination of finance capital" (1972, 408–9; Burlatskii and Galkin 1985).

Increasing social differentiation does not ultimately matter since it does not obliterate the fundamental division of society into those who own the means of production and those who do not. Still, the differentiation complicates matters enough to create some roadblocks to unifying all the nonowners in the struggle against the owners. Thus establishing the existing and changing extent of differentiation has a very practical importance to Soviets engaged in analyzing the current stage and state of the class struggle. These pragmatic considerations allow Soviet specialists to study social differentiation so long as they give recognition to the ideological expectation that it will eventually be replaced by polarization.

In developing more differentiated approaches, most writers have continued to reject as unscientific Western studies of social stratification simply because they do not relate individuals to the means of production in terms of ownership or nonownership. In particular, the existence of a middle class has been stoutly denied, as has the reality of any *significant* upward social mobility.[4] Because these authors define class as they do, there can be no middle ground between ownership and nonownership and thus no middle class in any meaningful sense. Given that, the only social mobility that can take place between classes is the relatively huge number of cases in which owners of productive property lose their ownership—or the insignificantly small number of instances in which nonowners manage to become owners of productive property. This is the very common downward mobility of the petty bourgeoisie, especially family farmers, and the relatively rare upward mobility into the ranks of the bourgeoisie of either the proletarians or people from the intermediate strata, the middle strata, or the elements.

Some analysts began to move cautiously beyond the fixation upon ownership/nonownership to determine membership in the two basic classes. They used Lenin's more expansive definition of class as justification (1958–1965, vol. 39, 15):

> Classes are large groups of people differing from each other by the place they occupy in a historically determined system of social production, by their relation (in most cases fixed and formulated in law) to the means of production, by their role in the social organization of labor, and, consequently, by the dimensions and mode of acquiring the share of social wealth at their disposal. Classes are groups of people, one of which can appropriate the labor of another owing to the different places they occupy in a definite system of social economy.

In Lenin's first sentence the owner/non-owner element is either almost or totally equated with a number of other ways of distinguishing among groups of people. The second sentence reverts to the more classical Marxist formula. On the basis of the flexibility inherent in the first sentence, Anatolii Mel'nikov extended somewhat the limits of the owner/nonowner factor and so produced a more realistic treatment of upward and downward social mobility as significant aspects of American life. Specifically, he had no qualms about identifying upward mobility—understood as obtaining a better job—as a widespread fact of life, provided that this was not taken to mean massive deproletarianization (Mel'nikov 1974).[5] Only by becoming a substantial owner of productive property, and not simply a small shareholder, can a person clearly and unequivocally quit the proletariat.

Of all the authors treating the American class structure Mel'nikov took most seriously the differences in status within the working class created by factors such as variations in the skill levels of different occupations, wages and salaries, the type of industry in which a person is employed, educational level, and ethnic origin.[6] Nevertheless, even if significant upward mobility occurs because of changes in these factors, the fact of ownership or nonownership of productive property, or of working for hire or not, remains basic in determining a person's ultimate membership in one of the two fundamental classes. Even though the income of some workers may increase markedly and they may move up in many real senses, the fact that they work for hire is for Mel'nikov still the key to comprehending the ultimate commonality of interests of everybody in American society excepting the capitalists, the big bourgeoisie, the ruling circles, the owners.

It is clearly significant that innovative analysts like Mel'nikov ultimately come to the same conclusion as other Soviet writers. But the no less significant difference between the two is that the former do not portray the American working class's situation as unrelievedly bleak and growing worse. Nor do they envisage as imminent a polarization of society into a handful of extremely rich people and a mass of extremely impoverished proletarians—the image typically created by earlier SMC analysts. Writers like Mel'nikov readily admit that some blue-collar workers are relatively well off, but they maintain that the status of these workers is precarious because they remain essentially and ultimately at the mercy of those owners whose means of production they are hired to operate.

In the meantime, however, it is possible to communicate a much more realistic picture of the differing conditions of the various parts of the working class than analysts of the SMC persuasion either could or would allow themselves to do. The SMC approach accentuated negative phenomena and encouraged analysts to write as if the negative were typical—or even universal.

A similarly differentiated approach was taken by Mel'nikov and others toward managers. They took as their starting point the fact that managers, just like workers, are hired by the owners, who may also remove them. These writers were very much aware of the analyses by Adolph A. Berle, Gardiner Means, James Burnham, and others, that power could exist without property and that corporate managers had just such power. Their counterargument was that, *whenever challenged,* the owners' ideas, policies, and power prevailed over the managers'. Moreover, they insisted that most top managers cannot usually be included in the category of the big bourgeoisie: along with the middle and lower level managers, they belong to either the petty bourgeoisie or one of the intermediate strata (Men'shikov 1969; Beglov 1971; Mel'nikov 1974).

This combination of simplicities and complexities in the discussion of class has resulted in various estimates of the overall composition of class structure in the United States. However, only two of these are comparable enough to contrast because of the unresolved issues mentioned earlier and the very serious problems involved in transposing American social statistical categories into Soviet ones.[7] Zagladina's percentages (unfortunately, she gives an absolute figure only for 1970) in Table 1 indicate that the working-class proportion of the population has not increased appreciably, while the petty bourgeoisie has declined markedly. Most important, the members of the intermediate strata have increased sharply in number, particularly those she has called the "toiling strata of the intelligentsia" (highly qualified specialists, scientists, physicians, attorneys, and dentists), who comprised 10.9% of the gainfully employed civilian population in 1970. The remainder of the intermediate strata includes middle-level administrative personnel, small stockbrokers, and traveling salesmen (Anikin, ed. 1972).

Zagladina does not draw the conclusions that flow from her statistics, namely, that the shrinking size of the petty bourgeoisie has not resulted in the significant expansion of the proletariat that

Table 3–1. Class Structure of Civilian Gainfully Employed Population*

	Mel'nikov 1971		Zagladina		
	Millions	%	1947 %	1960 %	1970 %
Working class/proletariat	56.7	67.4	73.9	74.3	75.1
Petty bourgeoisie	7.6	9.0	17.1	12.4	9.5
Bourgeoisie	3.5	4.2	2.4	3.0	2.9
Intermediate strata	16.3	19.4	6.6	10.3	12.5
Totals	84.1	100.0	100.0	100.0	100.0

*Except for S.M. Zagladina's percentages for the working class, which actually include unemployed workers and would therefore comprise 61 million persons in 1970. See Vozchikov and others, eds. 1974, where Zagladina gives and explains the percentage figure for the working class and says on p. 35 that it totaled 61 million in 1970.

Sources: Mel'nikov 1974, 299; Zagladina is in Vozchikov and others, eds. 1974, 30.

has long been predicted by Soviet analysts. Rather, the shrinkage has been accompanied by an unexpected growth in the *nonclass* social components, the intermediate strata. These striking changes were primarily the result of shifts in the occupational structure wrought by technological change, which, it should be stressed, will continue.

Mel'nikov's 1971 statistics show a surprisingly large bourgeoisie, at least to people steeped in reading ritualistic Soviet statements over the years about the "handful" of exploiters that dominate capitalist countries—three and one-half million is some handful! As compared with Zagladina's statistics for 1970 on the working class, Mel'nikov's calculations for 1971 show the diminished weight of that class when unemployed persons are not included. And Mel'nikov's data indicate that the intermediate strata are greater in number than Zagladina had suggested.

These shifts have had the significant effect of increasing the number of conflicts taking place within the classes.

Conflict Within Classes

Because the two basic classes are not completely homogeneous in their composition, the differences within each class create intra-class conflicts. The dimensions of this problem are significant enough to complicate the nature and actual conduct of the class struggle. In Marxian social analysis, classes are seen as passing through long phases of formation, development, and, finally, transformation. At various points within these phases the members of the classes manifest a higher or lower level of consciousness of their class interests than at other points. But the overall anticipated tendency is for an ever higher degree of class consciousness and solidarity to develop. Were these two indicators to reach very high levels, it would be a sign that a revolution could be in the immediate offing.

At any point in this developmental process a Soviet writer could analyze the performance of a class as a whole acting against the opposed class, or of the behavior of the major or lesser components of a class. Some of the smaller parts could play a larger role than their size would suggest in determining either the psychology of the entire class or the strategic power position they hold at a specific time in a specific place. In their analyses the Soviets stress one of these elements or combine them in various mixes. These differences in focus and approach create variety in the interpretation of the class situation in the United States.

The unexpected conclusion emerging from a survey of the Soviet writing on class is that almost as much attention has been paid to conflict within classes as to conflict between classes. Nonclass sources of conflict have received about as much attention as have class sources.

The Bourgeoisie

Since the bourgeoisie is the dominant actor in the SMC model and in the Soviet analysis of bourgeois democracy, some of its divisions and the resulting conflicts have already been discussed. These and other conflicts originate when the various factions within the bourgeoisie perceive their immediate or long-range interests differently.

The major divisive issues within the bourgeoisie have been the questions of the need for, the extent of, and the precise nature of state economic and social intervention.[8] The Soviets believe that the state must intervene in order to preserve the capitalist system, but the aims of such intervention are not always correctly perceived by all components of the bourgeoisie. Starting from the proposition that interest is the basis of political activity, Valentin Zorin concluded that "an integral quality of capitalists is the narrowness of thinking which is inevitably characteristic of them, and the inability to see anything further than the immediate interests of their business. How many respectable businessmen damned F. Roosevelt in horror, declaring him to be an advocate of socialism in the White House, at a time when Roosevelt's programs were the only salvation for American capitalism which had been undermined by the great crisis" (1964, 548).[9]

Zorin both condemned the archetypal individualistic capitalist and considered it a fact of life that governmental intervention in both the individual's and the corporation's affairs had become necessary to preserve what inevitably had to be, because of new conditions, a now limited individual and corporate initiative. World War II accelerated the process of intervention. In 1946, when to write in this vein was dangerous in itself because the Soviets still officially considered the state to be the absolute supporter of the entire bourgeoisie, Evgenii Varga cautiously noted that in the recent war "the bourgeois state as the organization of the entire bourgeoisie was on the whole compelled to try to subordinate by force the particular interests of particular enterprises and particular persons to the interests of carrying on the war" (1946, 18).[10] In war and peace both the degree and nature of state intervention created conflicts within the bourgeoisie.

Another major battle, also interest oriented, has been between those who favor using methods of force to keep the proletariat quiescent and those preferring to institute reforms and grant concessions (Marinin 1967a). These issues have been constantly addressed in Soviet discussions of bourgeois democracy.

Analyzing the process through which the interests of individual capitalists and firms are limited has been troublesome. Some authors started from the proposition that the monopolies have common or general interests (Boichenko 1970) and concluded that the state's function is to limit the interests of specific monopolies when they conflict with the common or general interest (Men'shikov 1964, ed. 1964; Varga 1968; Kovaleva 1969). But other analysts have maintained that there are times when the state does not limit some monopolies on behalf of the monopolies' general interest but rather does so on behalf of the predominant monopolies (Levin and Tumanov, eds. 1974). And Sergei Chetverikov suggested, taking a risky position, that there is no unity of views among the ruling circles as to what their general interest is (1974). This seems to have been another way of suggesting that perhaps there is no such thing as a general or common set of interests.

Other analysts opted for an explanation, based upon pandemic conflict among the bourgeoisie, vaguely reminiscent of the clash of interest groups at the basis of American pluralist theory: "The domestic and foreign political course of the U.S. government is worked out as a result of the behind the scenes struggles of groups of monopoly capital in the U.S.A. and the greater or lesser predominance at a given stage of the interests of one of the groups or of a coalition of groups" (Trofimenko 1959, 56). What distinguishes this approach from American group conflict explanations is that policymaking is strictly limited here to interactions among big business interests, and no one else participates.

Several of these approaches were combined to create a fuller range of possibilities: "Monopoly capital is itself not of a piece but consists of many financial–industrial coalitions which are in a state of constant and sharp competitive struggle among themselves." The economic rivalry has political consequences because "whichever coalition wins posts in the government uses them not only in the general interest of the monopoly bourgeoisie and against the workers but also in its own economic interests" (Zorin, ed. 1971, 371).

Another conflict within the dominating class stems from its division into the monopoly and nonmonopoly components. One method used by the nonmonopoly bourgeoisie to preserve itself from being completely overcome by the monopolies is antitrust legislation (Zhidkov 1976; Dragilev and others, eds. 1975). In addition, a group of American establishment writers, including Gardiner Means and Rexford Tugwell, who were critical of the growth of the monopolies' size, mounted an attack on the theoretical level (Kozlova 1966). The antitrust laws have been criticized as ineffective (Dragilev and others, eds. 1975; Bel'son 1960), but the "bourgeois critics" of monopoly were applauded for articulating what was seen as a growing protest against increasing monopoly domination launched by the farmers, the urban petty bourgeoisie, the intelligentsia, white-collar employees, and small and middle-sized entrepreneurs (Kozlova 1966). However, and this is typical of mindset attitudes, Kozlova criticized those critics on the grounds that their stated aim of reforming capitalism is unrealizable.

A number of analysts point out that in the struggle between the big and petty bourgeoisie the middle strata have tended to support the latter. Taken together, the petty bourgeoisie and the middle strata come close to constituting what has long been considered the "middle class" in the United States, or what Americans began calling "middle America" starting in the late 1960s, or "the new middle class" in the 1980s. But owing to the extreme political and ideological instability always characteristic of the middle strata, and nowadays common to "the new middle strata," they sometimes have not supported the bourgeoisie, either big or petty, but were attracted to various of the positions supported by the proletariat.[11] On the other hand, the middle strata have been identified as the mainstay of right-wing extremism. The major study of the American far right concluded: "Rich businessmen representing the top of the middle strata of the U.S. population constitute the backbone of the ultra right movement" (Nikitin 1971, 382).

In addition to these conflicts over domestic policy matters, the bourgeoisie has split over foreign policy issues. Depending upon what portion of their business interests lies abroad at any given moment or over time, and depending upon the extent to which their profits derive from defense contracts, the major corporations may or may not favor an aggressive foreign policy, expanding trade and improving political relations with the socialist nations, and they may or may not have supported the Vietnam War (Zorin 1964; Gromyko 1968; Zorin, ed. 1971; Anikin, ed. 1972; Shamberg 1968b; Bugrov 1970).[12]

However serious the intrabourgeois disputes and splits may be, the Soviets conclude that the American bourgeoisie has not been as deeply or seriously disunited as have many of its counterparts in Europe. In substantiation, they point to the numerous bourgeois political parties that exist in many a European country, whereas in the United States there have been two, and only two, significant parties representing the interests of the bourgeoisie—the Democrats and the Republicans. The reasons cited for the existence of only two bourgeois parties are the political weakness of the American labor movement (as compared to labor's strength in European countries) and the relative effectiveness of the American bourgeoisie's total control over the political system (Levin, ed. 1964b).

In treating the question of who controls the political system, a small group of analysts noted that because the monopolies' basic common interest in system maintenance activities has led to the creation of an American "political elite whose function is to ensure the stability of the existing order and the normal functioning of the entire state and sociopolitical mechanism and which is therefore obliged to take into account the interests and demands of all classes and strata of society" (Iakovlev, ed. 1969, 134). This statement was surprising and risky because the concept of political elite had long been attacked and rejected in Soviet writing. Allegedly, in the West this "vague" term (the elite) was used to delude the workers by masking the actual political control exercised by the ruling class, which supposedly was very clearly specified in Marxist writing.[13] The rare use of "political elite" by a Soviet writer in a positive analytical sense was a milestone.

The political elite concept was developed further by Fedor Burlatskii and Aleksandr Galkin in their groundbreaking study of sociopolitical leadership, another topic that had not been treated systematically by Soviet social scientists (1974). They argued that the political elite must take into account the interests of all classes in society because the electoral system provides feedback (an important concept that these authors helped introduce into Soviet writing). To ignore totally the interests of so many societal components might lead to very serious political trouble at election time (1974). In this formulation the extraordinary thing was the recognition that elections do act as a political weathervane, and that they are not merely the subterfuge that many writers in the SMC and bourgeois democracy traditions had made them out to be. Nevertheless, the analysts who maintain that a political elite exists have not advanced very far in clarifying the nature of the conflicts engendered within the bourgeoisie by its need to consider the interests of the nonbourgeoisie. These analysts had to discover and describe that functional need prior to looking at concrete activities and situations. The first steps in the latter direction are just being taken (Burlatskii and Galkin 1985).

Attempts at resolving the analytical problem posed by intramonopoly struggles have produced various explanations, none of which has proven satisfactory to Soviet Americanists for one or another reason. The narrowest and ideologically preferable solution, the concept of the bourgeoisie's general or common class interest, has been found wanting. The broadest solution in the form of the political elite concept ran into the limits of ideological tolerability, although lately it has enjoyed increasing acceptability. This is not an insurmountable problem, and one can have the best of both worlds. In an illuminating policy study of the American race problem Igor Geevskii produced a very realistic analysis of disagreements among the bourgeoisie. He analyzed intraclass conflict over the issue of racial discrimination and thereby controverted the usual Soviet depiction of ruling-class solidarity when dealing with the problem. Just to ensure that he not be accused of overstepping the boundaries of orthodoxy, he concluded his book by stating flatly, but without adducing any specific examples, that these disparities did not go "beyond the interests of the dominating class" (1973, 330). Such statements are a typical Soviet ploy intended to be ideologically reassuring. Their practical meaning is not easy to demonstrate, and Geevskii sensibly did not try.

The Proletariat

Since they identify the bourgeoisie as the exploiting class, mainstream Soviet writers have generally considered conflicts within it as positive and have analyzed them with alacrity, not to mention a certain relish. Conversely, conflict among the proletarians is viewed negatively, always in sorrow, sometimes even in bewilderment. Disapprovingly, it is normally discussed in terms of disunity or splits (*raskoly*—literally, schisms) in the ranks of the working class. This bespeaks the anger and frustration with which Soviet authors view the failure of the American working class to unite, and also the reluctance of the analysts to apply the term "conflict" to anything but the class conflict or to conflicts within the bourgeoisie.

The two main tests for membership in the proletariat are nonownership of productive property and working for hire as a wage earner or, with some exceptions, a salaried earner. Historically, Marxist writers normally used the nonownership criterion to identify and establish a person's proletarian status and then discussed working for hire in the course of their analyses of exploitation. But in recent Soviet writing on the American proletariat working for hire has become more important than nonownership.

This shift occurred in response, and as a counter, to Western theories asserting that large portions of the work force have been deproletarianized, are upwardly mobile, have attained a higher standard of living, have experienced embourgeoisement, and so on. If many American analysts were impressed by the growing numbers of white collars in the United States and took that as a sign of an exodus from the working class, most Soviet analysts maintain that significant numbers of white-collar employees are members of the proletariat because they still work for hire. Movement from a blue- to a white-collar job is considered a change in occupational status, not class status—it is a movement upward within the ranks of the proletariat. Nevertheless, the Soviets concede that significant consequences flow from the massive shifts from blue- to white-collar jobs because the quality of the proletariat is upgraded since more of its members are better educated and more highly skilled. Beginning in the 1960s, therefore, the Soviets have stressed that industrial workers comprise only a part of the proletariat, and a diminishing one at that.

To an extent the Soviet shift in emphasis toward the working for hire criterion responds to some significant changes in the source of income of a substantial proportion of the population since 1900. If at that time the absolute majority of Americans consisted of private owners of productive property (with small farmers, merchants, craftsmen, and small and medium-sized capitalists predominating), the proportions were dramatically reversed as small businesses collapsed and family farms were abandoned.[14] Millions of people who formerly would have been self-employed now worked for hire.

At the same time, care has been taken to establish that not all persons working for hire in the United States are members of the proletariat, a social class. Although members of the intelligentsia also generally work for hire, they are not included in the working class because in this instance the Soviets use the classification system they apply to their own society and consider them a social stratum. As is the case with all intermediate strata, they find within the intelligentsia conflicting developmental tendencies that result sometimes in proletarianization, sometimes in bureaucratization. There is even a tendency toward commercialization to the extent that some members of the intelligentsia in effect leave their intermediate social stratum and become substantial businessmen, thereby joining the ranks of the bourgeoisie (Mel'nikov 1974). Of course, higher managerial personnel also work for hire. But because they directly organize the production process (that is, the process of exploitation in capitalist society, as far as Soviet analysts are concerned), and since they receive huge salaries, bonuses, and stock options, they appropriate some surplus value just as the capitalists do. So the topmost group of managers, "despite the purely external aspect of having been hired, is turning into a growing element of the big, and even the monopoly, bourgeoisie" (Mel'nikov 1974, 210; Arzumanian and others, eds. 1963).

With these exceptions and qualifications in mind, it makes sense at this point to reproduce Mel'nikov's definition of the proletariat, the clearest one so far essayed in the Soviet Union: the proletariat is "the class of hired workers [*rabotniki*] who are deprived of the means of production and therefore live by the sale of their labor power, are subjected to capitalist exploitation, and fulfill purely executive functions in the spheres of production, exchange, office work, and services" (1974, 53).

For many years Soviet writers avoided systematically investigating differentiation within the American proletariat. Concerned primarily with tracking the struggle of the working class against the bourgeoisie, they developed an image of a monolithic proletariat based on the homogeneity of its class interests in that struggle. To be sure, they were aware of the disunity among the workers in economic and political struggles, but they ascribed that to the machinations of the class enemy (the bourgeoisie) as well as to the perfidy of both the labor aristocracy (the most highly paid workers) and the trade union leaders who sold out the interests of the workers and in effect sided with the exploiters. Aside from these elements, the remainder of the proletariat seemed of one, single piece. Mel'nikov was therefore forced to dredge up quotations from Marx and Lenin, relying especially upon some widely scattered remarks by Lenin, when he argued for a differentiated approach to the composition of the working class (1974).

The first tentative systematic studies that recognized differentiation within the American working class were published in the 1960s. Major advances were made in the 1970s. In the later studies the basic distinction made is between the people working in the sphere of material production (heavy and light industry, transportation, construction, agriculture) and workers in the nonproduction sphere (office workers and merchandising and service sector personnel). Another major distinction is between workers in industry and those in agriculture. Other divisions are made according to the branch of industry in which a person is employed, skill level, race, sex, geographical location and unemployment.[15]

Imposing though this enumeration may seem, the divisions themselves were not probed until recently. And there are no major analyses of some factors—race, sex, and geographical location, for instance. This curious situation arose because, until the late 1960s, the Soviets did not devote their attention to the working class as a whole but focused intensely upon what they called its "organized sector," the labor unions. As a consequence, the major cleavage that the Soviets perceive in the American proletariat is between union members and the majority, who belong to no union. By 1970 only slightly over 60% of all American manual workers (*rabochie*) and only a third of all persons working for hire were unionized (Shishkin 1972). The overwhelming majority of the proletariat has been unorganized—or, even worse, disorganized. The Soviets blame this on the indifference of the union leaders ("the union bureaucrats," in the preferred Soviet terminology) with expanding membership (Androsov 1971; Grechukhin and others, eds. 1970).

Within organized labor the basic split is between the leaders and the rank-and-file workers who have generally been portrayed as being increasingly in revolt against the leadership as their interests have diverged (Mkrtchian 1973; Lapitskii 1973). But even while noting that he shared this view, Lapitskii took a critical step warning against oversimplifying the nature and course of that struggle because, he said, the leaders were "sometimes" genuinely popular among the workers. He also cautioned against overestimating the significance of those struggles since many rank-and-file revolts against the leaders were better described as internal power struggles than as the battles between the progressive and conservative forces the Soviets were inclined to see (Lapitskii 1973).[16]

Working-class unity was also undermined by the uneven geographical distribution of unionized workers. Not only were most concentrated in a few regions, particularly the Northeast and Midwest, but by 1969 over 40% of union membership was concentrated in four branches of the economy: transportation, metallurgy, machine building, and construction (Lapitskii 1973; Androsov 1971). Fragmentation within the unions themselves was rampant: the myriad unions differed over questions of organizational structure, whether to join the AFL–CIO or remain independent, and in their liberal or conservative orientation (Grechukhin and others, eds. 1970; Lapitskii 1973; Androsov 1971).

Ethnic and racial factors created more divisions. The multiethnic composition of the American working class inhibited the growth of unity, particularly since historically there had been a hierarchy of workers based on ethnic origin with the WASPs on top (Geevskii 1962; Mel'nikov 1974). The union leaders primarily have been to blame for racial discrimination in the unions, then the monopolists, the "backward portion of the masses" or the "racial moods" found among the workers themselves, and, finally, racist propaganda (Lapitskii 1973; Androsov 1971; Grechukhin and others, eds. 1970; Nikitin 1971).

Changes in occupational structure produced further differences, which had the dual effect of expanding the number of proletarians but also contributing toward disunity within the proletariat. The proportion of "the industrial proletariat" among all hired workers declined from 52.8% in 1947 to 43.6% in 1970.[17] The watershed year was 1956: for the first time in American history there were more white-collar than blue-collar workers.[18] The Soviets have been careful to stress what they see as the real and positive significance of this process: "It is not the proletariat which dissolves into the 'new middle class,' as the bourgeois sociologists attempt to prove, but rather increasingly numerous groups of white collar employees are reduced to proletarian status" (Gauzner 1968, 71 [quotation]; Shishkin 1972; Mel'nikov 1974).

But no blessings are unmixed. Mel'nikov observed that this influx into the proletariat of people who were formerly petty bourgeois, along with the growth of the proletariat working in the nonproduction sphere, resulted in the penetration of bourgeois ideology into the proletarian ranks (1974). Commenting on some aspects of this problem in his major study of classes in capitalist societies, Semenov made an intriguing distinction between "the worker, the proletarian" and "the new hired laborer" (1969, 356). Placing the intelligentsia and employees in the latter category, Semenov refused to recognize them as proletarians, maintaining that his more conventionally and narrowly defined "working class," composed of proletarians in the strictest sense of the term, was a more progressive and revolutionary force than either the intelligentsia or the employees.

Even at the time of its publication this was very much a minority position among Soviet scholars, and somewhat old-fashioned. Yet Semenov was wrestling with a basic problem not addressed by the partisans of the broader definition of "proletariat." In it the intelligentsia and the employees practically disappear as intermediate strata, since most members of these components are considered to be proletarians. Given the important political roles these strata play, their repositioning creates serious problems in analyzing the class struggle.

Disunity within the proletariat has also been encouraged by the bourgeoisie through the incessant propagation of bourgeois ideas in the media and through attempts to buy off the more skilled workers—the worker aristocracy (Mel'nikov 1974; Androsov 1971; Vainshtein 1971). But because technological progress has been eliminating many of the old skilled jobs, the worker aristocracy has been in decline since World War II, only to be replaced in its "bought off" role by the worker bureaucracy—the union leaders. As technological progress has erased many differences between blue- and white-collar jobs it has also accelerated the segmentation of the working class (Mikhailov 1988).

The unions' political roles also create splits. Unions have differed in their degree of participation in politics generally and in their support for the Democratic party. Some have supported the Republicans; some have denied their support to any party in national elections; and, in New York City, some locals supported the Liberal party (Lapitskii 1973). Although the rank-and-file generally supported the Democrats, a disconcerting 15% supported George Wallace in 1968 with young workers constituting a significant part of that percentage (Lapitskii 1973; Grechukhin and others, eds. 1970).

The magnitude of American working-class disunity is most arrestingly demonstrated by the absence of an organized mass labor party. To the Soviets this means that "the organized sector" of the working class lacks the cohesion to organize and conduct its own independent political activity. Lacking its own political party, through which it could articulate and assert its interests on a nationwide scale, labor has been easily used and manipulated by the two major parties for their own purposes. This is the specific reason why the Soviets deeply regret that there is no labor party in the United States—for them the issue is fundamental (Androsov 1971; Shishkin 1972).

Curiously, little attention has been given to what the organizational characteristics and size of that party might be. It is therefore not clear whether that party would in fact be the American Communist party, following the model of the mass French and Italian Communist parties, a party on the model of the European Social Democratic parties, or a party separate from the Communist party but directed by it. If the increasing attention Soviet writers devoted to the American Communist party starting in the 1960s is any indication, it would seem that the first alternative is most likely.

There have been two paramount themes in Soviet analyses of the American Communist party.[19] The first stresses the party's leading role as vanguard of the proletariat in the class struggle. It quickly becomes evident that leadership is exercised mainly through the party's having an ideologically, tactically, and strategically correct program rather than through active organizational work among those to be led (see Boichenko 1970; Timofeev 1967). Many reasons have been given by Soviet writers to explain the party's lack of contact with its constituencies down through the decades, the chief of which is the defensive posture the party assumed because of the powerful attacks upon it during the 1950s in particular, and also because of the pervasive anticommunist mood fostered by the bourgeoisie in the postwar period. As the Soviets see it, the party itself is totally blameless.

The second basic theme in Soviet analyses of the American Communist party is the high level of disunity within it, a problem serious enough to be the subject of a lengthy book (Grechukhin 1975). The need to concentrate so much attention on managing dissension within the party inevitably weakened its capacity to exercise any kind of meaningful leadership over the proletariat.

In his report to the party's Nineteenth National Convention, Gus Hall identified two main negative consequences produced by all these factors. They are repeated by Soviet analysts: the party's membership was growing too slowly and the party had not yet managed to become the organizer of a mass struggle (Mostovets and others, eds. 1972). In other words, even the party's proximate aim had not been realized.

The Soviets contend that the composition of the working class has affected its political role. The numerous centrifugal tendencies identified in this chapter have undermined the labor movement's unity and have prevented the proletariat from organizing a successful class struggle. Rightly or wrongly, mainstream Soviet writers consider these phenomena to be temporary obstacles that will be overcome ultimately once the condition of the proletariat worsens sufficiently—however difficult it may be to establish precisely just what that level of worsening must be.

Meantime, the class struggle rages. But the specifics of that classic battle between bourgeoisie and proletariat turn out to be not so simple a matter as the Soviets had long thought.

4 HOW DO RULERS AND RULED INTERACT? THE CLASS STRUGGLE

In principle, Soviet writers could discuss all American politics as part of the class struggle. In practice, their writings on the class struggle cover a number of definite topics, some treated often, others receiving less attention.[1]

Despite the importance of class struggle to Marxist political analysis, there are few comprehensive Soviet studies of its American variant. Indeed, Petr Shishkin's landmark volume on the subject was published only in 1972—on the one hand rather late in the game, on the other not starting a trend, either.

The virtual demise of sociological studies in Stalin's time inhibited the development of full treatments of the class struggle, although the Soviets did analyze aspects that were salient during various historical periods. In the 1950s, for example, they studied the politics of the McCarthy era as a period of militant reaction. There was a shift toward economic problems in the early 1960s, then a swing to both political and social themes in the late 1960s, and a return to economic problems as the 1970s progressed.

The components typical of Soviet analyses can be structured out of this mass of shifting materials, and fundamental insights into the mindset can be garnered. As the Soviets explain it, the class struggle arises because the overwhelming majority of the people is in the exploited class: they do not own the means of production and they work for hire. Through their labor they add value to the commodities they produce or the services they provide, and they create profits for the owners of the means of production. The owners sell the commodities and charge for the services but return only a very small part of the profits as wages or salaries to the people working for them, thus exploiting the workers.

The exploited groups, particularly industrial workers, respond by engaging in an economic struggle to gain a larger share of the value created by their work. The chief weapon is the strike, used primarily by workers already organized into unions. The exploiting class responds politically by prevailing upon Congress and the state legislatures to pass antilabor laws either forbidding strikes outright or drastically limiting strike activity. These laws draw the government into the class struggle between labor and capital as a pseudo third party (in reality favoring capital) and tend to politicize the economic struggle. But full politicization is inhibited by the union leaders, most of whom undertake direct political activity only very reluctantly and limit it once they act. Moreover, whatever political activities do transpire are further limited and maneuvered into safe channels by the operation of bourgeois democracy.

The major conclusion the Soviets draw from this scheme is that labor's activities on its own economic behalf may now and then produce some substantial gains, but the political system continues to be controlled by the exploiting class. As a result the class struggle must be waged largely outside the framework of the political institutions and processes, taking the form of mass social movements. The strategy adopted in the 1950s by the American Communist party to conduct a successful class struggle in the conditions of post–World War II America was to forge an "alliance of democratic forces" and an "antimonopoly coalition." This would bring together the forces in American society that opposed the monopolies and their control of the political system as well as the policies the government pursued to bring the interests of the monopolies to fruition.

Bourgeoisie versus Proletariat

Exploitation and Countertrends

It is a classic Marxist tenet that capitalism is inherently exploitative and that the degree of exploitation grows over time. The basic form of exploitation is evident in both the high profits the owners of productive property receive and the low wages and salaries they pay to the people hired to operate these productive properties. Other forms of exploitation are unemployment, which deprives people of income or lowers their income substantially under compensation programs, overtime hours, speed-ups, moonlighting, the decline of real wages, automation, and wage and employment discrimination on the basis of sex (Mkrtchian 1973). Exploitation implies an ever-increasing impoverishment of the exploited groups.

Soviet analysts, however, have disagreed widely about how extensive the growing poverty of the American working class really is. They distinguish two forms of impoverishment, relative and absolute. Relative impoverishment results from a constant decline in the share of the total national income going to the working class as opposed to the increasing share that goes to the bourgeoisie. To establish the ratio between the two the Soviets take the total new value created in manufacturing industry in a given year and divide it by the total wages paid in the same period. Multiplying by 100 yields a percentage called either the rate of surplus value or the rate of exploitation.[2]

While the formula itself is simple, the Soviets have debated what the precise components of the formula's two elements ought to be, and a host of arguments over methodological questions has arisen (Varga 1968; Veber 1986). Nevertheless, the consensus has been that exploitation in the form of relative impoverishment has grown worse, particularly because of sharp increases in worker productivity. Although workers now produce much more per hour then ever before, their remuneration is proportionately less than ever.

But there have been disagreements over the extent of the increase in exploitation as well as over the nature of the exploitation and impoverishment. Particularly in the early 1960s, as Varga pointed out, many Soviet analysts overstated the extent and degree of these phenomena.[3]

Without becoming enmeshed in the technicalities involved or in the extensive criticisms that might be made, these are examples of conclusions two authors reach. Solomon Vygodskii calculated that in the American manufacturing industry the rate of exploitation was 125% in 1899 and that it increased to 312% in 1969.[4] Melaniia Kovaleva calculated the rate of exploitation at 145.6% in 1947 and 213.3% in 1964, the latter percentage representing the

$140,202,000,000 that the owners of the means of production received and the workers did not (1969). But then Kovaleva added to this all the taxes and collections taken from "the population" (excluding corporate taxes) and also made adjustments for price increases and concluded that in 1964 the rate of exploitation of workers in manufacturing industry reached "about 400%" (1969, 301). Calculations like these are one basis for the Soviet contention that exploitation in the United States is worse than ever despite gains the workers may have wrested from the capitalists.

The second form of exploitation, the absolute impoverishment of the proletariat, is the result of a decline in real wages. The major debate on this issue took place in the early 1960s between analysts who viewed the decline as constant and uninterrupted and those who saw it as intermittent and intermingled with periods of growth in real wages, though still showing an overall decline. Essentially, it was an argument between the proponents of Stalinist orthodoxy, Ivan Kuz'minov and Adol'f Kats, and the perennial gadfly, Varga. As was so often the case, Varga eventually carried the day, with at least Kuz'minov finally recognizing the validity of Varga's position.[5] And even Melaniia Kovaleva, in the last major restatement of many of the extremely conservative arguments, agreed that absolute impoverishment was not constant and uninterrupted (1969).

The dispute was based on analyses of trends and countertrends since the late 1800s. While not participating directly in that debate, and concentrating on the post–World War II period, Nikolai Gauzner determined that real wages in America had grown every year between 1947 and 1965 with the exception of 1951 (1968). If the real hourly wage in 1947 is taken as 100, the real hourly wage in 1965 was 141.1. But Gauzner qualified his analysis by devoting much attention to growing relative impoverishment—the extent to which labor productivity had outdistanced wages received. Gauzner attributed the growth in real wages to some recently created favorable conditions that allowed the workers to improve their position against the owners. He argued that the changed correlation of forces (balance of power) in the world arena between socialism and capitalism in favor of socialism helped make possible the higher real wages, albeit in ways that he avoided making clear. He made this ideological point to counterbalance his observation

on the growth of real wages that undermined ideological expectations (1968). Heightened labor union activity also contributed
to the growth in real wages (Vozchikov and others, eds. 1974).

Very few writers noted and attempted to explain the relatively
high general standard of living in the United States. Anatolii
Mel'nikov attributed it primarily to a labor force increasingly composed of skilled workers as well as to successes in the struggle of
the working class to attain a higher living standard. In addition,
he observed that the parasitism characteristic of advanced capitalism encourages the growth of the service sector of the economy,
which expands the services available to the entire population
(1974).

Igor Geevskii combined a number of explanations (1962). The
high standard of living exists because American capitalism developed in an exceptionally favorable environment (rich natural resources, large areas of free land, immigration of skilled labor) and
because the United States exploited foreign countries following
World War II. But to achieve that living standard workers were
forced to pay a high price in the form of excessive amounts of
physical and nervous energy expended on the job. Even worse,
the high living standard sowed "bourgeois illusions" among the
workers. They came to believe that capitalism could produce a
better life for them, which inhibited their accepting socialist ideas.[6]

Petr Shishkin coupled his brief observations on the comparatively high living standards with the remark, which he did not
develop further, that even this does not spare the American workers from severe exploitation, and they therefore remain an oppressed and exploited class (1972). Mel'nikov discussed this
situation at some length, contrasting widespread poverty in the
midst of relatively high wages (1987), while others documented
the complex ups and downs over time in the various components
of individual and family income and expenditures (Arbatov and
others, eds. 1988).

Melaniia Kovaleva neatly articulated the time-honored orthodox
position when she noted that even though the working class may
achieve some betterment of its situation under capitalism, really
fundamental improvement can be made only after the capitalist
system has been replaced by socialism (1969).

Stated otherwise, the Soviet mindset is deeply committed to the idea that whatever improvements the workers may achieve under capitalism the class struggle continues because the working class "is the chief object of capitalist exploitation and its toil is the source of the monopoly bourgeoisie's wealth" (Liven' 1975, 156). Another succinct expression of the mindset's conviction says: "Not only has the opposition of the basic interests of the toilers and the capitalists in the United States not disappeared . . . but on the contrary it has become even more obvious" (Baglai 1960, 83). Whatever its effects may be on American workers themselves, the high standard of living leaves mainstream Soviet analysts unimpressed. They continue to attack the notion that America can be described as a high consumption society for the majority of the people.[7]

The bourgeoisie attempts to camouflage exploitation by stressing cooperation, and downplaying conflict, between capitalists and workers. If in the nineteenth century capitalism tried to adopt a paternalistic image to diminish worker rage, the Wilson administration after World War I began to stress harmony between labor and management. Then a procession of variations on that theme followed: the "new capitalism" of Harvard professor Thomas Nixon Carver, union capitalism, profit sharing, social unionism, human relations, democratic capitalism, American exceptionality (the belief that Marxist analysis does not fit America's unique circumstances), people's capitalism, industrial democracy, the affluent society, and the like. The Soviets roundly criticized all these concepts (Timofeev 1967; Pavlov 1963; Khromushin 1969; Baglai 1960; Mshvenieradze 1985).

To assuage the proletariat's wrath the bourgeoisie couples ideological maneuvering with granting concessions to the workers through social legislation. Although the workers must struggle outside the political system, it grudgingly responds to the pressures they apply.

Additional concessions are won directly from the capitalists, particularly by the workers' "organized sector," through strikes. The Soviets study strikes within an established analytical framework (Mikhailov, ed. 1971; Shishkin 1972; Mkrtchian 1973). To determine the overall dynamics of strike activity, they collect basic data on the number of strikes per year, the number of participants in them, and the number of worker-days lost. Next they determine the length of strikes, concluding that after World War II and up to the mid–1960s strikes tended to last longer. They then identify specific periods of greater and lesser strike activity and the kinds of demands raised in the strikes, distinguishing between economic demands (e.g., higher wages) and noneconomic demands such as improved working conditions and the defense or advancement of union prerogatives. At this point they look at variations in the level of strike activity among different groups of workers as well as changes within each group over time. Here they compare steel workers, auto workers, teachers, and government employees. The final elements considered in the analysis are the geographical location of strikes and their timing in the collective bargaining process.

Strike activity, a constant part of life in the United States in the twentieth century, is considered the main arena for the economic struggle between labor and capital. Collective bargaining is yet another perpetual battle between the classes over the share of the social product of labor that is received by the owners and by the people they hire. The workers use it to expand their share, and when that fails they resort to strikes to diminish the degree of exploitation to which they are subjected.[8] This interpretation of strikes as directed against the economic system (and particularly the system of exploitation) stands in sharp contrast to conventional views in the United States, which rarely if ever link strikes with protest against the system.[9]

The Soviets view strikes as a decades-old economic struggle in which the monopolies eventually began to lose too much ground to the workers and therefore periodically turned for help to the state, which they controlled (Baglai 1960; Popov 1974; Sivachev 1972; Gromakov 1958). The state responded to these pressures when Congress adopted, and the executive branch put into effect, a series of antilabor laws. Typically of bourgeois democracy according to the Soviets, these laws established labor's right to strike but at the same time limited and undercut that right as much as possible. Overall, the effectiveness of strikes has been severely inhibited by all the labor laws starting with the Wagner Act up to and including the right to work laws adopted in several states.[10] Governmental intervention in labor-management disputes on behalf of management reached new heights in Nixon's New Economic Program of 1971–1972.

Political Activity

These events were critically significant: "The intensification of state intervention in the economy is the decisive reason for the transformation of the economic struggle between labor and capital into a political struggle for power" (Keremetskii 1970, 252). Sergei Dalin viewed the merger of the monopolies with the state as a major cause of the economic struggle's politicization (1961). It was in the 1950s and 1960s that the unions finally began moving beyond their traditional focus on economic issues and became concerned with expanding social and political rights during their campaigns against antilabor laws, racial discrimination, and the Vietnam War (Lapitskii 1973).

The Soviets have welcomed any shift on the part of American labor from economic activity toward political action as moving the class struggle forward markedly. On this point they follow quite literally Lenin's famous argument in his 1902 pamphlet *What Is to Be Done?* that struggle over economic issues produces only very limited results, whereas the political struggle, if assiduously pressed, will lead to the biggest prize—taking political power away from the exploiters and placing it in the hands of the proletariat.

The American working class's record has evoked frustration among Soviet analysts. Samuel Gompers started things badly in the late nineteenth century with his policy of "pure and simple unionism" or "business unionism." He denied the need for involvement in the complexities of politics and focused on the immediate economic concerns of the workers—precisely the opposite of what Lenin was to advise some years later. His pragmatism expressed in the slogan "An honest day's wage for an honest day's work" became the hallmark of American unionism and remained that until after World War II.[11]

The slogan's implications seem even worse to the Soviets than the refusal to engage in politics since earning an honest day's wage under exploitative capitalism is simply impossible. The slogan also implies a sharing of interests between worker and owner/manager, and indeed Gompers had in his day stressed the need for the two parties to cooperate rather than become locked in a struggle. For Soviet analysts there can be only diametrically opposed interests in this innately hostile relationship which breeds class struggle.

Nonetheless, despite adopting Gompers' ideology, the unions quickly became involved in politics. Still, the Soviets contend that union political activity was, and has remained, altogether too self-limiting (Lapitskii 1973; Grechukhin and others, eds. 1970; Rogova 1983). The Soviets would prefer to see a labor party created which would enable the workers to pressure the bourgeoisie directly during political campaigns and, more importantly, in the legislature. This is a far more meaningful and effective form of representation for the workers than the indirect method of lobbying (Lapitskii 1973; Rogova 1983). But desirable though a worker party may be, so far none has appeared. Instead, the union leadership consistently has supported the two-party system and has opposed forming a third party. Additionally, the concessions characteristic of the politics of SMC and bourgeois democracy have acted as a countervailing force to the development of class consciousness among the workers and therefore to the successful development of their struggle (Shishkin 1972; Lapitskii 1973; Androsov 1971).

Because the labor movement does not have its own political party and the union leadership refuses to entertain the idea of conducting what the Soviets call "independent political activity" through a labor party, the American movement is at a lower stage of development than the British, French, Italian, and Japanese movements that have such parties.[12] Admittedly, labor's political involvement has grown over the twentieth century through lobbying, the creation of the CIO's Political Action Committee in 1944, and even the adoption of programs of political activity such as the United Steel Workers' Legislative Education Program in the later 1950s (Shishkin 1972). But progress toward the goal of an independent labor party has been painfully slow.

In attempting to account for the "political passivity of the workers" and the "tendency within the worker movement toward conservatism and reformism," as the Soviets alternatively put it, a long list of reasons has been developed indicating that past performance has been weak and future promise is not very bright. Some causes are the workers' economic gains; the attacks launched against the Communist party, "progressive" unions, and nonconformists in general; "demagogic propaganda" that seeks to show the superiority of the private enterprise system and the open democratic society; the disorienting effect which the ideas of people's capitalism and the welfare state have had on the workers; the union leaders' active struggle against socialism and establishing a worker party; and the failure of the socialists to establish a mass base among workers and win their support for a worker party (Androsov 1971).

Anatolii Mel'nikov added as other causes the penetration of bourgeois ideology into the working class through the influx into that class of former petty bourgeois and white-collar employees, control of the media and their message by the bourgeoisie, the disunity produced by both the multiethnic composition of the population and the race problem, and the general disunity among the unions (1974). While noting the labor movement's overall conservatism, Burlatskii alone among the commentators saw a need to analyze the concrete circumstances of the various strata of workers to explain that conservatism (1970).

But neither he nor any other Soviet writer has yet produced such a differentiated analysis. And nowhere in Soviet published works is there a systematic, comprehensive discussion of worker gains. In fact, the most complete listing of them in any Soviet source takes up less than half a page (Vozchikov and others, eds. 1974). Rather, Soviet writers have concentrated on the bourgeoisie's social policies, already discussed, of keeping the workers quiet through granting concessions, and they placed even greater emphasis on the negative role played by the leadership of the major unions.

Soviet criticisms of unions and union leadership are directed at the mainstream unions and not the few unions labeled "progressive" by the Soviets. Nor were they applied to a small number of innovative mainstream leaders like Walter Reuther of the United Auto Workers. The remarks target the major leaders of the major unions, the backbone of the movement.

In a normal advanced capitalist society there would be a worker party (usually called a Social Democratic party) which claims to assert the workers' interests but, according to the customary Soviet analysis, in fact plays a conciliatory role, trying to reduce the level of class conflict. Because there is no such party in the United States, that mediating role is played by the union leadership (Androsov 1964). Put in the severe terms the Soviets often use to describe this situation, the union bureaucracy acts as the monopolies' accomplice, and the labor leadership's policies practically coincide with those condemned decades ago by Lenin: "However strange the words may sound, yet in a capitalist country the working class can also follow a bourgeois policy if it forgets about its liberating aims, tolerates hired slavery, and limits itself to concern over uniting with now one and then another bourgeois party for the sake of imaginary 'improvements' in its enslaved status" (1958–1965, vol. 22, 232).

The chief indictments against the labor leaders are that they try to keep the class struggle in the economic realm, not permitting it to become political, and that their objective is to stabilize relations between labor and capital through preaching class cooperation (Androsov 1971). But at least one analyst doubted that the union leaders could play that role successfully: "Having become essentially a part of the economic and political mechanism of the monopolistic state, it [the union leadership] at the same time cannot completely ignore the interests of the masses which it heads. The logic of the class struggle places it, even despite its desires, in opposition to monopoly capital" (Men'shikov, ed. 1964, 285). A much less hopeful writer charged that the leadership had lost its proletarian status and degenerated into an intermediate social stratum having its own particular interests which put it at odds with the union rank and file, the bourgeoisie, and the state (Men'shikov, ed. 1964).

In this vivid, outraged depiction, the union leaders are more embattled than the proletariat itself. Moreover, this condemnation naturally leads one to wonder how the rank and file can tolerate such leaders. Part of the standard Soviet answer is that the workers have been successfully socialized to expect and accept this sort of leader and have, in addition, been duped by the union leaders. The normally higher wages received by unionized, in contrast to nonunionized, workers also help keep the leaders in power (Geevskii 1962). Another reason is that the membership is passive and so is easily dominated by the leaders. Domination is facilitated when the leaders make deals with the owner/managers to obtain limited benefits for workers in exchange for continued work without strikes. The union treasury is then not depleted through paying strike benefits, the union becomes richer, and the leaders receive higher salaries. The workers, in turn, are often quite satisfied with the limited benefits obtained without a fight—and the existing union system is once more strengthened (Keremetskii 1970).

This line of analysis would seem to lead directly to a discussion of corruption in the unions, a topic on which source materials are hardly lacking. Yet that problem is not studied, most likely because the workers could begin to look *too* passive, and even permissive. That could create an undesirable pessimism when optimism ought to characterize those who know the victorious direction in which history is headed.

A similar ideological problem arises when the Soviets must note the absence of a labor party. Although American opinion surveys are cited to show that there was considerable rank and file support in the mid–1960s for founding a worker party (Lapitskii 1973), no Soviet writer has been hopeful about the future possibility. But it would be impolitic for any analyst to be actively pessimistic about this matter. Fundamental beliefs of the mindset are at stake. On the one hand, it holds that the working class cannot participate directly in the existing political system, but, on the other, the door must be left open for action by the workers to introduce socialism.

In their concern with the labor movement's pursuing independent political activity the Soviets advocate politics of labor, by labor, and for labor, with labor speaking on behalf of those working for hire, whether members of unions or not. Labor is envisaged as speaking without compromise, design, equivocation or any of the other modes of expression characteristic of bourgeois democracy. But since there is no labor party on the scene, apparently only the American Communist party has articulated that stance.

This state of affairs gives rise to an attitude, typical of the Soviet mindset, that leads to heated arguments between Americans and Soviets over whether workers are represented in American politics. We have already seen that most Soviet writers attacked the union leaders for choosing to act within the system and for actually becoming part of the system, while other writers claimed that those leaders are objectively forced to oppose both monopoly capital and the political system's managers. Looking beyond the leadership, the Soviets contend that neither the working class as a whole nor the rank and file union members are part of the bourgeois political system. Since there are no workers directly from the workbench serving in Congress or on the Supreme Court or occupying the presidency, and since there is no worker party, the closest that the workers come to being represented in the American political system is through union lobbies. But to equate the effectiveness of lobbying by the National Association of Manufacturers and other corporate lobbies with lobbying by the unions is seen as a reprehensible attempt to include the union membership as a whole (rather than just the leadership) in the bourgeois political system. "This conception [union lobbying] in and of itself is supposed to serve as a means of 'including' the unions in the system of the bourgeois state, and by that same token it is supposed to eliminate the class struggle and the subordination of the working class to the dictatorship of the monopolies" (Levin, ed. 1964b, 84–85).

The irony and sarcasm communicated by the quotation marks around the word "including" speak volumes. Because they are organizations of the working class the unions cannot be included as parts of a system that belongs to the bourgeoisie.[13] Nevertheless, the Soviets have made some rare statements implying a measure of inclusion—but still with the quotation marks: "The degree of 'inclusion' of the proletariat and all the toilers in democracy, just as the degree of freedom of each worker under capitalism, is determined to a significant degree by the gains of the workers themselves, by the real position of their organizations in a society's political system, by their pressure on the state mechanism, and by their level of organization and strength" (Guliev 1970, 32).

Even though the unions have achieved functional indirect representation within the government through the union leaders' membership in executive branch consultative committees, the rank and file must still make themselves heard through engaging in direct mass action as they did in the nation's capital on Solidarity Day in 1981 (Rogova 1983).

The standard Soviet interpretation asserts that not only are the workers and their organizations not part of the system (though the workers' leaders "essentially" are), but that all the gains which the working class has achieved through social legislation cannot serve in any way to legitimize the system that produced such legislation (Kalenskii 1969). Orthodox Soviet analysts condemn the "illusions," fostered by social legislation in bourgeois democracies, that the state is "above class" and that the state acts as a disinterested neutral third-party peacemaker in the struggle between labor and capital. But, they say, policies such as the wage increase guidelines adopted by the Kennedy administration, the general tendency to interpret labor laws and to apply labor policies in favor of business, and the notable lack of success of the labor lobbies in influencing both Congress and the executive branch toward a more prolabor position have been gradually dispelling that illusion and creating a more favorable climate for the idea of establishing a labor party (Keremetskii 1970; Grechukhin and others, eds. 1970; Shishkin 1972).

Nevertheless, the tendency has been for the illusions to hold sway over the masses, particularly through bolstering the widespread inclination in America "to confuse the owner with the overseer," to quote the expression which Valentina Liven' herself puts in quotation marks (1975, 225). That is, the state is used by the ruling class as a kind of lightning rod to distract the attention and anger that would otherwise be focused on the pervasive power of the large corporations. The professional politicians serve as overseers and bear the brunt of popular anger, while the real owners of the political system, the monopolists, rarely hold office (Burlatskii and Galkin 1974).[14] As a result, many Americans falsely feel "included" in the political system's workings. They avidly participate in the system's political battles, which are battles of the bourgeoisie, by the bourgeoisie, and for the bourgeoisie, battles which the Soviets believe to be unproductive for anyone but the bourgeoisie, save for those rare exceptions in which concessions are made.

Burlatskii addressed a particularly significant aspect of the state's role in "including" the nonbourgeoisie in the system in one of his chapters whose title is shocking from the perspective of the Soviet mindset: "The Power of the Monopolies and Its Mass Base" (1970, 212–50). To the extent that the SMC analytical framework has remained the cornerstone of orthodoxy, no Soviet would expect that the monopolies, the proverbially incorrigible handful of exploiters, could possibly develop a mass base of support. Yet Burlatskii wrote: "In our epoch the ruling classes, strata, circles, and groups cannot maintain their domination without the support of a mass base among the various strata of the population, which is created through the mechanism of social institutions (the parties, and the voting system, the press, radio, television, and the other mass communications media, the professional organizations, etc.) which assist them in strengthening their political and ideological positions among the masses" (1970, 217).

The need to manipulate this mass base effectively is the source of the public opinion and voting behavior research that is so widespread in the United States (Kalenskii 1969). The ruling class is interested in what and how people are thinking, the better to control their thinking and activity.

These parallel insights by two major Soviet students of American politics are significant as the sources of inspiration for later Soviet studies on American public opinion and political consciousness.

In the Soviet vision of the class struggle the ruling class has very considerable, even overwhelming, advantages over the proletariat. But they are overpowering only if sufficiently large numbers of people are taken in by the illusion that they participate in the bourgeois political system. The typical Soviet position on this question is that the "institutions of social struggle and social pressure" such as the labor unions and the strike movement are in the bourgeois political system but not *of* it. Functionally, they stand in opposition to the constitutional institutions of the political system (Burlatskii and Galkin 1974; Boichenko 1970). The class struggle takes place not so much within the system's institutions as outside them. But the struggle spills over into those institutions whose members simply cannot avoid doing something to control and channel the struggle lest it become unmanageable. In those institutions the representatives of the bourgeoisie fight these battles out among themselves, and the concrete outcome of the class struggle at a particular time and on specific issues is incorporated either into laws expressing gains for the working class or, more likely, into antidemocratic and antilabor policies in the interest of the ruling class.

Although in terms of SMC analysis worker gains are concessions which the bourgeoisie is forced to make, the institutional mechanism and processes through which they are made have been analyzed systematically only rarely and in books with small printings.[15] Soviet readers therefore know that concessions have been made, and they know why concessions have been made, but they are mostly in the dark about *how* they are made and what their content and extent are. To the degree that the Soviets believe that the workers are not included in the political system's institutions and processes it is almost pointless for them to consider these factors. Moreover, it could even be risky to do so since an investigation might well show that the interests of the workers are not quite so excluded as the mindset would lead the analysts to expect.

Revolution

Writing on the class struggle has focused almost exclusively on the struggle and not on expanding analytical frameworks or extending intellectual horizons in order to pose the question of whether capitalist systems can be reformed. Those are not the purposes for which this kind of writing is undertaken. The basic conviction is that reform would not change the systems in their essentials— whatever that may turn out to mean concretely. Rather, these irredeemably flawed systems must be fundamentally transformed into socialist systems through the class struggle either peacefully or through revolution.

Soviet specialists on American politics writing on the class struggle in the SMC tradition have had very little specific to say about the question of revolutionary transformation. Boichenko is the only Soviet writer on America in the past several decades to have devoted much space—seven pages—to revolution (1970).[16] But writers specializing in the analysis of capitalism in general, or revolution in particular, have addressed these matters. That is, the writers concerned with American politics most directly and concretely have not discussed revolution nearly to the extent that the theoretical generalists have. A brief treatment of revolution is relevant here chiefly because revolution has so often been considered the classic outcome of the class struggle.

Moscow's position on revolution changed dramatically in 1956 when the Soviet Twentieth Party Congress declared that revolution was not the only way of eliminating capitalism and achieving socialism—a peaceful transition was also possible. This was a basic shift to a position that the Soviets had bitterly attacked as revisionist for so many decades. It triggered an involved discussion probing the interrelation of the two possibilities, which became even more complex when the Chinese communists, who kept the older faith, now condemned the Soviets as revisionists for admitting the possibility of peacefully eliminating capitalism.

Richard Nordahl has divided Soviet theoreticians and ideologists who wrote on revolution in the 1950s and 1960s into "revisionist" and "neo-Stalinist" camps (1972). The first maintained that a peaceful transition to socialism is most likely in most, if not all, advanced capitalist societies. The second group held that revolution is practically inevitable. These positions were derived not so much from the analysis of concrete data as from the willingness or unwillingness to go beyond what had been the orthodox Soviet position for decades, one traceable to *What Is to Be Done?*

The three specialists on American politics who did comment briefly on the problem of peaceful or revolutionary transformation in the United States came to no single conclusion. In 1969 Valerii Kalenskii found that in no advanced capitalist country did a revolutionary situation exist. He envisaged the class struggle as continuing to improve conditions through winning concessions. Galina Boichenko contented herself with repeating the American Communist Party's Program adopted in 1969: whether peaceful or violent tactics will be used can be determined only when an actual revolutionary situation exists. At the time the program was adopted, none existed. Avgust Mishin, writing in 1972, was the only specialist to maintain that the parliamentary road to socialism is not possible in the United States. The reasons he gave are that the Communist party was weak; there was no social democratic party to advance the basic aims of the proletariat; and American democratic traditions were not as strong as those in England, Sweden, Norway, Belgium, Switzerland, New Zealand, and Australia. Since these countries did not suffer the disabilities Mishin attributed to the United States, he felt that the parliamentary road was possible in them as it was in Italy, France, and Finland because of the very strong communist and worker parties in those three countries.[17]

The one conclusion common to these three authors, who apparently coincidentally published between 1969 and 1972, was that imminent revolution was not to be expected in the United States. The class struggle had not yet intensified to a degree warranting that expectation.

The situation has not changed much in the interim. The class struggle therefore remains a matter of strikes, of the legislative battle among the factions of the bourgeoisie over the magnitude of concessions granted the workers or of the repressive measures taken against them, of a so far fruitless attempt to woo labor away from the two major parties in order to form an independent third party, and of trying to overcome a massive lag in worker class consciousness (Diligenskii and others 1985). The class struggle is an incremental process in the absence of serious economic crises and given the gains made by the workers in their standard of living. Changes in these contingencies would, of course, inflame the struggle, and the long-term Soviet expectation is that the tendencies inherent in the development of capitalism will encourage just that.

The Antimonopoly Coalition/Alliance
of Democratic Forces

During the general Soviet reevaluation of ideological orthodoxy following Stalin's death it was rediscovered that the proletariat was not alone in the class struggle with the bourgeoisie. The proletariat had sources of support.

Allies for the Proletariat

The idea that the proletariat could, and even should, forge temporary alliances with portions of the bourgeoisie in times of threatening danger or tantalizing opportunity had an impeccable pedigree. Marx and Engels had recommended the strategy occasionally, and the Popular Front tactics of the 1930s were more than just a memory to many Soviet politicians and ideologists attending the Twentieth Party Congress, which sanctioned the idea of peaceful transition to socialism.[18] Soviet theoreticians then concluded that peaceful transition could be accelerated if all the political forces in capitalist society suffering from the ravages of the monopolies united in an antimonopoly coalition and if they created an alliance of democratic forces from the segments of society favoring expansion of democratic rights (Arzumanian and others, eds. 1963).

The coalition would unify the proletariat with large portions of the intermediate and middle strata, the petty bourgeoisie, and even some of the middle bourgeoisie (Arzumanian and others, eds. 1963; Dokunin and Trepelkov 1963).

In practical politics the ruling elite cannot dominate the working class without also treading on the rights and prerogatives of the small farmers, the urban middle strata, and those in the intelligentsia favoring democracy (Guliev 1970). Moreover, in pursuing their aim of redistributing the national income in favor of themselves, the monopolies even infringe upon the interests of various strata of the ruling class, especially the middle and petty bourgeoisie. The latter, which support the monopolies specifically because they share an interest in retaining the private ownership system, are progressively alienated by the disadvantages they suffer at the hands of the monopolies and they become potential members of the antimonopoly coalition (Varga 1968).

The coalition's social base is therefore "the commonality of the interests of the entire people in the face of the handful of powerful monopolies" (Androsov 1971, 319). While the coalition would include disaffected elements from within the ruling class itself, trustworthy hands would remain in control: "Only the unification of the majority of the people around the working class and, consequently, only the leadership of the working class and its progressive forces headed by the Communist party can compel the reactionary forces of the dominating classes into capitulating to the will of the people" (Arzumanian and others, eds. 1963, 396–97).[19]

The idea of a possible peaceful transition to socialism had its enemies within the Soviet Communist party and among Soviet social scientists as well as within the communist parties of other nations, notably China. But once the concept was adopted in Moscow most other foreign communist parties followed the Soviet lead, quickly incorporated the idea of an antimonopoly coalition in their programs, and set about forging the coalition (Arzumanian and others, eds., 1963).

But the American Communist party, badly shaken by Khrushchev's revelations about Stalin at the Twentieth Party Congress and by the Soviet intervention in Hungary in 1956, was so besieged by internal problems that it adopted the concept only at its Eighteenth National Convention in December 1959 (Timofeev 1967). Since 1960, most Soviet analyses of the class struggle in the United States have devoted their attention primarily to the coalition/alliance aspect of that struggle. Coincidentally, that year introduced a turbulent period of a dozen or so years in American politics which seemed to provide an almost perfect context for creating an alliance of democratic forces.[20]

The actual direction taken by events in the United States in the 1960s led the Americanists to modify the theoretical framework produced by the Soviet generalist theoreticians and ideologists. Exercising judicious powers of hindsight, Iakov Keremetskii articulated well the consensus among Americanists at that point when he wrote that "the natural allies" of labor in the struggle against SMC were the Negro liberation movement, the youth and student movement, and the politically active intelligentsia (1970). Obviously missing here are the components enumerated previously that should constitute the backbone of the alliance from the theorists' viewpoint: the middle and small farmers and the middle and small urban businessmen, the "employees," and most of the middle strata.

These disparities point toward a still unresolved problem for Soviet social scientists when they deal with alliances. They predicted the formation of an alliance/coalition but never worked out a general theory of alliance or coalition formation and maintenance. While arguing that there are "objective factors" favoring the creation of a coalition, they have not taken systematic account of the fact that alliances and coalitions in politics in general, and in American politics in particular, have all too often been notoriously unstable and temporary—if and when they have been formed. American political scientists have produced a copious literature on this phenomenon in American politics, but these analyses have been ignored in the Soviet Union. In the case of the antimonopoly coalition/alliance of democratic forces the unity envisaged in Soviet writings was, and has remained, very much in the mind's eye of Soviet politicians, ideologists, and scholars. No coalition/alliance has yet been forged, and unity remains a goal not yet achieved even though Soviet analysts have written about it in deceptively real terms.

But even while accentuating the positive, Soviet writers normally have not eliminated the negative. They have not been unqualifiedly hopeful about the alliance's prospects for reasons originating in their own framework of analysis.

The principal reason for such hesitation is that the middle strata in capitalist society are supposed to play an important role in the unification process. But every Soviet analyst recognizes these strata to be highly unstable in their political perception, activity, and commitments. Depending upon circumstances and issues the middle strata may become allies of either of the two contending classes, but they do not remain very firm allies because their interests are constantly shifting.[21] Indeed, the class enemy heavily populates these strata comprised of the owners of small and medium-sized businesses in industry and the service sector, the more highly paid white-collar workers in the corporation and the civil service, the scientific and technical intelligentsia, physicians and attorneys, and the most highly paid skilled workers (Androsov 1971). When the middle strata grew rapidly in the 1960s, the Soviets did not perceive it as an unqualifiedly hopeful sign for the alliance/coalition, since it was precisely from among the income levels characteristic of these strata that extreme right-wing movements drew strong support (Nikitin 1971).[22]

Another problematic aspect of the alliance is rooted in the argument over whether the state represents the interests of the entire bourgeoisie or those of the monopoly bourgeoisie only. Attacking writers who contended that the entire bourgeoisie's interests were represented by the state, Kovaleva asked how it could be logically possible to speak of a broad antimonopoly coalition if that were the case (1969). Kovaleva was touching on a basic problem: the more representative the state is of the interests of the entire bourgeoisie, the less likely the middle and petty bourgeoisie are to join a coalition against the monopolies.

Because most Soviet analysts adopted the partial monopoly domination version of the SMC model following the mid–1950s, this dynamic ought to have been more widely recognized and debated. Evidently the partial domination model's proponents ignored the question because the coalition was not promising of quick success in the class struggle. It was left to an ideological conservative like Kovaleva, who favored the total domination version even in 1969, to raise the issue.

A final reason for caution about the prospects for a coalition in America was the memory of the difficulty experienced in attempting to establish a similar alliance through the Progressive party in the late 1940s and early 1950s (Mikhailov, ed. 1970, 1971).

Despite these reservations that were scattered throughout Soviet writings and are brought together here for the first time, the Soviet contention has been that objective conditions do exist for the unification of all the antimonopoly and prodemocracy forces. Politically, socially, and economically the concentration of wealth, power, and privilege in the hands of a small group of monopolists creates a counterreaction on the part of almost everybody else in the population in favor of a restoration of democracy and the rights trampled upon by the monopolies (Burlatskii 1970).

Moreover, as the number of persons engaged in nonmanual work sharply increases, the very fact of that growth undermines the formerly privileged position of white-collar workers, whose standard of living declines and begins to approach that of manual laborers. In protest, people in the nonmanual occupations increasingly adopt behavior long characteristic of manual workers—they engage in strikes, political demonstrations, and, in particular, they do what had earlier been unthinkable: they establish trade unions of retail salespeople, engineers, teachers, and the like (Dalin 1972; Shishkin 1972). These actions are taken as proof that the middle strata are being proletarianized. The monopolies therefore gradually lose those few, yet very important even though unreliable, allies they once had in the class struggle.

Labor, Blacks, Students, and Youth

The antimonopoly coalition/alliance of democratic forces has often been conceptualized as a union of the worker movement with "the general democratic movement," those political forces striving to expand democracy in any way. Specifically, the labor unions were to link forces with the black liberation movement, the youth and student movements, the anti–Vietnam War movement, the farmers' movement, the women's liberation movement, the Chicano movement, and the consumer and ecological movements.

The expectation was that the class struggle would be won through a fusion of social movements. But that did not materialize for two principal reasons: the Soviet's concept of movements was poorly conceived and the movements themselves were flawed.

The concept of social and political mass movements is another of those basic ideas often invoked in Soviet social science analyses but not studied adequately in the Soviet Union. Although mass movements of all kinds are discussed in great detail in Soviet writings, and, in the process, some clarification of the concept does occur, systematic treatments of its parameters are missing, as are attempts to do something so basic as to produce an extended definition.[23]

The closest brief specification that can be made begins with the highly ideologically charged definition of the term "the people": "In historical materialism, the people, or popular masses, are a social community comprising, at various historical stages, those strata and classes that, owing to their position in society, are capable of actively participating in the progressive development of society; they are the makers of history, the determining force in fundamental social transformations" (*Great Soviet Encyclopedia,* vol. 17, 605). Mass movements are generated because they are the only means the masses have to protest and overcome the monopolies' control of the nation's political institutions and processes, which by definition serve the interests of the bourgeoisie almost exclusively (Burlatskii 1970). For this reason one can only agree with Burlatskii's contention that the concept of political movements lies at the basis of the Marxist approach to politics (1970).

BLACKS

After the workers, the Soviets give preeminence of place in the general democratic movement to blacks due to their historically disadvantaged position, both politically and economically.[24] With the possible exception of the American Indians, they have participated less in the institutions and processes of bourgeois democracy over a longer period of time than any other segment of the population. The Soviets consider racism and the exploitation of racial minorities to be inherent in the capitalist system chiefly because both are in the general economic self-interest of the monopolies (Geevskii 1973; Mitrokhin 1974). It was estimated that in the late 1960s the monopolies made $15 billion to $17 billion in superprofits per year simply through wage discrimination against blacks (Nitoburg 1971).

Yet the general interest the monopolies have in maintaining racial discrimination sometimes breaks down in clashes of particular monopoly interests. If some monopolies sought to retain lower labor costs in the South and so contributed to continuing black disadvantage (Kalenskii in Tumanov, ed. 1967), other monopolies took various positions on racial problems based on differences in political interests, religious affiliation, and historical traditions going back to the Civil War period. But these reasons for the differences were secondary to the main one, which was the clash of economic interests, particularly between businesses in the Northeast and the South. The fact that some businesses were economically interested in partial improvements in the racial situation led to "pressure from above," that is, pressure from parts of the ruling class on the political system. That pressure explained why "the American government had more than once taken the initiative in the sphere of civil rights even in the years when there were no Negro uprisings" (Koroleva 1967, 129–30). Even the Ford Foundation had become much involved in studying racial problems and northeastern and western businesses seemed to favor ameliorative measures out of a concern over the continuing prospect of urban uprisings, the general decline of the ghetto areas, the low purchasing power of the ghetto inhabitants, and the animosity on the part of the latter toward white businessmen (Geevskii 1973).

In sum, continuing racial problems were blamed on big business, and at the same time partial amelioration of the blacks' conditions was attributed to the self-serving support given their cause by some big businesses. Geevskii therefore concluded that because the bourgeoisie had no single view on what the government's race policy ought to be, that policy was a result of power conflicts within the dominating class (1973).[25]

This is but one part of what amounts to an explanation of how progress can be made in a system controlled by forces ostensibly opposed to social and political progress. Another part takes into account the struggle by blacks for their own advancement and the aid they receive from the forces in society pressing for expanding democratic rights. This combination could force even reactionaries into making partial concessions. But just as was true of the labor movement, progress here was inhibited not only by the actions of the ruling class and the political system it controls but also by the disunity of black organizations pressing for change in race relations. The social heterogeneity of the participants in the movement created differences over the aims, tactics, and methods of struggle (Nitoburg 1971). Also, as in the labor movement, the leadership had not pressed forward vigorously. But in neither movement have Soviet writers probed in any depth the relationship between the heterogeneity of the membership and the nature of the leadership role the better to determine whether these might be correlated to some degree.

Lev Mitrokhin attributed some disunity to what he called the far-reaching class differentiation among Negroes (1974). And this is indeed the most basic reason Marxism gives for social and political cleavage. But the argument was made that class antagonisms among blacks are not as pronounced as might normally be expected because all, not just the poor, are the objects of discrimination. The black bourgeoisie therefore reflected, and continued to reflect into the early 1970s, the interests of all blacks because of the relatively narrow range of class differentiation among them (Vozchikov and others, eds. 1974).

As for those actively involved in the movement, the basic splits were between moderates and radicals, between the older black organizations favoring legalistic methods of struggle and those preferring direct but nonviolent action in the streets, those favoring integration and those declaring for separatism, and those opting for or against violence (Nitoburg 1971; Mostovets and others, eds. 1972).

These factors, according to the Soviets, had varying significance during the movement's phases of development. Initially the civil rights movement was a non–class-based coalition of blacks and whites governed and cemented by a bourgeois liberal ideology propounding a gradualism and tokenism that inhibited development of activism for a time. The eventual shift to more active methods of struggle and more radical economic demands made the non-class alliance untenable and pushed blacks toward a commonality of interests with the working class (Shishkin 1972).

But there were obstacles. Whatever other significance the urban riots of the 1960s had, they showed that there was a serious crisis in the movement, as evident in the gap between the black people in the street and the organizations' leadership. Mitrokhin called this the gap between the spontaneously created mass moods of the Negroes and programs and methods of social action more consciously formulated by organizations (1974). Much as the Soviets sympathized with the ghetto rioters, they criticized the riots for being spontaneous outbursts of despair and anger. Spontaneity of this sort is condemned (a loud echo of Lenin) because it lacks conscious direction and is more in the nature of a psychological acting out than the self-directed, thoughtfully formulated, effective political behavior that it ideally should be. Moreover, the indictment continues, in those riots there were many excessive and extreme actions by the participants, some of which were allegedly instigated by the police or the FBI and others allegedly by black "nationalist and extremist groups" attempting to direct the riots against whites in general (Vozchikov and others, eds. 1974, 121–22).

In the Soviet view, the way to correct these faults would have been to introduce a socialist consciousness into the ideology of mass protest—in other words, to raise the level of awareness and understanding of the participants in mass protests about the real cause of their grief (the capitalist system) and then point out ways for engaging in purposeful, knowledgeable, and appropriately controlled and dosed political activity to eliminate the cause (Mitrokhin 1974).

For the Soviets the evolution of the Black Panther party illustrated especially well the pitfalls of the movement and of spontaneously misdirected, as opposed to consciously directed, violence. The Panthers at first embraced the false idea of black separatism as the way out of the racial predicament, but they soon realized that it was capitalism, not the whites, which was creating the problems (Nitoburg 1971)—a progressive step. Still, in the fight against capitalism care had to be taken to exclude the ideology of black power, which could turn into black racism, and black nationalism, which did not link racial oppression to the overall political system (Nitoburg 1971; Mitrokhin 1974; Shishkin 1972).

The Panthers took a number of steps in the correct direction but failed to reach the ultimate destination the Soviet analysts hoped for, a genuinely Marxist understanding of the situation that would guide them toward appropriate political activity. Although at one point some Panthers, notably Eldridge Cleaver, claimed to be Marxists, the Soviets rejected their claim. Mitrokhin accused them of merely appealing to Marxist ideas to justify their sentiments of social criticism and specifically charged Cleaver with being unable to differentiate between accurate Marxist theoretical explanations for the blacks' plight and the attitudes spontaneously generated by the conditions of ghetto life (1974). Mitrokhin agreed with black American communist leader Henry Winston that both Panther extremes on the questions of the class struggle and black liberation—Huey Newton's concept of waiting for a black uprising and Cleaver's philosophy of revolution right now—were wrong (1974). Newton's later conversion to the idea of black capitalism was a matter of even greater concern, with some Soviets attributing a decline in Panther membership to his shift in position (Mostovets and others, eds. 1972).[26]

In discussing black power ideology Aleksandr Fursenko cited the Gallup and Harris polls in 1969–1970 to establish that black power, which had been an especially popular concept earlier among black youth, had lost its attraction and that improving their lot through violence had lost credence among the majority of black respondents (Fursenko and others 1974). Borrowing an expression from John Foster Dulles, S. Sergeeva called black power an attempt to deal from a position of strength—but the movement by itself lacked sufficient strength and could attain it only in alliance with other forces in society also working for a fundamental transformation in American life (Mostovets and others, eds. 1972). It is in this context that Fursenko's positive evaluation of the Reverend Dr. Martin Luther King must be understood: his greatest merit was his unswerving advocacy of joint black–white efforts (Fursenko and others 1974).[27]

Problems internal to the black movement made it less effective than it might have been. But the movement did not exist in a vacuum, the political system's operation influenced its fate. Here there is a revealing divergence in Soviet analyses, with writers on the class struggle minimizing or even ignoring the positive role periodically played by political institutions and processes, whereas writers who tended toward policy analysis took that role into account to a greater degree.[28]

In his analysis of governmental racial policy Geevskii noted that the black vote was critical in electing John Kennedy and that for the first time in history the presidential candidate who received the majority of white votes (Richard Nixon garnered 51% of them) had lost. In spite of that support, Kennedy's racial policies at the beginning of his administration were typical of bourgeois liberalism. Insignificant concessions were made (which no longer satisfied blacks) and care was taken not to offend southern Democrats in Congress (1973). Fursenko's analysis was quite different. He took into full account the fact that the correlation of forces in Congress was generally against Kennedy on many issues, including race, and that part of Kennedy's strategy was to do what little he could on the race issue and basically wait for his second term to make major moves. Fursenko felt that these considerations were well understood by the black leaders who then counterpressured the administration by organizing the March on Washington in 1963. That event, along with the campaign in Selma, Alabama, the March on Montgomery, and the generally increasing popular dissatisfaction with the do-nothing policy regarding race helped change the balance of forces in Congress and forced the administration to introduce a bill extending voting rights (Fursenko and others 1974; Geevskii 1973).

State–monopoly capitalism analysts have interpreted these and other gains as concessions wrested from the bourgeoisie through actions undertaken outside the political institutions and processes (Vozchikov and others, eds. 1974). Other Soviets maintained that some gains were achieved through and in the political system. They recognized that the blacks became a significant force in the nation's political life. Specifically, in 1969 some 1,200 blacks held elective posts, including 29 mayorships, and the migration to the cities had raised the degree of their political influence in presidential and congressional elections (Mostovets and others, eds. 1972). Blacks were achieving greater representation at all levels (Vozchikov and others, eds. 1974).

Additional within-system gains were made in the realm of justice. A series of civil rights acts, executive orders, Supreme Court

decisions, and lower court decisions "to a significant extent" over-
came the formerly widespread system of judicial inequality. Also,
some of the governmental agencies created during the 1960s actually succeeded in improving certain conditions for some blacks,
and those employed in these agencies managed to help the cause
even though they were not in leadership positions and so did not
determine the overall nature and thrust of these agencies' activities
(Geevskii 1973). Shifts in public opinion helped make these many
advances possible. Polls taken in 1964 showed that the majority
of Americans in both the North and the South favored expanding
black civil rights, a notable change from the situation in the 1940s
and 1950s (Geevskii 1973).

In summing up their attitude toward these results most analysts
made some attempt to balance achievements and remaining problems. Eduard Nitoburg, for example, noted the increased numbers
of black voters and officeholders and the removal of the classical
forms of discrimination. But inequalities remained and the disparity in the standard of living between blacks and whites continued
to grow (1971). The civil rights laws were great achievements, but
the laws were halfway measures (Vozchikov and others, eds. 1974).

Although these limited gains were worthy of qualified praise,
the fact was that the movement lost momentum and ultimately fell
apart. Its cohesion was undermined by a combination of factors:
severe repressive measures taken against urban rioters by the white
power structure, granting some civil rights through legislation, Nixon's tougher attitude toward the movement, the well-developed
class differentiations among Negroes, which inhibited unification,
and the wrong strategies often adopted by the movement or parts
of it—whether one of reform (rather than working for a fundamental sociopolitical transformation) or the counterproductive
strategy of violence (Vozchikov and others, eds. 1974; Mitrokhin
1974; Fursenko and others 1974).

Increasing black–white cooperation in political campaigns, white
support for black strikes, and black civil rights organizations' encouragement of unionization by unorganized black workers held
out the hope that the coalition/alliance might come to pass (Vozchikov and others, eds. 1974).

But it was not forged. Links between blacks and whites were
weak because of discrepancies in their socioeconomic status. Many

white workers supported discrimination out of fear that they would lose their jobs to lower paid blacks, and the monopolies cultivated these anxieties the better to undermine worker unity. Many labor unions refused to allow blacks into training programs, especially the rail, construction, and metalworker unions. Moreover, since in the Soviet view the majority of black workers mistakenly perceived the conflict of antagonistic classes as a race conflict, it turned out that the fight for civil rights was led by the black bourgeoisie, the black intelligentsia, and the black clergy rather than the black workers, whose leadership and ideological influence were insignificant (Mostovets and others, eds. 1972; Koroleva 1967).

Yet the potential for an alliance remains since the race problem was not resolved. The civil rights laws, which did not go far enough anyway, were not effectively administered, and the economic status of the blacks in general had not improved much if at all up to the mid–1970s (Vozchikov and others, eds. 1974; Luzik 1976).

Soviet studies of the black movement illustrate a number of problems besetting social science analysis in the Soviet Union. In the absence of systematic theoretical studies on the phenomenon of movements, Soviet considerations of individual movements have rarely moved beyond a discussion of the preconditions of a coalition/alliance and the tendencies favoring one. They have not come to grips with the difficulties in organizing and maintaining coalitions. A very hesitant and tentative beginning in tackling the problem was made by Lev Mitrokhin when he briefly and circumspectly discussed the role of "the subjective factor" in political analysis (1974, 197–98).

Mitrokhin's point was that people do not always act in the ways that Soviets would anticipate they should on the basis of Marxist–Leninist expectations. Subjective feelings and perceptions sometimes prompt people to act against their objective interests. Mitrokhin commented that in their analyses of the black movement Soviet authors concentrated overwhelmingly on analyzing what they considered to be objective social processes, factors, and conflicts and said very little about subjective factors. Soviet analysts believed that blacks objectively ought to be in an alliance with labor because their basic interests in opposing the monopolies coincided. But they were not, and Mitrokhin contended that some of the causes lay in subjective perceptions of the situation found in both the mass black consciousness and the ideology and programs of black leaders.

Mitrokhin did not identify those perceptions, much less analyze them. And he quickly ended his discussion of the topic. He was approaching the limitations put on Soviet analysts by their need to conform both to the ideological orthodoxy of the moment and to the conventions of Soviet academic writing. When the Soviets analyze a capitalist society, objective factors are easy, and safe, to write about because they are positive features of the ideology, whereas subjective factors do not conform to ideological perspectives and expectations. Mindset attitudes have so far discouraged systematic investigation of subjective factors because they raise issues that could easily lead to questioning the validity of the ideology.[29]

Nobody has considered whether some objective factors may conflict with other objective factors, thereby canceling each other out. For example, the Soviets have contended that the monopolies are objectively interested in exploiting the blacks more than any other group. Yet Valerii Kalenskii quoted John Kennedy, who SMC analysts felt best expressed the general interests of the monopoly bourgeoisie, as saying that one reason for mounting an attack on racism was to enable the economy to maximize the use of America's human resources and so encourage economic growth (Tumanov, ed. 1967). The lesson here is that if there are objective economic reasons for retaining racial discrimination, there are no less objective reasons for eliminating it, as American sports organizations seem to have realized quite some time ago—much to their profit, if not to the satisfaction of many blacks.

The Soviets regard the black contingent in the coalition/alliance as beset by problems similar to those troubling the unions: its level of political consciousness and understanding has not been high, and it has been ill-served by its leadership. The great Soviet ideologically inspired hope for blacks lay in the action to be taken by black workers, but in view of problems faced by the labor movement in general there does not seem to be much promise in this expectation.

A major qualitative shift for the better occurred in the 1970s when the Afro-American movement (as the Soviets then began calling it) moved from demanding formal equal rights to demanding equality of results. But in the 1980s the movement became fragmented because the better off blacks were able to take advantage of gains in civil rights to improve their status while the poorer ones were hard hit by recessions. In addition, the national movement withered as greater attention was given to local situations. And with 1% of elected officials at all levels of government being black by the mid–1980s, the movement's leaders made greater use of elective institutions to tackle the blacks' socioeconomic problems (Geevskii and others, eds. 1986).

STUDENTS AND YOUTH

Students and youth are the third component of the coalition/alliance researched in some detail, although much less so than labor and blacks. As an analytical category youth cuts across other movements, so that its role in the labor, peace, and civil rights movements has been considered as well as its role in the radical student movement (Vozchikov and others, eds. 1974).

Soviet scholarly interest in youth affairs followed the course of the movement's rise in the 1960s and its fall in the early 1970s. The main dissatisfactions motivating it in the late 1960s were identified as higher unemployment rates and lower wages than among older people, unequal access to higher education and the uneven quality of university education, control of higher education by big business through university boards of trustees, the role of the military–industrial complex on the campuses, and the Vietnam War and the higher draft calls it produced (Iakovlev, ed. 1969).

Behaving in true SMC and bourgeois democratic fashion, the establishment attempted to turn the student movement into the tried and true channels of mainstream bourgeois politics through transforming movement politics into liberal politics (Mostovets and others, eds. 1972). The establishment tried to replace action with talk.

As usual in movement politics, there was also an enemy within— many of the movement's leaders. The left element in the student movement, which ought to have been pointing the way, at one juncture wrongly turned toward "petty bourgeois radicalism," which encouraged what the Soviets criticized as ultrarevolutionary moods, utopianism, anarchism and adventurism. There was too much excessively premature talk about revolution and even some outrageously premature attempts at instigating revolution. But the student leaders finally did the correct thing in turning toward an alliance with the workers—only to encounter resistance from union leaders and heightened attempts by the political system's managers to deflect the students into participating in bourgeois politics, especially through working in election campaigns (Shishkin 1972). The alliance was also inhibited by elements of anarchism, Trotskyism, and Maoism expressed in the idea that the students and not the workers were the vanguard of the revolution (Vozchikov and others, eds. 1974; Iulina 1971). Small wonder, then, that there was not one Soviet analyst who was at all hopeful about the prospects for the New Left movement of the 1960s and 1970s.

With respect to what was called "the general youth and student movement," however, a few studies dealing with the situation in the early 1970s predicted heightened activity because the economic, social, and political oppression that had activated the movement in the first place was growing worse (Mostovets and others, eds. 1972; Zorin, ed. 1971; Vozchikov and others, eds. 1974). But in 1974 Aleksandr Fursenko recorded the movement's sharp decline, attributing it to the absence of strong organization, the lack of firm contacts among whatever organizations that did exist, the presence of anarchist and extremist elements within the movement, the punitive measures undertaken before and during the Nixon administration's law and order campaign, lowering the voting age to eighteen, and the work of the Scranton Commission on the causes of unrest and violence (Fursenko and others 1974). Here again the Soviets see a mix of responses and policies reminiscent of those used in controlling labor and blacks.

The last major study of the student movement focuses on its consequences, namely the creation of a counterculture expressing itself in negative attitudes toward the quality of bourgeois life, and especially toward the traditional values associated with the Protestant ethic. The criticisms of American society articulated by the student movement have forced bourgeois ideologists to recognize the crisis of values which has befallen bourgeois society and have raised the level of consciousness of youth in general, thus creating a prerequisite for the further development of the antimonopoly movement (Novinskaia 1977).

The most recent study of the youth counterculture maintains

that the counterculture stimulated some young people to become socially and politically active, "objectively" readying them to join the antimonopoly coalition. But before that optimistic point is made, there is an extensive realistically critical analysis of the numerous negative elements (the subjective ones) among the profusion of subcultures within the counterculture (Baichorov 1982). It would be hard to envisage how the widespread attraction of youth to various religious sects, narcotics, escapist music, and downright nihilism will produce the objective result.

A new stage in the study of youth affairs was reached in a book making extensive use of American public opinion surveys to study youth attitudes on social and political problems (Emel'ianov 1986). Methodologically innovative, its conclusions hardly differed from previous writings. The author reports that although youth remained intellectually critical of the political system in the 1970s and 1980s, their interest in politics had diminished and they were apathetic. Apolitical attitudes are generated by the stress on individualism and consumerism. There are feelings of helplessness and hopelessness among youth about the possibility of changing things through elections, and there is a sense that politics is too complex to understand. As for the youth movement in particular, there is no one overarching issue around which to organize a national, inclusive effort. Rather, young people are separated and fragmented because there are many individual movements organized around a multitude of issues (Emel'ianov 1986).

Assessing the Democratic Movement

The Soviets have given relatively little attention to the farmer, women's, and Spanish-speaking agricultural workers' movements.[30] The fates of these individual movements and of the general democratic movement are contingent upon the degree of internal cohesion and the nature of the political system's responses to the movements' expressed dissatisfactions, demands, and concrete activities. In his study of the labor unions Vladimir Androsov warned in a veiled way against underestimating the effect of the system's responses. State–monopoly capitalism measures constitute a significant countervailing force against the workers' achieving an appropriately anticapitalist class consciousness, not to mention developing an intensive struggle against the capitalists (1971). Similarly, as long ago as 1958 Boris Gromakov attributed the political passivity of the working class to its having achieved "relatively large successes in the economic struggle" (10). "Great harm was done the worker movement by F. Roosevelt's 'New Deal' reforms, which were carried out in a period when the class struggle was intensifying" (Geevskii 1962, 86).

Yet there are limits to the policy of granting concessions and engaging in social maneuvering. The Kennedy–Johnson social programs engendered negative reactions in "millions" of Americans because they saw these programs as resulting in higher taxes and a higher cost of living while failing to halt mass black protests. These were the concerns of middle Americans, who felt that they contributed more to government than they received in services, feared losing the higher standard of living they had attained through so much effort, and simply disliked big government and big unions (Androsov 1971).

The Soviets also argued, making the best of a bad situation, that while some movements may have declined in the 1970s, the growing knot of unresolved problems activated other movements (Geevskii and Salycheva, eds. 1978). However, they stopped short of weighing the relative political significance of the various movements in order to determine how great an impact this factor might have.

Finally, there is the problem of the American Communist party's role in forming the coalition/alliance. Soviet authors avoid analyzing the party's activity in forming the coalition/alliance. It is safe to assume either that the writers do not wish to publicize these sensitive activities or that the party's concrete organizing activity has been rare or ineffective—or all three. In their brief treatments of the party's relationship with one or another movement the analysts state categorically that the party has given much attention to the democratic movement in its programmatic statements and considers it to be an important element in the broad antimonopoly coalition the party is working to organize (Vozchikov and others, eds. 1974).

Taking the long view, the business of organizing the coalition is only an early stage in preparing the masses for the ultimate revolution (Mostovets and others, eds. 1972). A leading Soviet writer on revolution warned against making the mistake of confusing the struggle for extending democracy with the socialist revolution. The struggle for democracy was at best a step toward revolution or a form of transition to revolution (Kovalev 1974).

Conclusion

The coalition/alliance is a specific form that the class struggle takes at a particular stage of development of capitalist societies, the stage at which the United States now is. The Soviet studies of the co-alition/alliance and its component movements show how complex and contradictory the class struggle has become in the eyes of the Americanists. In particular, they see internal struggles sapping the strength of the classes just as the tendency of the middle strata to shift their support from one class to the other and back again weakens them. For a long time the classic assumptions that there are only two or, at most, three classes and that antagonisms be-tween them are the most important facts of life prevented the Soviets from understanding the full ramifications of social structure in the United States and especially how it serves to modify and moderate the class struggle as it had been portrayed.

The Soviet studies of the class struggle show how far from a revolution the United States has been and remains because of historical factors such as the easy availability of land and rich natural resources, and of more recent factors like SMC policies of granting concessions and the favorable position of the United States in the world market following World War II.

Despite the barriers to forging the coalition/alliance the Soviets have concluded that some of the historically important buffers are disappearing: some domestic natural resources are nearly ex-hausted and America's world market position began a decline in the 1960s. But no analyst has rushed to make predictions of im-minent doom on that basis, most likely because earlier Soviet intimations of the impending dissolution of the American system in the depression years proved premature.[31]

Yet the analysts remain quite clear about the long-range ten-dencies in development of the American economic, social, and political systems, which will, they believe, eventually result in heightened exploitation and polarization coupled with a declining living standard and continued inability of the nation's political institutions and processes to resolve a host of problems such as poverty, unemployment, housing, medical care—and the list goes on. The fate of the youth movement is an example. The movement was given a major impetus by the Vietnam War in the short run, but then it declined. It did not disappear, however, and the long-term factors motivating the movement—the general crisis of capitalism and the crisis of values in the United States—remain and are expected to lead to the movement's resurgence (Salycheva, ed. 1974).

For Soviet analysts the continuing but long and drawn out process of polarization coupled with the failure to resolve the nation's economic, social, and political problems serve as guarantees that the class struggle will both persist and, indeed, intensify.

Americans often wonder where mainstream Soviet perceptions originate, and these first four chapters have provided one set of answers. Another set will emerge in Part III.

Continuity and Change in Soviet Analyses of American Politics

5 SOVIET INTELLECTUAL CONTEXTS AND THE INTERPRETATION OF AMERICAN POLITICS

As the politics of a capitalist country, American politics are supposed (in both senses of the word) to fit the mindset's mold. At the same time many Soviet writers find much to criticize about the way American politics are studied using the concepts of SMC, bourgeois democracy, and the class struggle.

How and why did this conventional Soviet analytical framework come into being? How and why did it change in some ways but remain constant in others? How do these continuities and changes affect the study of American politics?

In cultural terms and most broadly conceived, the mindset is produced by the reciprocal interactions of the ideology with reality, of belief with experience, of commitment with flexibility, of prescription with adjustment, and of the Marxist–Leninist value system with "life." Ideas and ideals often take on a life of their own. But on a less abstract level, and because they do not exist in a vacuum, these interactions are mediated by psychological factors. They live, as the saying goes, in hearts and minds, as a mixture of feelings and intellect in individuals.

Moreover, abstractions become concrete when they are embodied in institutions, in established processes and procedures, and even in events such as holidays, which are ritualized celebrations of ideas or are commemorations of events exemplifying cherished values. In the name of ideological values, sociopolitical conventions—mindset attitudes—spring up to preserve and advance those values on a daily basis.

The interrelationships in which ideals and ideas shape people

125

and are shaped or reshaped by them, especially as they affect an entire society, are highly complex. For one type of person, established ideas and ideals may have a life-directing force, but other people infuse ideas and ideals with new content, and others may even abandon them. The ways in which political and social institutions operate may either reaffirm traditional understandings of ideas and ideals or they may modify or even transform them. Gorbachev's policies aimed at transforming Soviet society are prime examples of these interactions. As he lamented: "We understand with our brains that it is necessary to change. But the system doesn't let us" (198).

This chapter focuses on that microcosm of Soviet society composed of specialists on American politics and social scientists in general, as they interact with formulators and interpreters of the ideology (particularly political leaders and their administrative executors) whose joint activities contribute heavily toward creating the predominant intellectual ethos in the Soviet Union.

The specialists' responses to traditions, modes of operation, and changing needs of the institutions within which they work play a significant role. Institutions tend to lend an institutional personality to individuals, which in turn creates functional groupings or discernible schools of thought. But in some cases the personality of an individual may be so strongly developed in its own right that there is considerable variance from the expected institutional personality and even from the predominant intellectual ethos. This is the stuff that both hidebound conservatives and radicals are made of, but it is what also explains the more limited creativity that changes the intellectual ethos incrementally but decisively.

History, Political Leaders, Institutions

Mainstream Soviets continually make the point that the social sciences in their country have developed under the guidance of the Communist party. More accurately, the political leader who has controlled the party's ideology has done the guiding. He has at times been assisted, influenced, or temporarily supplanted in that role by the major spokesman responsible for articulating the current orthodoxy. Considerable influence can be exercised by party functionaries in charge of various Central Committee departments and by the heads of some academic institutions and research institutes together with their senior advisers. Groups of scholars and individual social scientists who have contended among themselves (to the degree possible under specific circumstances) over the direction in which the social sciences ought to develop also have an impact.

This interactive network creates a problem for the political leadership. Leaders deliver commands to bureaucratic organizations which have interests and perspectives that can be at variance with those commands to some degree. The leader and his supporters in the bureaucratic organization must devise strategies to assure compliance. Concurrently, the opponents adopt strategies to modify or even obviate the force of the commands. This old conflict is being played out in new ways under Gorbachev.

Difficult though it may be to keep score of these matches, in general "the party's" guidance has won out. But often that has been so because in the long run "the party" has changed position on hotly debated issues in social science research. Thus some research institutions and researchers who resisted an earlier command, sometimes at great cost to themselves, in order to pursue a particular line of inquiry have ultimately found themselves vindicated. "At great cost" sometimes meant repression and the end of individual careers or the summary disbanding of research institutions. More often, however, there was no such drama, but only a host of problems reminiscent of the tribulations peculiar to government-related research in any number of nations.

Over the decades these processes have worked themselves out in the Soviet Union in some peculiar ways. The available evidence indicates that Lenin originally intended the social sciences to play a domestic educational role in spreading the new ideology and to attract foreign Marxists to Bolshevism. Soon after his second stroke incapacitated him, the Twelfth Party Congress (April 1923) mandated that social science research centers give greater attention to current economic and political problems in foreign countries (Eran 1979). In the remainder of the 1920s these questions were studied in the context of the more liberal Soviet understanding of Marxism, which was later replaced by Stalinist orthodoxy.

The chief center of study of the United States was the Institute of the World Economy and World Politics. It was mainly concerned with the operation of the economy, particularly the agricultural sector, as exemplified in the articles published in the institute's monthly, *Mirovoe khoziaiastvo i mirovaia politika (The World Economy and World Politics)*. Politics was given far less attention, most going to presidential and congressional elections, less to Congress.[1]

The scholars at the institute developed plans for a massive, comprehensive thirteen-volume study of the United States stressing basic research in the social structure, economy, politics, and geography. But the onset of the Great Depression was an attention-preempting event that returned the institute's focus to economics and associated topical matters. At the same time the party reasserted its interest in following current events.[2]

A major exception to the switch in focus was an extraordinary study by V. Lan (pseudonym of Veniamin I. Kaplan), whose title translated into English is *Classes and Parties in the USA: Essays on the Economic and Political History of the USA*. The book contained a wealth of information, and its analysis was relatively dispassionate by contemporaneous Soviet standards. The volume was the most significant piece of basic research on American politics published in the first two decades of the Soviet Union's existence.[3]

In the 1930s Americanistics were relatively little affected by the kind of turmoil that afflicted many academic disciplines. Only a decade later did the institute experience similar havoc. It was disbanded in 1947, its monthly journal ceased publication, and its prominent head, Evgenii Varga, went into near seclusion following his partial confession of error (Barghoorn 1948; Schlesinger 1949; Shulman 1963). V. Lan, the institute's chief specialist on American politics, experienced a similar fate.

Because the institute had not given much systematic attention to American politics, these measures, however severe, might not seem to have had a significant impact. Yet something very important was lost in that the relatively dispassionate and factual approach to American politics disappeared. For a while outright vituperation reigned (examples are in Barghoorn 1950) and then calmer but still strongly negative studies predominated. They concentrated on American diplomatic history, an area hardly touched earlier, with the object of proving how incorrigibly imperialistic the United States had been starting in the late 1800s (Mills 1972). Whatever the merits of these contentions, this was the era when Stalin's personality cult and Politburo member Andrei Zhdanov's attacks on "objectivism" in favor of ideologically driven studies produced the nearly full degradation of Soviet scholarship. In the early 1950s the first of many books appeared analyzing American domestic politics as systematically as the SMC framework would allow.

The narrow, negative, and polemical Stalinist orthodoxy was imposed on the study of American politics late by comparison with other fields. But it was no less traumatic. That orthodoxy fell victim to the needs of successor political leaderships.[4] Khrushchev's destalinization drive initiated criticism of the recent narrow orthodoxy and led to the reestablishment and rapid initial growth of sociology as an academic discipline. Sociology quickly became the cutting edge of Soviet social science in general and of the study of politics in particular. Soviet scholars were able to make contact with their Western and world counterparts and became more familiar with Western social science. Ultimately the Soviet Association of Political Science was established, creating the strange situation that still exists: there is an association, but no academic discipline called political science.

Another need was recognized in Khrushchev's day but received major attention only in the Brezhnev era. In 1967 the party's Central Committee ordered a dramatic acceleration in developing the social sciences. The aims were to create larger data banks on, and improved ways of interpreting, Soviet life, international affairs, and economic, political, and social events and processes in foreign countries.

This effort produced an immediate landmark result in 1967 when the first Soviet academic institution devoted exclusively to the study of the United States was established: "The Presidium of the Academy of Sciences of the USSR has resolved to organize an institute on the USA as part of the Economics Division. G. A. Arbatov, Doctor of Philosophical Sciences, has been appointed the institute's director."[5] In 1970 the Institute of U.S. Studies began publishing its monthly, whose translated title is *USA: Economics,*

Politics, Ideology. The institute's purview was thereafter broadened to include Canada, and its name was changed to the Institute of United States and Canadian Studies—IUSAC.

The significance of these arrangements is understandable only if we take a closer look at the institutions within which the United States and its politics had been studied earlier. Since political science did not exist and sociology was not restored until the late 1950s, politics had been studied within other academic fields: political economy, economics, history, philosophy, and a very important Soviet discipline called state and law. Until some long overdue progress was initiated in the early 1970s, state and law was a particularly narrow, legalistic, and formalistic way of studying politics which treated how institutions are organized on paper, how they are supposed to operate on paper, and how the decisions they make appear on paper.

This combination of disciplines produced the outpouring of SMC analyses in the 1950s and 1960s.[6] In the academic institutes representing these fields there usually were departments of world economics or world history that might have either an American Sector or a Section on Bourgeois Countries housing several specialists on the United States. Between 1947 and 1968 these specialists were scattered throughout Soviet universities and research institutes. The greatest concentration of specialists on American politics was in the Institute of State and Law and also in the Institute of the World Economy and International Relations, founded in 1957 as successor to the one disbanded in 1947.

Since both the ideology itself and the entire Soviet tradition of organizing academic institutions had linked the study of politics and economics, the Arbatov institute (as Soviets often refer to IUSAC in conversation) was understandably placed in the Academy of Sciences' Economics Division. In view of the political sensitivity involved in studying the United States it is also not surprising that an accomplished, flexible ideologist with considerable journalistic experience was named the institute's head.

The establishment of IUSAC led to only a partial concentration of Americanists within the institute. That fact's significance is too often missed or misunderstood in the United States. The selective concentration is simply inevitable because of the physical impossibility of housing all Soviet specialists on the United States in

Moscow. But it also reflects the institute's delimited roles in studying the United States and its politics, a matter that needs elaboration since the institute has been the most visible center of
American studies in the Soviet Union and, in many respects, the
most important one. This status is largely attributable to the entrepreneurial talents of Dr. Arbatov and to his position as a major
adviser to the political leadership at the Soviet–American summit
meetings in the 1970s and 1980s.[7] Insofar as they deal with American domestic politics, the institute's publications show that IUSAC
concentrates on analysis of current events and trends and secondarily on basic research. The institute's monthly deals almost exclusively with topical matters. Its articles characteristically identify
the major issues being discussed by American politicians and political analysts, the various interpretations of these issues by the
politicians and analysts, and the likely direction events will take
in politics and the economy.

The monthly's content is relatively free of Marxist–Leninist vocabulary and ideological analysis. The important exceptions were
the one or two special articles included in each issue up to the
mid–1980s for the benefit of persons studying in the Communist
party's in-house educational network, and clearly labeled as such.
Overall the monthly contains factual data and their interpretation,
both familiar to any American reader. Morton Schwartz, a major
interpreter of the institute's significance, commented quite correctly on the "relatively speaking more realistic," "better informed," and "more sophisticated" nature of the institute's
analyses when compared to some other Soviet writings (1978,
2–3).

A fuller assessment of the institute can be based on additional
observations. First, the improvements noted by Schwartz are not
so much due to the independent efforts of Soviet analysts as they
are a result of the institute's researchers' having been authorized
to summarize and then interpret to a limited degree some ongoing
discussions in the American press. This is a form of research in
the service of the state or, more accurately, the party. While better
than not having such a possibility at all, this Soviet reflection of
debates in American periodicals rarely gets down to the basics of
the issues involved.

A second associated question is the limited availability of the monthly, whose 1970 inaugural issue was printed in 22,000 copies. Its press run grew until it peaked at 38,000 in February 1978 and remained at that plateau through 1981. In January 1982 the run precipitously declined to 33,640 copies (almost the 34,000 it had been in January 1978) and gradually fell to 30,000 in February 1984. In January and February 1987 it suddenly rose to 32,000, then it stabilized at 31,000 until it declined to 26,000 in early 1989. Whatever the reasons for these ups and downs (and they could be as simple as a shortage of paper or as complicated as politics), the result is that relatively few people have access to this unique source of information.

Third, the institute also directly sponsors the publication of two kinds of books in line with its role in basic research. In one type the ideological component is strong enough to make the volume indistinguishable on those grounds from hundreds of others (Iakovlev, ed. 1976 and Beglov 1971 are examples). In the other type ideology plays such a minor role that, on the whole, the book comes close to being indistinguishable from typical American books on the subject (Zamoshkin and Batalov, eds. 1980 and Petrovskaia 1982 are examples). The factors behind these variations are to some extent as disparate as the particular ideological orientation of each writer within current permissible limits and the general need to conform to the publishing profile or posture of the institute and the specific publisher, not to mention the preferences of individual editors. Moreover, in view of what has happened in past decades, and taking into account the range of possible political eventualities in the Soviet Union, it is safest and most generally useful for a writer and a publisher to have a mix of more and less ideologically charged publications. In the long run this sort of publication profile may serve as a kind of insurance policy for an author, editor, and institute depending on the impact of politics on scholars and scholarship in the future.

Whatever the reasons behind it, the fact that the institute does sponsor some rather heavily ideological books, and that its monthly for many years normally contained one ideologically based article, should serve to modify any overly optimistic evaluation of its position and role in studying the United States. The institute operates in a context called the Soviet Union, and while the institute is shielded from some of the environment's conventions and may seek to modify particular aspects of the environment, it must inevitably reflect something of the context precisely in order to ensure its otherwise unique place within it. The institute's monthly has reflected the changing Soviet mood regarding U.S.–Soviet relations, as a comparison of the tone and content of its editorial articles in the early 1970s and 1980s would show.

The institute's influence upon the Soviet environment is severely limited in a particularly important area. It plays only a secondary role in broadening the ideological framework in terms of which politics in general, and American politics in particular, are interpreted in the Soviet Union. The institute's publications largely ignore the problem of modifying the ideology. The monthly concentrates on factual materials, and many of the books sponsored by the institute avoid drawing new ideological conclusions or criticizing older ideological orthodoxies. But there are important exceptions. Ziabliuk's book on lobbying broke new ground (1976). And even greater strides were made in studies of American public opinion and political consciousness (Petrovskaia 1982; Zamoshkin and Batalov, eds. 1980). The study of these important topics has become the institute's major focus. The institute also played a key role in producing a factual 542-page encyclopedic handbook on the United States printed in 240,000 copies (Arbatov and others, eds. 1988).

Perhaps just because it has been politically sheltered since its foundation in order to fulfill its mission of keeping track of current events and trends, the institute has not been *the* major force in expanding the bounds of ideological orthodoxy. Other Soviet institutes and universities and the individual scholars working in them have made numerous much more important contributions to the development of the ideology in general, the social sciences, the Soviet version of political science, and, specifically, Americanistics and the study of American politics. Unexpectedly, even some institutional bastions of conservative orthodoxy have participated in these creative processes. As its copyright page indicates, Anatolii Mel'nikov's (1974) innovative book on American class structure was sponsored by the Higher Party School and the Academy of the Social Sciences that are attached to the Communist party's Central Committee.

The question of IUSAC's role in widening the limits of ideology takes on a different aspect when the publishing activity of its members as individual scholars is considered. Many of their books published without the institute's sponsorship have contributed greatly toward expanding either the ideological boundaries or, more simply, the scholarly conventions of studying American politics, as in the case of Geevskii's (1973) book on the race problem and a book on the American political system edited by Nikiforov (1976). As a strategy, the institute itself maintains a rather low profile but arrogates to its members the role of leaven in the more widespread processes of incremental ideological development or modification of the mindset.

The influence of IUSAC on the Soviet political leadership also requires consideration, difficult and obscure as that topic may be. To begin with, the leaders are steeped in the essentials of the Soviet mindset's characterization of American politics. They have received more than the usual Soviet exposure to the negative features of American political and social life treated in Chapters 1 through 4. As they go through the training given in the party's own educational network they are exposed to materials on the United States like those in the special articles in IUSAC's monthly intended for those moving up in the party.[8]

Assuming that Soviet political leaders relate to experts in much the same way as leaders do in other countries, the following scenario seems realistic. Once they reach even middle-level leadership positions, future Soviet top leaders move into a situation typical of that status in any large organization. Increasingly, they "cannot hope to go beyond 'executive understanding'—typically skimming memoranda prepared by assistants" (Rosovsky 1987, 35). And apparently they depend on briefing books and oral briefings of all sorts unless their avocation is studying some aspect of American life.

Given the press of other matters, the leaders have no time for deep study. Academic experts on the United States prepare reports for "upstairs" that are channeled through directors of institutes, who transform the reports into a form deemed appropriate for submission to staff assistants of major political figures. The assistants transform that input into the kinds of memoranda that produce "executive knowledge," or as I have suggested, "briefing knowledge."

It is safe to assume that only rarely in this process do experts, advisers, or staff members attempt to speak truth to power. They have every incentive to communicate what the boss wants to hear and, chosen as they are, they probably actually believe what the boss wants to hear.

In this normal bureaucratic scenario Soviet experts on the United States are "clearly on tap, not on top" (Gustafson 1981, 158). To continue the image, they must tap into the mindset and try not to look too "American" for their own safety's sake. It is small wonder that American politicians and diplomats who have met Soviet leaders report on how generally poorly and stereotypically they have understood American politics and society (Huber 1988).

A different sort of expert and normality appeared when Aleksandr Yakovlev, a propaganda specialist and former ambassador to Canada, and Anatolii Dobrynin, longtime ambassador to the United States, joined a leadership already steeped in mindset attitudes. The early effects of their contributions were felt at the December 1987 summit in Washington: a welcome improvement in U.S.–Soviet relations coupled with an increase in the effectiveness of Soviet dealings with the United States from the vantage point of advancing Soviet interests. Yakovlev operated in the public relations realm helping create a media blitz; Dobrynin and his team of former Soviet embassy staffers in Washington worked in the area of detailed policymaking and implementation.

Even allowing for the summit's positive results, there was also uncertainty about whether the Soviets' basic attitudes had changed or whether they had put on a show. In either case, there are few grounds for expecting significant changes in the Politburo's substantive attitudes that remain typical of the Soviet mindset. Certainly the Gorbachev openness policy has not yet produced any noteworthy shift, great or incremental, toward comprehension of American politics and society in Soviet publications.

The addition of Yakovlev and Dobrynin to the top decision-making bodies, and the respective staffs they brought with them, probably served to diminish Arbatov's confidential advisory role as head of IUSAC, though not his public relations role as spokesman. In the daily policymaking interactions of the Soviet leadership Yakovlev and Dobrynin (until his retirement) with their policy inputs have been on top. Arbatov is rather more on tap. He remains the chief public figure representing Soviet Americanistics in interviews, whether alone or accompanying Gorbachev. And, of course, Georgii Shakhnazarov's position as Gorbachev's personal adviser and Fedor Burlatskii's friendship with Gorbachev put them closer to the top than Arbatov.

IUSAC's monthly publication demonstrates an obvious caution in changing its approach to information about American politics and society despite Gorbachev's openness policy. The first and most startling departure was translation of an article by Felix Rohaytin (1987), the Wall Street financier, on the troubled relationship of America's domestic and foreign economic policies. A second article contained a wealth of information, by Soviet standards, on the average American family's income and consumption patterns, and compared them with Soviet conditions (Zaichenko 1988). One article argued in favor of overcoming stereotypes in perceptions of the United States (Zubok 1988); another suggested radically improving Soviet arrangements for conducting cultural exchanges (Borisiuk 1988).

A fifth article ranged more broadly and deeply, the first one fully in the spirit of *glasnost* (Batalov 1989). Here was an attack on ideologically "primitivized" and "vulgarized" Soviet images of the United States that were produced on instructions (*ustanovki*) to present a "corrected" picture of life in America through "unmasking" and "rebuffing" positive images of the country (3–6). Batalov asserted that this continuous stress on the negative deprived the Soviets of the opportunity to borrow elements from American experience that would be useful in democratizing socialism in the Soviet Union. He singled out election practices such as declaring one's own candidacy, the development of leadership capacity (in the sense of the ability to defend one's positions against the government), the study of public opinion, learning the art of dialogue as opposed to "Stalinist monologues," and involving youth in the "practical school" of political campaigns (9–11). Finally, Batalov advocated utilizing American political science methods to study mass movements, socialization, political culture, and the structure of power.

A sixth article (Samuilov 1989) drew some unusual and overdue lessons from the Watergate and Irangate affairs. These were crises created by the operation of the separation of powers mechanism, which initially made possible the expansion of presidential power but then enabled Congress to check the expansion. More than that, the mechanism prevented the rise of an authoritarian regime and provided a means of restoring and preserving the rule of law.

The rate at which these kinds of articles are published will probably accelerate since five of the nineteen members of the editorial board were replaced in January 1989. (Arbatov was one of those replaced, probably because of his recent election to the new Supreme Soviet as a full-time legislator.) A radical step was taken when readers' strong mixed reactions to Zaichenko's (1988) article and his response to them were printed in the monthly's June 1989 issue.

In view of IUSAC's general record of caution, and perhaps also Arbatov's own, it is not surprising that it took so long for the monthly to address themes that had been articulated for some time by Gorbachev, especially "political culture," "pluralism," and "checks and balances"—preceded in each case by the word "socialist." There is a telling contrast here with the influential Aleksandr Yakovlev who, as the eminent Sovietologists Seweryn Bialer and Loren Graham point out, favors taking selective elements of the American political experience and applying them to the Soviet Union, in particular using the New Deal as a model for reforming a system without abandoning its basic values (Keller 1989). It would seem that the institute could have done more sooner.

Finally, it is noteworthy that, given Gorbachev's and Yakovlev's generally critical attitude toward the United States, there has been no appreciable increase in the number of negative books about the United States that began appearing in the late 1970s and continue to come out regularly.[9] A new book from Arbatov's institute contains an astonishing statement that may suggest why: even though the overwhelming majority of Americans knows about the many negative aspects of the system of representation, they do not question its existence—and it has lasted a long time. So the Soviets ought to study the system rather than continue unmasking it (Borisiuk and others 1988). Apparently, there are useful lessons to be learned from the system's success that could be applied to the Soviet experience, a conclusion shared by Aleksandr Yakovlev.

To return to academic institutions, Americanistics developed so rapidly, and Americanists became so much more widely scattered geographically, that in the mid–1970s coordinating bodies were established like the Scientific Council on Economic, Political and Ideological Problems of the United States, headed by Arbatov, and the Scientific Coordinating Council on Problems of American Studies, headed by Nikolai V. Sivachev of Moscow State University.[10]

These bodies and the institutions whose work they coordinate will, naturally, remain under the guidance of the party. On the other hand, they and the researchers working in them will also influence the party, its leaders, the attentive publics, and even the public at large.[11]

The overall extent to which the Americanists have influenced the top leadership is unclear and debatable (Huber 1988). Just how and in which directions they will influence is problematical because ultimately no institution in any country can be expected to escape the effects of the twentieth century's seemingly normal political swings between liberalism and conservatism (or left and right radicalism) in the polity at large. At times in the Soviet past those swings have been, and once again may be, substantial if not excessive in either direction. In the Gorbachev era the swing has been in a radically liberal direction. But neither can institutions escape the effects of the individuals working in them nor can the ideology itself escape the varying degrees of modifying manipulation by individuals and groups.

Individuals, Ideology, Academic Traditions

A major factor in determining why the Soviets interpret American politics in their unique ways is the process whereby an individual interprets reality through the mediation of a philosophy of life, a world outlook, a set of guiding or orienting principles, an ideology. Alternatively, a person may modify all these in light of their perceived conflict with reality.

A significant element in these two processes is that individuals must make public ("publish," but in a broader sense) their own "private" interpretations of reality in the context of a politico-intellectual system, or a net in Karl Deutsch's sense. Their interpretation must be expressed within the confines of discourse encouraged, tolerated, or forbidden by a real, existing system.

The essential question here is: What limitations does a system place upon an individual or a group intent on working out and publishing a new or different idea or principle, an entirely new value system, a new world outlook that calls into question the validity of an old idea or even an entire existing politico-intellectual system? In what ways are people encouraged, allowed, or forced to systematize their attitudes and findings in order to make their publication possible? The differing answers to these questions incorporated into the operation of various political systems create vastly different environments, each with its own limitations and incentives, within which the individual can publicly interpret reality. Yet despite the attempts of systems and their managers to mold and channel people, certain individuals manage to retain their individuality.

For purposes of analysis individuals may be divided into two temperaments, the fixed and the flexible, depending on the characteristic way they orient themselves toward values and the very process of thinking. Philosophically, this represents the difference between persons primarily concerned with conserving knowledge and those in favor of raising doubts and criticisms in order to expand knowledge. Put in other ways, some people prefer to have the answers, others like to raise questions; some need to have the truth, others are interested in falsifiability; some thrive on certainty, others on uncertainty; the ideal attracts some, the empirical others; some focus on being, others on becoming.

In the context of religion it is the difference between belief and disbelief, orthodoxy and heterodoxy, a dogmatic as opposed to a creative attitude; denomination-centeredness as opposed to ecumenicity. In politics it is usually the difference between conservatives and liberals. And in the most general terms it is the difference between no and yes, between closedness and openness, narrowness and breadth. In the social sciences the difference is between those preferring to repeat the old or most recent eternal truths and those seeking new probabilistic truths, between having found the definitive as contrasted with the search for the suggestive, or between adhering to established principles and reflecting on their relevance or workability.

For the fixed temperament the source of truth is particularistic—in Soviet conditions it is "the classics of Marxism–Leninism," the writings of Marx, Engels, and Lenin. For the flexible temperament the source is universalistic—truth may be found anywhere.

When analyzing politics the two temperaments represent the contrast between people who believe in the predictable inevitability of definite political outcomes and those believing that the outcomes are only more or less probable. The fixed temperament favors stability, continuity, and maintenance; the flexible is attracted to change and experimentation. (Obviously, there are exceptions. A revolutionary's fixed temperament favors drastic change—at least before the revolution.)

Many elements help create these temperaments: personality, upbringing, peers, education, life experiences, responsiveness to the spirit of the times, personal or community trauma, and many others. A combination of individual and environmental factors is at work.

In the Soviet Union the temperaments have had to express themselves within the changing parameters officially established by the political leaders, the party, professional organizations, and place of employment.[12] The flexible temperament was allowed much greater scope in the 1920s than in the 1930s. In the 1940s and early 1950s the fixed mindset reigned supreme. The 1960s and 1970s provided many more possibilities for exercising flexibility, capped by an explosion in the 1980s. Yet many partisans of the fixed temperament remained entrenched in positions of institutional authority, new generations came of age that included individuals who either had a fixed mindset or developed one, and some restraints on flexibility remained.

The interaction of these factors can be illustrated up to a point by contrasting the roles of two Soviet analysts exemplifying the temperaments. Valentin S. Zorin's major contributions to explicating the total monopoly domination version of SMC analysis in the 1950s and 1960s were documented in Chapter 1. He remained faithful to that mode even while he was on the editorial board of IUSAC's monthly, a publication which (with exceptions) downplayed the ideological factor in its articles.[13] In recent years Zorin has been better known as moderator of one of Moscow television's main current events talk shows where one of his roles is to add

ideologically correct comments to statements made by Americanists he is interviewing that he considers too venturesome. Traditionalist that he is, he has not contributed to developing the newer
modified versions of SMC. He is of the fixed temperament.

It is generally true that since the mid–1960s the stronger tendency
among Soviet academic analysts was in the direction of flexibility,
openness, and development. Fedor M. Burlatskii, a political so-
ciologist, has been the outstanding practitioner of this art. His
daring proposal in 1965 that political science be established as an
academic discipline received some support, but at the time nothing
came of it, a nonevent revealing much about the relationship between politics and academe in the Soviet Union. Burlatskii then
published a key book in 1970 that initiated the process of incorporating many Western social science methods and ideas into the
study of politics in general.

It was only after the Soviet Association of Political Science
hosted the Congress of the International Political Science Association in Moscow in 1979 that much greater progress became
possible in Burlatskii's seemingly endless campaign to introduce
variant methods into the Soviet study of politics (Shakhnazarov
and Burlatskii 1980).

The situation was complicated. Some adherents to the old orthodoxy remained in positions of institutional influence but published rarely because they were out of tune with the political and
academic times, while partisans of the officially encouraged movement to expand the orthodoxy operated under a significant re-
straint on that very expansion created by pressure coming from
the old believers. Clearly this was a case where the political culture
tended to support the fixed temperament, whereas the interests of
the political leadership encouraged flexibility. As had been normal,
the two temperaments coexisted. But while normally only one had
been in official favor at a time, to be replaced by the other eventually, by the early 1980s the two came into a state of more nearly
balanced official favor and their partisans exercised mutual re-
straint in criticizing each other. With Gorbachev as leader flexibility generally burgeoned, but not in Americanistics.

These peculiarities also derive from some typical Marxian analytical methods connected with the words "laws," "relations,"
and "tendencies." Whether of the fixed or flexible temperament,

mainstream Soviets agree that capitalism evolves according to its own inherent laws of development, which were discovered by Marx and Engels. Mainstream analysts agree that capitalism will disappear and will be followed by socialism and communism. But they disagree over how the various components of the capitalist system interact and how they are related to each other in both theory and practice. They also disagree over how rapidly a given capitalist system is moving in the directions preordained by its laws of development.

To outside observers these disagreements may seem to be hairsplitting, tempests in a theoretical or methodological teapot. But to the participants (especially those of the fixed temperament) they have been the stuff of scholarly and political life in the Soviet intellectual environment. If in a more tolerant environment analysts who disagree can be described as "miles apart," disagreements among Soviet writers before Gorbachev's incumbency were more accurately measured in feet or inches, and sometimes in even lesser intervals. Yet as the Soviets perceived matters, they saw themselves as miles apart in their disagreements.

Believing that Marxism is a science and that Soviet Marxists have the total truth about the essentials of reality, Soviets possessed of the fixed temperament find it disconcerting to introduce non-Marxist methods of analysis, and even terminology connected with those methods, into Soviet intellectual discourse. To do so seems to question the credibility of the ideology as the total truth about the essentials of reality. To the flexible temperament, incorporating selected methods and terms is acceptable because it improves analytical capacity without necessarily undermining the validity of the ideology. This is useful to political leaders, who can adapt the methods and terms to make them more compatible with the ideology (Brown 1984).

The key problem lies in determining what does and does not undermine the ideology. There has been no hard and fast answer to this question, but some elements contributing to resolving it are clear enough. Outside those critical times when the political leadership opts for making radical changes in the ideology (as Stalin did when imposing his brand of orthodoxy, as Khrushchev did when pressing for destalinization, and as Gorbachev now does in pressuring for "new thinking" and "socialist pluralism") the leadership as a whole has had a vested interest in keeping the ideology as intact as possible. They have avoided bringing in *too* many new elements. This happens because the ideology is perhaps the main legitimating factor underpinning the entire Soviet system and its leaders. Deeply embedded in the ideology, especially in the ideology's vocabulary, are some basic and some residual conceptual and affective elements. Consequently, when the political leaders discuss American domestic affairs in their public writings and speeches delivered at home they almost invariably use the terminology characteristic of the SMC mode. So frequent are the references to the monopolies, the ruling class, and so on, that, if one were to confine oneself to these materials in doing a study of Soviet perspectives on American politics, it would seem as though the flexible temperament did not exist and that we were back in the early 1950s.

Roughly the same can be said about the Soviet mass media after taking into account whatever improvements in coverage of American domestic affairs may have been made (Mickiewicz 1988), and also the most recent trend toward negative reporting, especially about human rights, which started in the late 1970s.

This mixed situation reflects both deeply held beliefs and differences in levels or realms of discourse. The leaders' public statements are largely programmatic discourse, expressing the ideological orthodoxy of the moment or, more rarely, setting a new ideological direction to be taken. Characteristic of this discourse has been a mixture of orthodox fundamentalism and what has been called "creative Marxism" in the Soviet Union. What the leaders consider to be the basically true elements of Marxism–Leninism are mixed with innovations and changes in emphasis they deem desirable at one or another time. For this reason it makes sense for the leaders to welcome the existence of scholars and ideologists representing both temperaments who may operate in a less public realm of discourse. Under appropriate circumstances either can be useful to the leaders. But at any particular time, or with regard to a specific issue, one temperament may be favored or deemed undesirable.

In written public discourse prior to Gorbachev's openness strategy the use of the terms "discussion" and "debatable" was a signal that the creative development of ideology was in progress. When

a very new and different approach was being made toward an
ideological issue by a writer its provocative nature or *diskussion-
nost'*, was noted by the editor, as if to alert the readers to expect
the unexpected. As the new approach evoked extended discussion
it became a controversial issue, or *spornyi vopros*. If the approach
proved acceptable to scholars, theoreticians, and political leaders
alike, it became part of the creative development of the ideology.
But if the approach was finally deemed "incorrect," it had to be
abandoned in public discussions, at least. The new approach to
the issue might or might not have a future, and only the future
would tell.

In sum, the interactions of many individuals in institutional set-
tings have produced incremental ideological change, and the decisions of political leaders have either produced or legitimized
much more radical change in the ideology. But these same kinds
of interactions have also accounted for the continuities that are
embedded deeply in the ideology's framework, in its terminology,
and in the temperaments and interests of some individuals. If one
were to make a final judgment about the dominant tendency in
the Soviet version of the ideology it would have to be that, until
the Gorbachev era, this version has encouraged, has been supportive of, and has tended to inculcate the fixed temperament.

There have been two formative and two catalytic contexts within
which Soviet analysts have studied American politics. The first
formative context was Lenin's version of Marxism, particularly his
theory of imperialism. This term is ingrained in the mainstream
mentality and has been used countless times by Soviet analysts and
political leaders, less so in the Gorbachev era. State–monopoly
capitalism perspectives are intimately connected with the Soviet
concept of imperialism. The second formative context was Stalin's
version of Marxism–Leninism, one that James Scanlan has insight-
fully suggested could better be called "Engelsism–Leninism" because of its narrow rigidity (1985, 22). This version applied to the
United States became SMC analysis.

The first catalytic context was destalinization, which in academic
life meant identifying and overcoming some accretions introduced
in the second formative period. This context served both to move
the Soviet analysis of American politics back toward what it had
been in the 1920s and early 1930s and to move it forward into

using some Western sociological approaches in political analysis. The second catalytic context comprises the attempt, so far unsuccessful, to establish political science as a Soviet academic discipline. Still, this attempt has contributed significantly toward introducing a richer variety of methods and means of analysis into the Soviet study of politics (Brown 1984). Gorbachev has created a third catalytic context that has not yet affected Americanistics in a major way.

I have already commented on several articles about American politics and society written in the spirit of *glasnost*. These are just a beginning. Concerning books on American politics, so far the beginning consists only of the last three pages of a new book on the history of American political science (Fedoseev 1989). Appearing in a volume that was otherwise orthodox and conservative, those few pages advocated among other things: adopting a respectful attitude toward other political systems; recognizing the right of each nation to choose its own political system; freeing Soviet analysts from myths and stereotypes; establishing free access to foreign writings on politics; establishing political science as an academic discipline in the Soviet Union; and founding a journal devoted to political analysis.

Effects on the Study of American Politics

What the Soviets think of American politics is to a large extent a product of *how* they think about American politics. Continuities and changes in Soviet interpretations of American politics are the product of the dynamic interaction of the ideology, academic traditions, and forces favoring modifications.

Overall, Soviet analysts have been faithful to certain elements of the ideology. Most important, they have remained conscious and determined critics of capitalist systems, a stance that has long been characteristic of all Marxists, non-Soviets included.[14] The Soviets call this critical attitude either "adherence to the class principle," according to which Marxists must criticize and even condemn the class enemy and all his multitudinous wrongdoings, or *partiinost'*, adherence to the Communist party's current version of orthodoxy.

To some greater or lesser degree mainstream Soviets are anti-capitalist. They never claim to be impartial to or about capitalism and they never claim to be procapitalist, even, and perhaps especially, when they go so far as to adopt market mechanisms to improve the functioning of their socialist economy. Their criticism of capitalism has been grounded in the continually reiterated belief, originated by Engels, that Marxism is the only truly scientific theory that really explains everything important in philosophy, history, economics, and politics.[15] It seems likely that this attitude will be modified soon, and the materials in this book will help to document rather precisely the extent and degree to which that happens.

A second continuity with Marx and Engels is the conviction, seemingly contradictory but easily comprehensible to a Marxist's dialectical way of thinking, that in capitalist societies politics simultaneously derive directly from economics, yet they are to some degree (apparently small and rather indefinite) autonomous and can even have a manipulative effect on economics.[16] A third continuity is the proposition that in capitalist societies politics is an outgrowth of the class struggle. Power is concentrated and centralized in the state, and it is nonsense to speak of the separation of powers.[17] This point will probably lose its validity in view of Gorbachev's positive attitude toward the "socialist separation of powers."

The chief continuity with Lenin derives from his analysis of the effects of both imperialism and the growth of monopoly upon politics in capitalist nations.

These continuities have been expressed in qualitatively different ways at various times. In general, the critical stance has always been the preferred analytical posture. But criticism can be minimal (as in IUSAC's monthly), or so violent as to be effectively an indictment (as in publications in the late 1940s and the 1950s), or so unremittingly negative as to stretch one's credulity (as in the more strident of the SMC analyses). But it may also be moderate, measured, well taken, and even right on target. Perhaps the best example of the latter is the Soviet attack, commencing in the early 1950s, on the expansion of presidential power.

On this point, coincidentally, differing beliefs have made strange analytical bedfellows over the decades. The original attack on this expansion had been made in the 1930s by American conservatives, while liberals supported the expansion. However, the liberals eventually attacked the expansion in the 1970s when they discovered that the presidency had become imperial, while the conservatives now viewed the expansion more benignly and even positively, particularly in the Reagan years.

There are three more continuities whose paradoxical importance lies in the changes they have produced in Soviet perceptions: dialectical reasoning; the linked analysis of economic, social, and political developmental tendencies; and the practice of citing extensively Marx, Engels, Lenin, party "documents," and the current party leader.

The mind trained in dialectical reasoning is inclined to analyze in terms of the dynamic interaction of opposites. The interactions of the proletariat and bourgeoisie that are most important for the Soviets are viewed as manifestations of the laws of the historical, economic, and social development of capitalism. These stress that in the long run capitalism will inevitably disappear together with its bourgeois political system. But the Soviets also analyze the medium- and short-run tendencies that show up in the interactions of the warring classes. At this level they consider factors and activities that do not point in any inevitable direction or result in an inevitable outcome. Tendencies toward disunity within the working class, for instance, can have a markedly negative effect on its struggle with the bourgeoisie. When coupled with dialectical reasoning, analysis of such tendencies presents the Soviets with opportunities to weigh, judge, and balance (within oscillating limits) and not be attacked for engaging in bourgeois objectivism while so doing. Under this dispensation it was possible to introduce modifications into primitive SMC analyses of American politics even during the 1950s when it was risky to do so.

The critical nature of Soviet analyses is a source of both strengths and weaknesses. It serves to concentrate the attention of analysts upon a delimited range of issues and, like a searchlight, to illuminate them brightly and in detail—but only in prescribed, almost ritualistic ways. Although this procedure can generate some neatly focused insights, it can also create a form of tunnel vision, confining and restricting the analyst and creating at least a strong preference, if not a mandate, for directing research exclusively toward proving the truth of the ideology.

The Soviet scholarly tradition of extensive quotation and citation of "the classics," of the "documents" issued following meetings of top party bodies, and of "authoritative" works and statements generally creates a conservative bias. But it can also serve as a method of legitimating change. Because these sources have by now been cited millions if not billions of times, it is impossible to determine how often they have been used to defend conservative ideological positions, to advance innovative ones, or to serve as an ideological insurance policy by showing that an innovative writer is familiar with the sources of orthodoxy and that there is something in those sources to substantiate the innovations the writer is making.

In the Soviet Union this practice has been attacked periodically as *tsitatnichestvo,* quotation-mongering. But that has not seemed to diminish its incidence appreciably and for very good reason in the Soviet mind. What Marx, Engels, and Lenin have written about politics in general, and politics in capitalist countries and in the United States in particular, has been much more important to generations of Soviet analysts than what anybody else has written about those politics. A cautious trend away from this scholarly convention has been developing since the 1960s, but it remains ascendant, even though the number of exceptions is slowly increasing.

The specific mechanism used to legitimate a change in perceptions lies in discovering that a new perception has always actually existed in "the classics" or had been proclaimed recently in authoritative statements by the current leadership. As is well known, the Soviet leaders have often changed their minds (sometimes at the instigation of experts or scholars) about what "truth" is, and this has been a most important source of change. Another source of modification is built into the ideology since the idea that economic, social, and political reality is constantly changing is basic to Marxism as an analytical system. Marx himself found it difficult to define his analytical terms or to keep a definition stable once he had stated it. He often modified his understanding of what a thing "is" after he considered how it related to various other things (Ollman 1976). In their own analyses Soviet writers use these variances to suggest or substantiate changes in interpretation.

Additional differences within "the classics" themselves that the

Soviets can use for similar purposes originate in the disparities in approach and conclusions between Marx and Engels (see Levine 1975), not to mention the question of Lenin's contributions to the development or modification of Marxism. These three theoreticians unquestionably have much in common. But the differences, great and small, found in the 105 thick volumes comprising their collected works nevertheless have been the source of either occasioning or legitimating change in Soviet perceptions. The extent to which one or the other has been the motivating factor is difficult, and probably impossible, to establish in the case of individuals and groups of analysts, let alone an entire intellectual tradition.

Until the 1970s the ideology and domestic Soviet political dynamics combined to discourage incorporating non-Marxian approaches and insights into the Soviet study of politics. Since then analytical techniques of Western social science have been adopted slowly because of the lingering tendency to dismiss them as unscientific, un-Marxist, or as techniques used by bourgeois scholars in an attempt to explain away the negative aspects of political life in the West.[18]

With some important exceptions, Soviet scholars have specialized in developing and changing their conventional analyses in an extremely incremental manner, hesitatingly, very qualifiedly, and at times obscurely. New insights, and especially appraisals differing from the conventional wisdom, have normally been scattered throughout a book or even throughout an entire body of writing dealing with a specific topic.

To an extent, some of these characteristics are the hallmark of scholarly writing everywhere. But there are two differences that complicate the Soviet case. First, while Soviet analysts may have thought about the unthinkable, and even talked about it in private, they could not publish it except under the conditions just noted or, only very rarely, in the form of clear, definite, and, by Soviet standards, forthright statements. Under *glasnost* there is a change for the better, but in Soviet social science it remains inadvisable to make what would be called in the West analytical breakthroughs. Only a few Soviet books on American politics and society can be called breakthroughs—Geevskii on the race problem (1973); Mel'nikov on the social structure (1974); Chetverikov on policy-making (1974); Fursenko on the political history of the 1960s

(1971). But not one of these volumes initiated a trend. The break-throughs produced no follow-up.[19] Second, it is an unwritten rule (to which there are increasing exceptions) not to attempt to sys-tematize scattered unconventional insights or appraisals outside of the usual forms of ritualized systematization in the modes of SMC, bourgeois democracy, and the class struggle.

Advances in analytical perceptions are normally submerged in a sea of orthodox materials. It therefore becomes problematical for Western analysts to determine what the real position of some authors is or what effect, if any, has been produced on the Soviet study of American politics by a number of insights scattered throughout the Soviet literature on the subject.

These preferences and requirements heavily influenced the way American politics was studied before the early 1970s. They shaped Soviet views of American politics even when modified by the highly incremental introduction of new perceptions and methods of analysis.[20]

A disturbing illustration of the consequences flowing from these preferences is the fact that only five studies describing the Amer-ican political system as a whole have been published as books in the Soviet Union since 1917. The first volume was published in 1930, three in the 1950s, and the latest in 1976. With the exception of the 1976 study, which exemplifies the effects of introducing modifications into the standard Soviet way of discussing the topic, the books are written for the most part in the state and law tra-dition. They are formal descriptions of how the national govern-ment is organized and operates according to the Constitution. Since the Soviet writers are considering a *bourgeois* political system, criticism is naturally part of their job (or simply of their convic-tions), so that the political system's organization and operation come under attack using SMC and bourgeois democracy as touch-stones. In partial contrast, the 1976 volume considers the formal-ities and also criticizes, but it additionally explains the system's operation in more informative functional terms and treats some old issues in new ways.

It has either not been considered important to publish general studies of this kind, or perhaps it has been too intellectually un-satisfying or professionally risky. Perhaps the mindset, the learning net, could not flex enough to produce such a study. Ultimately, the Soviets felt they had to translate the fifth edition of Dye and Zeigler's textbook (Dai and Zigler 1984) to make up for what they find it difficult, and perhaps even impossible, to do.

The preference accorded SMC and bourgeois democracy analysis is certainly an important reason for the dearth of these comprehensive studies. The Soviet failure to take American political science seriously until recently is another. It was only in the early 1960s that note was taken of the existence of political science in America as a discipline, and at once it was misidentified as a branch of sociology and attacked for allegedly being a vehicle for whitewashing the highly imperfect political system.[22] While remaining critical of American political science, Soviet writers have made increasing use of studies by its practitioners, its vocabulary, methods of organizing and investigating source materials and data, and even some of its analytical frameworks to a limited extent.[23]

These trends are best illustrated in the new ways that some Soviets have treated two ideologically sensitive aspects of American politics that are particularly difficult for the mindset to understand. One is the theory and practice of the separation of powers, together with checks and balances, as basic organizing and operating principles as well as deeply held values in American politics. The other is lobbying as an important part of the political processes connected with the theory of representation in government and practical, real access to it.

There are several conventional Soviet attitudes toward the separation of powers. Marx's assessment that the very idea is as absurd, in principle, as trying to square the circle has frequently been repeated while noting that, in practice, the separation of powers is just another bourgeois subterfuge for concealing the ruling class's undivided domination (Gromyko 1957; Guliev 1970; N.V. 1971b). In terms of the state and law approach it is simply impossible to separate "state power" since the approach provides for only one undivided sovereign power, and that is the state.[24] Finally, because all governmental bodies and posts are in the service of the bourgeoisie, president and Congress have the common task of defending the capitalist system—they are not so much rivals as partners (Solomatina 1972; Savel'ev 1976a).

This combination of ideology and constricting legalism created a Soviet intellectual tradition making it practically impossible for an author to take the separation of powers seriously in print for several decades. The most significant exception was Iosif Levin, who cleverly noted that although the separation of powers had been important in the American past, the development of SMC had undermined it but had not completely eliminated its role since in some future situations the ruling class might find it necessary to use Congress as a means of circumventing the president should he somehow not do the will of the ruling class (1951).

So sensitive an issue was this that Levin was criticized sharply some years afterward for making even this hedged statement (Gromyko 1957). But "life itself," as the Soviets are so fond of saying, finally showed the analysts that the separation of powers was indeed significant, although not in the way Levin had envisaged. The Watergate affair and the eventual resignation of President Nixon were a process and a result directly contravening long-established Soviet interpretive orthodoxies respecting the relationship between president and Congress. A new approach soon became possible in which the separation of powers was taken either as being fundamentally significant or as being significant with some reservations, especially that the principle and process continue to remain secondary to the continual strengthening of presidential power.[25] Ultimately, though, it was possible even to draw in print the obvious conclusion that may have been made in private by a few Soviet analysts: Watergate had contributed toward strengthening Congress (Kokoshin 1981).

These were major steps in developing a better informed and more realistic understanding of how American politics works. Roughly the same happened regarding the theory and practice of checks and balances, and for similar reasons. One group of writers stressed that the theory's purpose and function are to conceal the fact that the three branches of government are actually never at odds but rather serve the interests of the bourgeoisie in equal measure (Gromyko 1957; N.V. 1971a). One author discovered a particularly perverse form of checks and balances, claiming that Congress passes progressive legislation knowing that the other branches will effectively cancel it.[26]

Some writers began to controvert the standard SMC suppositions that the president dictated to Congress, and that Congress had once and for all been degraded.[27] Other analysts found that there had been a perceptible balance between president and Congress either from time to time or over time (Chetverikov 1974; Savel'ev 1976a). And then a position was developed that dialectically incorporated the best of both worlds: the separation of powers and checks and balances really do involve a partial sharing of functions; this is what makes the government work flexibly and effectively and is at the same time a manifestation of the oneness of the oligarchy's class interest and actions (Nikiforov, ed. 1976).

A similar process has affected the perception of lobbying. Soviet analysts had always stoutly maintained that the workers were in no way part of the bourgeois political system, that they could not and did not participate in it in any meaningful way, that they could in no way be "included" in the system, and that the proletariat could influence a system controlled by the ruling class only through strikes, mass movements, and the like. For these reasons it was conventional to argue that only business, and particularly big business, engaged in lobbying. The general assumption was that lobbying normally involved bribery and was therefore innately unsavory.[28]

The process through which the Soviet learning net and publication system achieved and presented a fuller understanding of lobbying is instructive. Some writers were aware that the labor unions engaged in lobbying but could mention it only in passing for the first time in 1960 (Arzumanian and others, eds. 1960). Another tack was to raise the issue delicately in a footnote, observing that in Soviet writing the term lobbying was used in a negative sense, whereas in the United States it was used positively—even by the Communist party's newspaper, *The Daily Worker*—to describe the process of getting progressive legislation passed (Guliev 1961). Guliev later dubbed these uses the broader sense of the term (to include unions) and the narrower sense (including only business), thereby initiating a process through which the broader usage very slowly gained greater currency in Soviet analyses.[29]

Other writers recognized labor's lobbying activity but concluded that, when compared with the magnitude of big business's efforts, it is very limited in scope and effect, and some maintained that lobbying by labor is so meaningless that it is significant only negatively in that it creates an illusion of worker political participation (Kalenskii 1969; Lapitskii 1973; Chetverikov 1974; Liven' 1975; Nikiforov, ed. 1976).

The one Soviet book devoted entirely to lobbying quite expectedly says little about lobbying by labor and concludes that whatever successes may be achieved by the unions, and by those leftist and other progressive organizations that do engage in lobbying, they do not undermine the monopolies' domination of the political system (Ziabliuk 1976). The most thorough study of union lobbying unexpectedly states that by the 1960s a highly organized effort had in fact been developed that was very well connected with the powers that be in Congress. But it was soon rendered obsolete by changes in the organization and operation of Congress connected with the post-Vietnam diffusion of power in that body, especially the weakened authority of committee chairmen and the erosion of party discipline (Rogova 1983).

This evolution of views still leaves the troublesome question of just what effects these insights into the separation of powers, checks and balances, and lobbying may have upon that relatively small number of Soviet readers who have access to the studies containing those discoveries and who also have the patience to follow the course of such belated and scattered revelations. Clearly, whatever the impacts were, they would have been heightened by a better knowledge of the American policymaking process than most Soviets have, and here I am excluding the subsets and subdivisions of the mindset that are better informed. After all, these basic characteristics of American politics have their greatest effect in the policymaking process. But the quantity of materials published by Soviet writers on the policy process in America is too small for anybody in the Soviet Union solely dependent upon these sources to achieve even a vague perception either of how the process works or of the arguments among American analysts over how it does or does not work.[30]

These imposing gaps, so detrimental to achieving a better understanding of American politics, are the result of a mechanism triggered by ideological commitments and also the propensity to downgrade American political science. That discipline may have finally been "discovered" and then utilized qualifiedly and hesitatingly in the Soviet Union, but so far the policy studies aspect of the discipline has not had a significant impact.

Conclusion

This chapter has sketched out the elements of a sociology of knowledge focusing on the learning mechanisms most relevant to the Soviet academic community as it has related to the ideology, the political leaders, and the Soviet academic institutional network and its intellectual traditions. These are the specifically Soviet contexts that in some very practical ways have delimited what Soviet writers have been able to "know" about American politics—or, more accurately stated, what they could say in print that they know about those politics. Soviet scholars, like their counterparts everywhere, write to preserve and advance knowledge, and they do so under conditions and restrictions imposed by their specific academic discipline, their institutions, their colleagues, and their publishers. Like scholars elsewhere, they write to get published, to be promoted, to establish a professional reputation, and to enhance a career. These factors have been known to stop people from becoming too venturesome the world over.

All these circumstances, those peculiarly Soviet plus the more universal ones, affect the choice of research topic, analytical strategy, and the presentation of results in a manuscript—which must then be approved by the Soviet writer's proximate colleagues, editors, editorial reviewers, the censor, and, finally, the critical public. The thrust of these checks and balances is to favor making highly incremental and atomized advances in published knowledge and to avoid the kinds of aggregation of data and generalization of findings that may lead to breakthroughs in knowledge.

These tendencies are further encouraged by the highly specialized and compartmentalized ways in which Soviet research is organized and conducted. A multitude of narrowly focused studies that avoid addressing basic interpretive issues is fostered, and breakthroughs are actively discouraged. When a rare breakthrough is made, the tendency is for commentators to avoid assessing the impact of the "discovery" upon the ideological framework for analyzing American politics. A final factor reinforcing this ten-

dency is the apparent prohibition upon publishing positive socioeconomic data indicative of the general American standard of
living or the productivity of industry and agriculture. This is little
different from a similar prohibition on publishing various negative
data about Soviet domestic affairs (Dewhirst and Farrell, eds.
1973). Under *glasnost* the latter situation has changed substantially, but the former remains essentially unchanged.

Connected with these sociological considerations, which may
also be viewed as a system of political control over scholarly life,
are some problems relating to the philosophy of science. The way
in which scientific research is conducted in any country is intimately
connected with the nature of the society supporting such research.
In the Soviet Union a fundamental issue in all scholarly research
is the relation of the official ideology's assumptions, claims, conclusions, and predictions to science (Lubrano and Solomon, eds.
1980). The official Soviet position has been to equate Marxism–
Leninism with science in the sense that the ideology has been
viewed as the one and only truly scientific world outlook.[31] This
prescription remains in force even though it has been necessary to
bring Soviet science (by ideological definition the most advanced
science since it is based on Marxism-Leninism) more into line with
world science and then, very reluctantly, to make adjustments in
the ideology.[32]

It is not easy to conceptualize or comprehend the process
through which any scientific community, and also the larger society
of which it is a part, either retains or changes its understanding of
what is regarded as real, verified, true, scientific knowledge.[33] If
this is true of the hard sciences, the problems in the social sciences
are infinitely more complex, if not insurmountable. For those Soviets (and who, indeed, knows how many of them there are?) who
believe that Marxism–Leninism is the quintessence of science there
are no problems. For persons so believing, a scientific study of
American politics can be done only by concentrating on the concerns and methods characteristic of SMC, bourgeois democracy,
and the class struggle. In such a study the knowledge contained in
"the classics" must be treated in ways analogous to the deference
accorded Holy Writ among religious believers. Conversely, "bourgeois" perceptions of politics must be treated extremely critically.
These are seen as conscious or unconscious distortions of reality

quite simply because they are non-Marxist. That is, by Soviet definition they are unscientific.

The logic of belief just described is difficult for nonbelievers to accept, if only because of its circularity. But there is a more universal and basic problem: the beliefs of other people are unbelievable. A person may respect them but still not believe them. This is one of those self-evident truths palpably demonstrated literally every day in pluralistic societies, but it is very often forgotten when the following question is asked: Does anybody in the Soviet Union *really* believe the official interpretation of American politics?

Put this way, the question is the naive product of Westerners' frustration with Soviet mainstream views. The more realistic question is: Do enough Soviets believe *enough* of that interpretation? The answer has to be yes for the very compelling reason that American, French, British, Italian, and other Marxists interpret American politics in essentially the same ways as do the Soviets. They use the class approach and historical materialism. In other words, some people who are either on the American scene, or who are closer to more information about that scene than the Soviets, share their primary views, and yet it occurs to few, if any, Westerners to ask whether those people really believe what they say they believe.

Just why the genuineness of the beliefs of one's own home-grown Marxists is apparently so readily accepted while doubts are raised about the authenticity of very much the same beliefs held by mainstream Soviet Marxists is something of a mystery.[34] It may, of course, be that there is a good deal of cynicism in what looks to be Soviet ideological commitment. But in that case Alfred G. Meyer's unusual observation about these two seemingly incompatible things that sometimes coexist bears recalling: "Perhaps they even support and reinforce each other" (1985, 112). The likeliest explanation comes from Nikolai Engver, a member of the new Soviet Congress of Peoples' Deputies, who commented upon some prevalent attitudes among his fellow deputies: "People here have such an undemocratic, authoritarian way of thinking that they view as pathological things that occur naturally in the civilized world" (1989).

The mainstream pattern of Soviet belief as enshrined in Soviet academic life creates a well-known problem. It is difficult for the believer to learn, or admit that anybody can learn, from sources other than those that are taken to be true by definition. For Soviet students of American politics several notable consequences follow. In particular, a problem identified by Varga years ago remained troublesome for decades in that Soviet analysts tended either to rehash "the classics" without paying too much attention to current data or to write very heavily factual accounts without relating them much to Marxist theory (1929). Although the first tendency has diminished somewhat, the second is still prevalent in IUSAC's monthly.

Essentially these were the consequences of knowing too much about the object of study even before serious study was undertaken, which helps explain why the separation of powers was not taken seriously for so long and why the *Federalist Papers* and the significance of the ideas contained in them for studying American politics were ignored for all practical purposes.[35] Finally, these attitudes have made it difficult to produce systematic studies of how American political institutions are organized and interact with one another as well as with society at large and specific parts of it. This is really a matter of how data are organized on the basis of one's intellectual sacred cows. In the Soviet Union these are SMC, bourgeois democracy, and the class struggle—ideas that hardly ever appear in American mainstream writing on politics.

Soviet analysts have almost totally ignored an important alternative or collateral way of studying those politics which is used in numerous American mainstream texts. It is not necessary to agree with either the particulars or even the general content of these American books in order to understand that their overall organizational framework is a suitable vehicle for clarifying certain relationships and activities that the Soviet tradition of writing on American politics ignores, overlooks, or underrates.

But for reasons connected with the nature of the Soviet mindset, the Soviets overlooked and then misidentified American textbooks on politics. Until the late 1950s a few Soviet researchers seemed to be aware of only one textbook, the various editions of Harold Zink's standard work (1942–1951). But the Soviets did not have an understanding of the nature and purpose of such textbooks as late as the 1970s. Even at IUSAC Vladimir Savel'ev, a specialist on Congress, assumed that he was discussing a specialized mono-graph, and not a textbook, in his review of Dye and Zeigler's *Irony of Democracy* (1970) for the institute's monthly.[36]

Soviet specialists avoided writing general systematic studies of the political system and overviews of American political institutions and processes such as the Congress, the presidency, the Supreme Court, elections, and policymaking. On the basis of what has been published in the Soviet Union people dependent upon those writings could not possibly achieve an understanding of how the institutions are organized and how the political processes function. For that very reason IUSAC's monthly published a special article (Vlasikhin 1985) summarizing the basics of the political system's organization and operation in response to a subscriber's complaint about not having a clear overall picture of American political institutions and processes.

Traumatic events in American politics (such as the Nixon resignation or adoption of the Jackson–Vanik amendment to the Trade Act of 1974), which flew in the face of the conventional Soviet wisdom, encouraged, enabled, or even required that some long overdue steps be taken to start filling some of these gaps in the publications on American politics.

One must, in the final analysis, be grateful for whatever progress is made against such stiff odds. But even these serious incentives to change have not been enough to move published Soviet interpretations in radically different directions. In the language of to-day's Soviet politics, there has been no significant restructuring of Soviet perspectives on, and little new thinking about, American domestic politics.

That remains true even though Gorbachev has begun to use terms like "socialist system of checks and balances," even though there has been an announced policy of separating the powers of the Soviet Communist party from the government's, and even though there has been visible lobbying going on at the sessions of the two new Soviet legislatures. Given the new applicability of information about American politics to Soviet political life, all this is bound to have an effect upon how the Soviets write about American politics because of the growing market for such data. As it is, one Soviet who ran for deputy in the March 1989 contested elections used campaign techniques he had read about in the Russian translation of Robert Penn Warren's *All the King's Men* (Murashev 1989).

The conceptual obstacles to introducing more elements from American experience at a faster rate are strong. Boris Yeltsin's comment while visiting America to study its democratic system illustrates the simultaneous Soviet attraction and doubt: "You have more than 200 years' experience with democratic government, although [it is] bourgeois democracy" (*New York Times,* September 10, 1989).

6 AMERICAN POLITICAL INSTITUTIONS AND PROCESSES: SOVIET EVALUATIONS

The concept of an information-patterning system is particularly significant to the Soviets' treatment of institutions and processes. The Soviet "learning net" willed two things, first that American politics be analyzed from ideological perspectives, and second that increasing amounts of hard data about American politics be incorporated.

In either case, or in combination, over the decades so many Soviets have presented their materials on elections, political parties, the president, Congress, and the Supreme Court in such a scattered way that it is difficult to reorganize them under these conventional headings. There have been rare exceptions to this scattering effect, but the Soviets have not yet written the kinds of systematic, general, critical studies of American politics produced in the United States by Mintz and Cohen (1971), Dye and Zeigler (1970–1987), Greenberg (1989), Parenti (1980), and many others.

The earliest major American attempt to systematize the widely dispersed elements of information was Frederick Barghoorn's *The Soviet Image of the United States: A Study in Distortion* (1950). The book's title and content were very faithful to the unrelievedly negative and abusive spirit in the Soviet materials of the mid- and late 1940s. A much later study (Gibert 1976) attempted with less justification to establish that there was one, and only one, orthodox Soviet viewpoint by giving little attention to the differences and innovations that appeared in Soviet publications in the 1960s and early 1970s.

John Lenczowski was able to differentiate two Soviet ap-

proaches, the traditionalist and realist, in studying the domestic
determinants of American foreign policy (1982). His conclusion
was that the differences between these approaches tend to be minimal, despite the obviously more sophisticated analyses of the real-
ists. Most important, there is an overall consensus regarding basic
issues which tends in the direction of orthodoxy or conservatism
(1982).

Other writers have also identified two distinct Soviet approaches,
the conservative and liberal (Nordahl 1972; Schwartz 1978). But
they stress the variety of ideas advanced by liberal Soviet writers
on a broad range of specific topics. Innovative ideas and sophisticated approaches are highlighted to show how far the Soviets
have developed beyond traditional SMC stereotypes. These analysts perceive a more liberal consensus than does Lenczowski.

The most complex attempt at ordering Soviet approaches was
made by Franklyn Griffiths, who discerned four images of American politics in Soviet writing: subordination of the state to the
monopolies, sawed-off pluralism, pluralism, and a state-centric
image (1972). Each image is associated with an analytical school
of thought, and individual Soviet analysts are placed within one
or another school on the basis of the identifiable thrust of their
writings. But Griffiths found that many authors could be placed
in more than one school. The problem of placement was further
complicated when Griffiths took into account factors like the individual Soviet analyst's organizational affiliation, generation, conservative or moderate bias, role performance, and position in the
group interactions revolving around policy debates.

Owing to the diffused, fragmented, episodic, atomized, and incremental ways in which the materials on American politics have
been distributed throughout Soviet writing as a general rule, sys-
tematizing them is a problem. It becomes even more complicated
to the extent that Neil Malcom's observation is true: toward the
late 1970s Soviet analysts had increasingly tended to develop individual and personal views and approaches, and even idiosyncratic
ones (1984).

The Soviet authors' hesitation about making generalizations that
might lead to the creation of readily identifiable schools or approaches reflects several of their concerns. There may be a preference or need to work within an ideological consensus that

expands or contracts. There is reluctance to go out on a limb and be proved wrong by the future course of events in American politics. There is also fear of leaving themselves open to attack by proponents of any new Soviet orthodoxy that may appear. It does pay to be cautious, and particularly to hedge one's bets. These requirements produce a form of writing in which sweeping, ideologically correct generalizations are made, usually early in a book or article. But these seemingly universally valid statements are sooner or later followed by numerous qualifications and even suggestions that alternatives to the generalizations may also have limited validity.

In keeping with the concepts of information processing and information patterning, it is more effective to shift the focus from authors and, instead, to evaluate individual Soviet publications on American politics. There are six categories of writing that contribute to forming the Soviet reader's understanding of American politics. Each category represents an actively encouraged or passively tolerated Soviet method of presenting publishable data on American political institutions and processes. For the moment we can assume that there are varying degrees of validity among the categories and discuss the question of validity fully in the following chapter.

The first type of writing comprises the elementary SMC, bourgeois democracy, and class struggle approaches. These analyses are ideologically conservative, supremely Marxist–Leninist, and characteristically treat institutions and processes either in highly ritualized ways or almost in passing. These can be called ideological writings.

The second type makes episodic, scattered, incremental additions to and corrections of the first type. A very limited amount of this is, in fact, found in the ideological writings themselves. But the additions and corrections are made to a greater degree (and sometimes to a much greater degree) in this second type, to be called incremental writings.

The third type conveys large quantities of heavily factual materials, often on narrowly specific topics, without much of an attempt either to build cumulatively on similar previous writing or to theorize about the materials. In the 1930s, before the SMC model was developed, V. Lan's studies of American elections used this approach. In the 1970s the same kind of knowledgeable re-portage was revived by, and has been characteristic of, IUSAC's monthly, which much more often than not carries articles treating a broad range of relatively narrow topics rather than articles that attempt to generalize.[1] In the process, a good deal of information is conveyed, but the readers must already have much contextual information at their disposal in order to know how to interpret the data meaningfully. These are factual writings.

The fourth type consists of nonincremental breakthroughs, or at least major advances, that may have been hinted at in incremental writings or even factual writings but were never made explicit there. In these writings, large bodies of new or previously ignored data are presented and significant advances are made in explaining political phenomena. These will be called innovative writings.

The fifth type comprises the five Soviet books on the American political system plus the few books devoted to political institutions and processes as well as the large number of articles on the same subjects. They are topical writings.

Finally, there are translations of American books on politics which partially fill some gaps in Soviet writing. Examples include radical critiques of the American political system focusing on the exercise of power and influence (Mintz and Cohen 1971) or liberal critiques as in the case of John Kenneth Galbraith's *The New Industrial State* or Senator J. William Fulbright's *The Arrogance of Power*. As already noted, the translation of Dye and Zeigler's textbook on American politics was a major event.

Chronologically, the initial Soviet focus in the 1930s was on elections and parties. In the 1950s and 1960s greatest attention went to the presidency, and in the 1970s and early 1980s greater stress was put on Congress, the liberal–conservative split, and analyzing public opinion and political consciousness. In the 1980s there was a sharp increase in studies of the Supreme Court.

Thematically, the major thrust in Soviet writing following World War II has been on the centralization of political power through the decline of federalism along with the expansion of presidential power and the accompanying growth in the power of executive branch nonconstitutional agencies like the CIA and the National Security Council at the expense of Congress and some older executive branch agencies (Levin, ed. 1964a, 131ff treats the growth comprehensively).

In terms of sheer volume of output, the history of the two major parties has received most attention, followed in declining order of consideration by elections together with the study of public opinion, the presidency, Congress, and the Supreme Court.

Parties and Ideologies

V. Lan's comprehensive history of American political parties, a combination of ideological and innovative topical writing, was a book ahead of its time (1932, 1937). It required half a century for a similar volume to be published (*The U.S. Two-Party System* 1988). Many narrowly focused topical historical studies have appeared on the Democratic party's policies between the 1930s and the late 1970s (Pechatnov 1980a, an incremental-factual book), Republican policy in the Eisenhower administration (Zorin 1960, an ideological work), the battle between conservatives and liberals in the Republican party during the Kennedy and Johnson administrations (Nikonov 1984, an incremental-factual book), the Democrats and the working class (Moroz 1971, also ideological), the reformism of the Democrats and the traditionalism of the Republicans (Iakovlev, ed. 1976, 305–433, 434–527, an incremental study), and the similarities in the policies followed by the Republican and Democratic administrations in the 1950s and early 1960s (Zorin 1964, again ideological).

There are also two important collections of articles, one on the origin and development of the parties from the 1790s to 1920, the other on party activities from the 1920s to the mid–1970s (Sivachev, ed. 1981, 1982). Both are incremental-factual. Finally, there are numerous articles scattered throughout Soviet scholarly periodicals as well as chapters in jointly authored books, especially those devoted to the study of political parties in the major capitalist countries, and sometimes even in books on other topics. In fact, the best short, factually oriented overview of the American party system appeared in a collection of articles on sociopolitical movements (Vozchikov and others, eds. 1974, 266–304; also Nikiforov, ed. 1976, 88–124).

Obviously missing in Soviet publications is a systematic study of American party organizations and activity that would approximate V. O. Key's classic *Politics, Parties, and Pressure Groups*. Many elements of the information that such a book would contain are spread throughout the historical works mentioned in the preceding paragraphs, but no author has organized them comprehensively. It is important to recognize that this is not as minor a matter as it may seem. Since Soviet scholarly books very rarely contain a subject index, it is extremely difficult for readers to develop a comprehensible picture of topics not treated systematically in individual chapters.

Consequently, it is the predominating themes in these Soviet studies that are impressed upon the Soviet reader's mind: Who controls the parties? What is the nature and function of the two-party system? Are there differences between the parties? How does the liberal–conservative cleavage affect the parties? What impact do all these factors have on the conduct of elections?

The question of who controls the Democratic and Republican parties was answered in a particularly forceful way by V. Lan in his chapter "The Bi-Unitary Party of Big Capital" (1937, 463ff). Since Lan agreed with Marx's and Lenin's contention that both parties were controlled by the same class, they were best described as a two-in-one phenomenon. The Soviets today view them as *bourgeois* parties controlled specifically by the big bourgeoisie, the monopolists.

Two arguments are used to substantiate this contention. One, a favorite in primitive-type SMC analyses, demonstrates that the monopolies totally control both policy input and output: the policies obediently followed by the parties at the behest of the monopolies naturally benefit the monopolies (Zorin 1960; Moroz 1971). Less virulent variants state simply that the parties' activities and policies clearly show whose interests they represent (Levin, ed. 1964b, 17) or that the two-party system as such serves monopoly capital (Shamberg 1968a, 77). The second argument is essentially that money talks (Danilenko 1985; Seregin 1972; Guliev and Kuz'min 1969, 73–74) and that heavy contributors to party coffers call the tune here just as effectively as do large stockholders in corporations (Beglov 1971, 391–92).

The two parties perform several functions. At the level of fundamental political purpose and basic principle, in all capitalist countries the main function is to ensure that the ruling class prevails in the struggle for power between the bourgeoisie and the proletariat. A secondary struggle goes on between the bourgeois parties and among the social groups comprising them, but this intramural battle is of a qualitatively different order in that it threatens neither the economic nor the political power of the monopolies (Levin, ed. 1964b, 8–10).

Functionally, the party system of any capitalist country is considered to be a "transformer" of a unique type, turning the universal right to vote into the perpetuation of the political control of the monopolies (Levin and Tumanov, eds. 1974, 112; Mishin 1954, 46; Levin, ed. 1964b, 14–15; Burlatskii and Galkin 1974, 208–14). In the United States, this is accomplished primarily through creating the illusion of a hot battle between the parties so as to create the further illusion that there is a real choice between them (Shamberg 1968a, 77; Moroz 1971, 14; Mishin 1954, 55; Zorin 1964, 131). In this way, the two-party system has succeeded in attracting into its orbit people from all classes (Lan and others, eds. 1966, 50). The financial oligarchy is therefore able to play the game of politics and always win (Beglov 1971, 502) and to juggle political power without losing it (Mishin 1958b, 125). This is achieved mainly through social demagogy, the Democratic party's manipulative specialty, which is used to discourage the workers from forming an independent mass party and to keep the liberal intelligentsia within the party system (Androsov 1971, 64–65, 73–74, 339–40; Moroz 1971, 16–22, 62; Beglov 1971, 387; Lapitskii 1973, 46ff).

The battle between the parties is completely utilitarian and is decidedly not one of principle (Krylov 1968, 88). The voter chooses not so much between parties as between personalities who, moreover, sometimes switch parties (Bel'son and Livantsev 1982, 99). Indeed, the party battle has been described as a kind of division of labor between the parties (Iakovlev, ed. 1976, 301). Its purpose is to deflect the attention of the American people from problems that create dangers for the ruling classes (Petrusenko 1970, 14). Essentially, this repeats what Lenin said about America's rulers and their two parties in an often used quotation: "They deceived the people, they deflected them from their vital interests by means of the spectacular and pointless duels of the two bourgeois parties" (1958–1965, vol. 22, 193).

The Soviets give two answers to the question of whether there are any differences between the parties—no and yes. No because both are bourgeois parties controlled by monopoly capital, because their electoral platforms do not differ in principle, and because the differences in their preferences regarding policy implementation do not outweigh their agreement over policy aims (Glagolev 1960, 95; Gromyko 1957, 38ff). In addition, bipartisanship, especially in foreign and military policy, shows clearly how little difference there is between the parties (Nikiforov, ed. 1976, 139–40).

The answer is also yes—there are meaningful differences. For one thing, the parties' roles differ. Ideological writers stress that if the Republicans are more open in their defense of the monopolies' interests than the Democrats, the latter's task is to play the demagogic role of defending the little man and seeming to attack the monopolies, but in reality the Democrats have acted as chief legitimator of the promonopoly policies adopted by the Republicans (Zorin 1964, 420–21, 500–505).[2] Since their roles differ, the parties' "tactics, methods, and ways of operating" also vary (Zorin 1964, 134 [quotation]; Moroz 1971, 18–22). The Democratic party, for instance, specializes in subordinating social movements to its own interests (Pechatnov 1980a, 30–60). This is tantamount to saying that the movements are thereby subordinated to the interests of the ruling class.

More normally, the Soviets cast the Democratic party in the role of chief concession maker from the time of the New Deal (Sivachev 1964; Pechatnov 1980a). This role differs from the almost purely demagogic one characteristically found in the ideological analyses. Studies of this goal give greater attention to the substantive material results of the alleged manipulation and focus more on the incentives thereby created for people to adhere to the system. This role at least partially originates in what was called "the fundamental difference" between the parties: the Democrats have a "so-called" left wing, whereas the Republicans do not (Gantman and Mikoyan 1969, 32).

The parties' social bases and social constituencies have differed over time, which affected the policies they pursued. Originally, when the two-party system was formed the social base of both was relatively uniform in its class composition (Levin, ed. 1964b, 66–67). But later it became quite varied (Cherniak 1957, 168; Bel'son and Livantsev 1982, 99).

Some analysts maintain that this shift has made little difference. Beglov contended that although the social composition of the parties may differ at the lower level, the variation disappears almost completely at the top leadership level since members of wealthy families divide among themselves the job of belonging to one or the other party much as they divide the task of belonging to this or that board of directors (1971, 376–85). But other writers say that because of their particular social base of support the Democrats have had to advocate more liberal domestic policies than the Republicans (Androsov 1971, 296). Yet Pechatnov has noted that labor's solid support for the Democratic party makes it the major instrumentality for linking the workers to the system's political processes—which is, he takes pains to point out, controlled by the monopoly bourgeoisie (1980a, 233).

Various writers have produced lists of the differing post–New Deal party constituencies based on factors such as wealth, occupation, geography, race, religion, and ethnicity (Levin, ed. 1964b, 38; Anikin, ed. 1972, 276–87; Fursenko and others 1974, 52; Nikiforov, ed. 1976, 105). They are like similar enumerations by American political scientists. The fact that the parties share some of these constituencies has been noted, as has the fact that since World War II some 30% of union members voted Republican in presidential elections (Lan and others 1966, 47; Popov 1972).

Much attention has been given to shifts in these sources of support and to changes in policy that both preceded and followed these shifts commencing in the 1960s. Since "the parties include representatives of all classes, they are forced to take into account to some degree the interests of more than just the monopolies alone" (Marinin 1967, 20 [quotation]; Lan and others, eds. 1966, 45). The nature of the struggle within, between, and outside the parties produces party policies that resulted from factors like the collision of interests within the bourgeoisie, the sentiments of the social strata which are identified with either party, and the level of activity of the social movements in the nation (Vozchikov and others, eds. 1974, 271–80). Because each party needs a mass base, it must support policies that appeal to its respective base (Shamberg 1969, 27). Since the 1930s this had produced both Republican conservatism and Democratic liberal reformism through the granting of concessions. The major difference between the parties, apart from a number of lesser differences, was their stand on the government's regulatory role in the socioeconomic sphere (Nikiforov, ed. 1976, 140).

Labor's dissatisfaction with the Democratic party's inability to go further than it did in representing labor's interests (because as a party it really represented the interests of the bourgeoisie) prompted some major labor leaders to consider creating a separate party in the late 1950s and early 1960s (Shishkin 1972, 212–16). This sign of the worsening "crisis of liberal reformism" pushed the Democratic party toward a greater conservatism (Pechatnov 1980a, 68–71). Together with the escalation of the war in Vietnam, the crisis began to alienate the liberal intelligentsia (Androsov 1971, 128–29). Whereas the Democrats had once been Keynesian innovators, they now became conservative defenders of the status quo because advocating further reform meant adopting some version of socialism, as John Kenneth Galbraith and Hans Morgenthau eventually pointed out (Pechatnov 1973; Iakovlev, ed. 1976, 409–11). The conservatism continued into the Carter administration and actually deepened because there was so little room for maneuvering to obtain concessions. This produced further disaffection among labor, blacks, and liberals (Pechatnov 1980a, 203–8, 215–18, 229–32). The age of limits was being felt full-force. There could be no more guns *and* butter, and the monopolies allegedly communicated their conservative strategy and policy goals to the Democratic party through Samuel Huntington's article in a Trilateral Commission report (Pechatnov 1980a, 200; Huntington's report is in Crozier and others 1975).

As for the Republicans, following World War II they experienced a long and bitter intramural battle over both justifying greater governmental intervention in theory and actually practicing it in the Eisenhower administration—although not necessarily in that neat order (Iakovlev, ed. 1976, 496–501). Given the rejection of a return to the Republicanism of the 1920s signaled by Goldwater's defeat in 1964, the Nixon administration was forced to adopt the neo-Keynesian policies of the Democrats, which boiled down to continuing SMC economic regulation in the face of the deepening general crisis of capitalism (Iakovlev, ed. 1976, 516–26; Glagolev 1974).

Both parties had no choice but to do much the same thing. Now, however, Tweedledum and Tweedledee faced a sharply deteriorating domestic economic and international politico-economic situation that undermined the very possibility of engaging in the kind of concession making that depended on economic growth (Pechatnov 1980a, 236). The two parties also began to look more alike in that they grew weaker as organizations and their social bases eroded. Both parties became more differentiated (Gadzhiev 1983, 198). The attempts by the parties to portray themselves as real alternatives in terms of ideology, policy, and image was unsuccessful because of the factional splits within each party, weakened organizational control, the intractability of economic problems, and the inability to produce an effective leader (Anichkin 1977; Pechatnov 1981; Valentinov 1982).

To be sure, in the 1980 campaign the Republicans offered both an attractive candidate and what looked like an attractive alternative to the average person in the very simplicity of Reagan's promise of restored economic growth with its attendant full employment, without inflation (Pechatnov 1980b, 50; Glagolev 1980, 56). But President Reagan's concrete program, while it was an implicit recognition of the crisis in both SMC-type regulatory policies and their Keynesian theoretical base, was not itself a retreat from SMC regulation. Regulation would continue, but to the even greater benefit of the monopolies and detriment of the have-nots (Bobrakov 1981, 47–50; Geevskii 1981). The reasons had been articulated decades before by Dalin: the monopolies that had long supported the Republican party and were against governmental regulation of the economy nevertheless were in favor of government subsidies, accelerated depreciation, profitable government contracts, and oblique governmental influence on credit and money supply policies (1961, 343–44).

This bankruptcy, as the Soviets call it, of both parties' policies created a crisis in the two-party system. Its main characteristics are voter apathy, a weakening of party identification and affiliation among the people, increasing absenteeism in elections, growing fragmentation and splits within the parties, which complicates leading them and also complicates executive–congressional coordination in policymaking, and the rise of third parties and of social movements outside the party system since the parties had failed to deal with mass concerns (Fursenko and others 1974, 315–20; Manykin and Sivachev 1978; Zorin and Savchenko 1979; Kokoshin 1982, 55–73).

The resolution of this crisis lies in the formation of a new party, whose characteristics were discussed in Chapter 4. But in what one Soviet ideological writer called "the paradox of 1968," the new party that did appear was George Wallace's American party— not a party of the future, but one wanting to turn the clock back and yet supported electorally by 17% of the workers and their families (Shamberg 1968b, 96). Only several years later did a more realistically inclined author partially resolve the paradox: "It is necessary to admit that on the whole the American worker is still highly conservative" (Berezhkov 1973, 9).

The Soviet answer to the question of whether there are substantive differences between the two parties in terms of their policies has so far been "no" within the fairly well-defined parameters of Soviet analytical approaches. These same approaches have discouraged Soviet writers from paying much attention to questions of party organization, and here the absence of a V. O. Key–type book is sorely felt. Nevertheless, they have not neglected the issue entirely.

Kokoshin remarked that the two parties are not organizations in the usual Soviet meaning of that term since they are very decentralized, they do not have an established program, and their mass base consists of coalitions including divergent strata of the population (1982, 55). The parties do not even have a clearly formulated ideology or a formal constitution, they do not provide for official, personal membership in the form of a party card, and having neither permanent members nor dues, they lack an independent financial base (Bel'son and Livantsev 1982, 93; Levin, ed. 1964b, 56; Iu. Zolotukhin 1976, 93).

Some of these perspectives are at variance with other Soviet views on party organization. One thinks, for example, of the typical primitive SMC perception of the commanding role of the national committees. Moreover, there have been some changes. At least the Democrats produced a party constitution of sorts in 1975 (Nikiforov, ed. 1976, 91; Pechatnov 1975). And some modifications and specifications have been made, as in the observation that although permanent membership on a mass basis may be lacking, there does exist among wealthy contributors a very real sense of permanent party identification that is tantamount to membership (Beglov 1971, 380–85).

The Soviets have always been concerned with locating the center of power within the parties. Decades ago, Lan rejected the contention that it was to be found in the national conventions and, typically of Soviet thinking on the matter, he placed it in the national committees and the parties' administrative apparatus (1937, 528–29). Through the 1950s the Soviets continued to insist that the committees and the apparatus controlled the local party organizations, especially through distributing financial largess in the case of the national committees (Gromyko 1957, 52–55; Mishin 1958b, 123–24). But after the 1960s it became possible to maintain that the national parties were coalitions of autonomous state parties, that the national committees were more coordinating than directing bodies, that organized party activity practically ceased once the campaign was over, and that such autonomy was based upon the local party organizations' having independent sources of financing for their election campaigns (Fursenko and others 1974, 50–51; Zolotukhin and Linnik 1978a, 31–32; Fedosov 1968, 111).

A potential countertrend was identified in the temporary prominence of the Democratic National Committee in the 1950s under the activist chairmanship of Paul Butler (Galkin 1982). Moreover, the national committees and their chairmen increased in importance as they attempted to bring order out of the parties' fragmentation, and even chaos, created in the 1960s and 1970s when the parties were under severe pressure from mass social movements and scandals like Watergate and its consequences (Lebedev 1974; Nikiforov, ed. 1976, 92–94; Manykin 1978).

Additionally, by the early 1980s the parties began to cope with some serious tendencies working against their control of elections such as the multiplication of primaries, the heightened role of political consulting firms and political action committees, changes in financing presidential elections, and the growing importance of the media in identifying and publicizing presidential hopefuls. In response, both of the national committees bolstered their roles in elections below the national level, transforming the party's organizational apparatus into something of a service bureau for candidates who traditionally would have had little if anything to do with the national committee. The national committees also created training programs for candidates, strengthened the links between party and academe, and sought to limit the proliferation of primaries (Pechatnov 1982).

The question of party organization was also affected by the nature of the problems confronting the nation, and a dilemma was being created. Retaining the traditional decentralized party organizational modes did not facilitate coping with today's complex domestic and foreign problems. Yet the growing centralization and the existing pressures to engage in more long-range planning could put an end to the process of the uninterrupted integration of alternative ideas into the system. That very process had been the means through which the monopolies dominated the political system (Manykin 1978, 52–53).

The most recent Soviet observations are that the party realignment in the late 1970s and early 1980s in the direction a more conservative consensus failed to resolve the country's many problems. The resulting disillusionment with the parties diminished their influence among the now better educated voters since it was harder for them to manipulate voter consciousness and behavior (*The U.S. Two-Party System* 1988, 345–96; Darchiev and Kortunova 1989).

The Soviets have also tried to answer the question of whether ideology differentiates the parties. The answers are rather muddled. At the level of fundamental principle, ideology does not and cannot differentiate the parties in the Soviet view since both are bourgeois. Nevertheless, the liberal and conservative orientations within the parties have sometimes been significant in affecting the degree of political flexibility shown by the parties, especially on the issue of governmental intervention in the economy (Tumanov, ed. 1967, 133; Zamoshkin, ed. 1967, 154–55).

But some analysts maintain that whatever differences there may be between liberalism and conservatism, they are not basic: the two philosophies are not antithetical (Levin and Tumanov, eds. 1972, 50; Valiuzhenich 1976, 311). There are more similarities than differences between liberals and conservatives despite all the attacks they have made on each other, and in the 1960s a trend toward convergence in the two orientations was apparent (Zamoshkin, ed. 1967, 163). The liberals' reaction to the turmoil of the 1960s showed that they feared real democracy (but not bourgeois democracy) more than they feared reaction, and such fear of revolutionary mass movements proved once more that liberalism favors the ruling class (Valiuzhenich 1976, 236). The ultimate function of liberalism is to undercut social protest movements through making minimal concessions to the masses (Geevskii 1973, 191).

If there is little substantive difference between liberals and conservatives in principle, in practical terms whatever differences there may be are moderated by the variations within each orientation. These run along a spectrum from radical liberalism and radical conservatism through moderate versions of the two, which has been the subject of an extensive innovative sociological study (Zamoshkin and Batalov, eds. 1980). Approximately these same differentiations have been reflected in the spectrum of political orientations of prominent Republicans and Democrats since World War II, as discussed in one highly ideological study (Zorin 1964, 140–50). There seems to be a Soviet consensus on this issue.

Other analysts have concluded that centrist groups within both parties predominate, using compromise as their major political instrument (Fursenko and others 1974, 57). There is a centrist bloc in Congress that is neither liberal nor conservative and is joined in voting on one or another issue by both conservatives and liberals (Nikiforov, ed. 1976, 147–48). This centrist phenomenon tends to moderate liberal–conservative differences. In combination with the existing liberal–conservative continuum, it serves to muddle the political perception of many Americans, leading them to think that there is no way out of the policy dilemmas created by the rather limited alternatives offered by the two philosophies and their political proponents (Zamoshkin and Batalov, eds. 1980, 420–21).

Although there are many Soviet studies of liberalism and conservatism, most have been only tangentially concerned with the relationship of these orientations to the political parties. The earliest major analyses were cautious attempts at establishing and clarifying the differences between the orientations (Zamoshkin, ed. 1967; Iulina 1971). The latest major studies have probed the differences more deeply in updated treatments (Mel'vil' 1980; Mikhailov 1983). Two books have pushed the Soviet exploration of the world of ideas beyond the liberal–conservative confines through focusing narrowly on right-wing extremist thought (Nikitin 1971) and through essaying a comprehensive treatment of the entire left–right spectrum, excluding only the American Communist party (Zamoshkin and Batalov, eds. 1980).

The most recent publications on conservatism and liberalism have focused on the untenability of the policy prescriptions of both, making the point rather forcefully that neither can work in the face of changed domestic and international conditions (Mel'vil' 1981). Most importantly, liberalism lost its appeal in the 1970s. Its optimistic social philosophy that a transformed capitalism can end economic crises fell victim to the crises of that decade, as did its technocratic schemes (like the Great Society) for putting the optimism into practice (Valiuzhenich 1976, 3–8; Mel'vil' 1980, 5; Pechatnov 1980a, 199–200).

Ideally, from the Soviet perspective this ought to have led to the growing realization among Americans that the two-party system, and the one class whose interests it continues to represent, ought to be abandoned in favor of a party and an ideology offering more radical, and more certain, solutions to life's many problems. Instead there was a turn toward conservatism, a familiar pattern in American politics and a frustrating one for the Soviets.

In their explanation the shift took place at the level of the monopoly ruling circles (Pechatnov 1980a, 200, 224–25; Plekhanov 1979) and at the level of "the politically active bloc of the population" (Mel'vil' 1981, 36–37). Its effects were seen in the moderate conservatism of the Carter administration (Pechatnov 1980a, 185–232) and especially in the election of Ronald Reagan. But there was no such turn at the mass level according to Plekhanov, who cited a paper presented at the 1978 American Political Science Association's national convention to show that the mass electorate had shifted to the left (1979, 21–22). When events took a different turn, and Reagan's 1980 and 1984 victories showed that enough people who actually voted thought otherwise, newer American public opinion surveys were used by Mel'vil' (1981, 1986) to demonstrate that mass attitudes had not turned solidly conservative even though they contained a contradictory mix of liberal and conservative ideas.

In sum, the ideological picture has become somewhat diffuse at the mass level, but most Soviets have lately perceived a clear tendency among the elites toward conservatism. However, another conclusion was reached in the broadest ranging Soviet study of political consciousness in America. The future would see the continued reproduction of the "various approaches, positions, tendencies, and expectations forming a more or less broad, internally heterogeneous spectrum of types of political consciousness close to the one that took shape in the United States during the 1960s and 1970s" (Zamoshkin and Batalov, eds. 1980, 438).

The expectation is that America will become more like Europe through filling in what were formerly gaps in the ideological spectrum. This could lead to a profusion of political parties on the European model, but no Soviet writer has said this will happen. At least one writer suggested that the liberals, in order to escape the blind alley they are in, could adopt social democratic ideas and become a real alternative to the conservatives. But he did not suggest creating a new party (Zamoshkin and others, eds. 1984, 37–41). The Soviet perception is that the American two-party system is in crisis, is in a blind alley, but has not yet reached the end of its rope. The increasing similarity in both the ideologies and the policies of the two parties is a sure sign that the traditional kind of maneuvering that has sustained the party system for so long is now unworkable. Yet somehow the system continues to manifest considerable staying power.

Elections

Of all the major topics in the analysis of formal political institutions and processes, the Soviets gave earliest and greatest attention to elections. The impetus was Lenin's remark, including his emphases, that the study of political campaigns in capitalist countries "yields *objective* material on the question of the views, feelings, and consequently also the interests of the various *classes* of society" (1958–1966, vol. 22, 331). The study of elections also yields data on the strategies used by the ruling class to consolidate its position under bourgeois democracy. "In the conditions of universal suffrage the big bourgeoisie cannot achieve the election of candidates amenable to it without attracting to their side voters from the other classes and social strata" (Boiko and Shamberg 1973, 84).

Soviet perspectives on the significance of voting differ depending on the strength of each analyst's adherence to SMC. For primitive SMC analysts like Zorin the voters almost do not count:

> The American two-party system, loudly advertised by bourgeois propaganda and passed off as the height of democracy, in reality does not provide genuine possibilities for expressing the will of the people. In being forced to "choose" between two evils, between the candidates of the two parties of the American monopolies, the voters are to a significant extent stage extras in an electoral farce which is acted out according to the monopolies' script. (1964, 429)

In contrast to this perception of total manipulation, other analysts have noted that since "in America political power is, above all, power over the minds, moods, and actions of millions of voters," policymakers are forced to address seriously problems like environmental pollution and urban crime that affect more than the interests of the bourgeoisie alone (Nikiforov, ed. 1976, 235–36). And, finally, regarding the role of the working class itself: "The unions have great strength in the industrially developed states which yield the largest number of presidential electors and members of Congress. All that forces the bourgeois parties to take into greater account the demands of the unions (the organized workers together with their families yield about 30 million votes)" (Androsov 1971, 303).

Typically, no Soviet has yet attempted a major systematic analysis of elections. Only recently was a detailed, inclusive methodology for studying elections in capitalist countries worked out (Burlatskii and Galkin 1985, 269–83). But it has not yet been applied.[3] The overwhelming mass of Soviet treatments is composed of articles on individual elections published during or just after a specific election. This means that the candidates and the issues in individual elections have received much attention, but questions like the role of critical elections and voter realignment have not. My analysis of Soviet approaches will reflect the variously weighted factors in Soviet writing: ideological, incremental, factual, and innovative approaches; problems and shortcomings in the election process; campaigns and campaign strategies; and the role of labor.

The Soviet mindset's preference is to stress that each party when in power pursues domestic and foreign policies that are antidemocratic or antipopular. The eventual voter disaffection results in a victory for the "out" party. This explains the defeat of the Democrats in 1952, and even 1956, and of the Republicans in 1960 (Lan and others, eds. 1966, 48; Zorin 1964, 428–29). In the perception of ideological writers, elections do not change much of anything because no significant policy shifts follow in their wake, and the problems that existed before a given election remain afterward (Zorin 1972b, 31). Whichever candidate becomes president is invariably placed in the "rigid confines of the state machine which doesn't allow any particular deviations from the course already charted by the financial oligarchy in domestic and foreign policy" (Beglov 1971, 526). Indeed, during the campaigns themselves sensationalistic efforts are made to distract the voters from the really troublesome issues, as was the case in the Eagleton affair in 1972 (Zorin 1972a, 24).

Ideological interpretations highlight the role of the monopolies in elections. Beglov listed the respective wealthy families that have historically been president makers for the Democratic and Republican parties before noting that grooming a presidential candidate begins at the initiative of a regional group of capitalists who then recruit support for him from other capitalists. They especially seek the support of Wall Street, which Beglov assumes speaks with one voice, and the candidate winning Wall Street's support is at once superior to his rivals (Beglov 1971, 416–19). Although there is generally disagreement among the monopolies over who the candidate should be right up to the conventions, in 1952, for the first time in a long while, the Rockefellers, the Morgans, the Mellons, the DuPonts, and the Fords all supported the same candidate—Eisenhower—even before the convention (Beglov 1971, 428).

Using his distinctively bombastic language, Zorin identified a concerted effort by the monopolies to put the Republican party in power in 1952: "In this unanimous decision, which expressed the general interests of the American monopolies, the unity of American monopoly capital in the fight for its basic aims was extraordinarily graphically embodied" (1964, 174). However, with the election won, a battle naturally broke out among the monopolies over seizing key appointive posts in the Eisenhower administration.

But since Republican losses in the 1954 and 1958 off-year elections showed that the promonopoly policies were rejected by the popular masses, "the bigwigs of big business decided not to obstruct the movement of the pendulum of American political life from swinging to the side of the Democrats" (Zorin 1964, 202, 421 [quotation]). The decision was made in secret, but Zorin felt able to document it in the shifts in support by the radio and television companies and the press as well as in the preelection pessimism of Republican leaders (1964, 421).

Typically of ideological writers, Zorin fails to take into account the normal loss of congressional seats by the party holding the presidency in off-year elections, and he conveniently neglects to consider the real significance of the closeness of the popular vote in 1960 when he asserts that the Republican policies of the Eisenhower administration provoked a massive rejection by the popular masses.

Some further weaknesses in the ideological writings are illustrated in the treatment accorded Senator Barry Goldwater and Governor Nelson Rockefeller. Zorin viewed Goldwater's nomination in 1964 as a defeat of Wall Street by the newer financial groups of the Southwest, the Midwest, and California (1964, 573–79). Yet this did not cause him to modify his earlier universalistic statement about the need for Wall Street's support. The election results did constrain him to modify another of his positions. While welcoming Goldwater's resounding defeat, Zorin was alarmed that the more than 25 million people who did vote for Goldwater constituted a mass base of support for his extreme views extending well beyond the handful of people in "the most aggressive groups of monopoly capital" that ideological writers like Zorin had normally assumed were supportive of far right views (1964, 594–96).[4]

If Zorin proffered no explanation for how and why the supposedly all-powerful Wall Street could allow a candidate like Goldwater to take the nomination, Beglov attempted one in attributing his success to a combination of support from the midwestern and far western "outsiders," the apathy of the usual East Coast president makers, the disorder in their ranks produced by Rockefeller's candidacy, and the attractiveness of Lyndon Johnson to many on Wall Street at the time (1971, 452–83).

The ideological writers' chief oversight, directly attributable to their particular form of analysis, lay in failing to perceive the critical new development introduced into presidential elections in 1960 by John Kennedy and repeated, though in modified form, by Goldwater in 1964. The nomination was effectively decided before the convention either through winning primaries or through winning delegates at the state party conventions. The ideological writers' treatment of Nelson Rockefeller is similarly flawed. They attribute his failure to win the nomination in 1960 and 1964 to the unwillingness of the other monopoly groups, especially the Morgans and DuPonts, to tolerate the inevitable expansion of the Rockefeller empire that would follow his acquiring the presidency (Gromyko 1968, 58; Zorin 1964, 408). Wall Street could not and would not back one of its very own.

Yet some Soviets either gave equal weight to other factors or even preferred them as explanations for Rockefeller's failures. In 1960 his popularity waned because of his divorce and remarriage, and that caused him to vacillate and finally decide not to run (Gantman and Mikoyan 1969, 164). In 1964 the same factor forced him to withdraw from the race after seeing his unpopularity demonstrated in the California primary (Fursenko and others 1974, 69; Lan and others, eds. 1966, 74). These analysts were essentially reinstituting in the 1960s and early 1970s a way of studying elections that had been characteristic of V. Lan's articles in the 1930s. The difference was that now a balance had to be struck (or could at last be struck) in such writing between SMC considerations and a mixture of fact and inference characteristic of American commentaries on elections.

So Shamberg could maintain that in the 1964 election there was for once a real choice for the voter between presidential candidates and electoral platforms (1965, 60). And Men'shikov could intimate that John F. Kennedy was as much beholden to the electorate as he was to the monopolies (1964, 26–28).

It took about a decade for this form of writing to evolve into incremental/factual writing. Initiated in articles published in the monthly *World Economy and International Relations* (in Russian), this process was markedly enhanced once the Institute of United States and Canadian Studies' monthly, *USA: Economics, Politics, Ideology,* began publishing in January 1970. It is well to recall here that the materials in this monthly are very often summaries and abstracts of, or reports on, discussions in the American print media, so their non-Soviet quality is sometimes notable. Shorter articles of this quality have become standard in newspaper reports on presidential campaigns, even in the staid *Pravda* (Vasil'ev 1988; Sukhoi 1988a, 1988b; Kolesnichenko 1988). This sort of writing on elections has been confined to articles, and no major topical book in this vein has appeared. Soviet readers wishing to familiarize themselves expeditiously with the many complexities of American elections have no convenient comprehensive source to consult.

There are several notable traits in incremental/factual writing. A few articles of this type contain the most comprehensive treatments of elections so far published (Zolotukhin and Linnik 1978a, 1978b; V.P. Zolotukhin 1976; Nikiforov 1973; Anichkin 1972). Typically, they concentrate on campaign issues, strategies, and tactics rather than on deducing, as ideological writers do, what the monopolies "obviously" want or need at the moment. There are attempts at concretizing some SMC themes, especially the role played by campaign contributions, or at correcting other perceptions, particularly the role played by labor.

Scattered throughout these writings are important ideas, insights, comments, and data of various sorts that most often are left undeveloped and unconnected. Years ago, for example, Pechatnov used awkward language to hint at a theory of critical elections while at the same time bowing to ideological necessity: "The party battle in the United States, despite all its superficial character and pragmatism, nevertheless reflects, although with some distortions, the course of profound social processes, especially at certain historical stages. In the twentieth century such were the campaigns of 1912, 1932, 1948, and 1964" (1973, 52). This line of analysis has not been carried forward, even though it was recognized that in the 1960 election for the first time in American history the candidate receiving the majority of white votes had lost (Geevskii 1973, 141) and that the 1968 election heralded a major change in priorities from foreign policy to domestic issues (Zorin, ed. 1971, 13).

Another example is Kokoshin's observation that recent trends showed that congressional elections were becoming more of a local than a national event (1982, 57). Perhaps, one might note, the trend was not so recent; but the important point is that here was a challenge to the old assumption in ideological writings that only national parties, only national elections, and only the national policy concerns of the big bourgeoisie were of much significance.

On rare occasions, elections are compared. If 1968 indicated a polarization since the voters tended to move both left and right, 1970 showed a movement toward the center (Zorin 1970, 45). It would be interesting to see the Soviets do a study of American attitudes toward change as exemplified in such voting behavior that would also take into account an insight communicated by Valentin M. Berezhkov, editor of *USA: Economics, Politics, Ideology:* "The Americans are in general a circumspect people, and, as I was told, although they understand the need for changes, they prefer that they be made gradually, for they fear that otherwise things might get worse" (1973, 5).

As contrasted with the attitude of the ideological writers, incremental analyses find that elections are important. Savel'ev noted that a number of cold-warrior senators failed to win reelection because of shifts in voter attitudes away from those typical of Senator Joseph McCarthy (1976a, 114). The 1966 election put the Democrats on notice that popular attitudes toward the party's domestic and foreign policies had changed (Anikin, ed. 1972, 293). Subsequent elections identified the specific problems troubling the voters: the Vietnam War, the economy, racial conflicts, soaring crime rates, disenchantment with the American political system's capacity to solve problems coupled with growing distrust in the two-party system resulting in apathy as shown in lower participation in voting, and, finally, Watergate and the resulting battle between president and Congress (Zolotukhin 1972, 60; Popov 1976, 55–56; Vladimirov 1974; Lebedev 1974). Inflation was designated the "superproblem" (Anichkin 1974, 57).

Recognition of these factors still leaves open the important question of the political system's effectiveness in coping with them. If effectiveness means resolving the problems, then the failure to do so noted by the incremental analysts is reminiscent of the conclusions reached in ideological writings. Manipulation of issues, rather than resolving problems, is considered a feature of the system's operation, as when both parties addressed the environmental issue in ways calculated to avoid dealing with it (Petrusenko 1970, 12–14). The system continued to present the voters with little or no choice in 1980 since both presidential candidates were judged unpopular (Anichkin 1980, 51), and the positions of both favoring increased arms expenditures offered no meaningful alternative (Popov 1980, 64). Because there is no difference in principle between the parties, Americans more often than not vote for the lesser evil (Petrovskaia 1982, 123), and when voters do not see an alternative between candidates, they tend to boycott the election (Popov 1980, 64).

Soviet concern with voter absenteeism produced a major insight that was mentioned in passing: the role of class is clearer in explaining absenteeism (the blue collars tend not to vote) than in explaining differences among those who do vote. "Class differences are manifested among the active part of the electorate only indirectly and to a limited extent. They operate via contradictions within classes that are reflected in the activity of the two bourgeois parties" (*The U.S. Two-Party System* 1988, 393–94, 394 [quotation]).

The handful of articles devoted to midterm elections is important beyond its number for many reasons. Races within states get much more attention than during presidential elections; it is recognized that many governors and state legislators are up for reelection; note is taken of jockeying for the impending presidential nomination; there is an awareness that the party with an incumbent president always loses congressional seats in these elections; commencing with the 1974 election these articles began to give more attention to public opinion polls; and one would hardly know from these articles that the monopolies existed—the role of the parties themselves is featured (Zolotukhin and Linnik 1978a; Anichkin 1977, 1970; Pechatnov 1983; Zorin 1970; Petrusenko 1970). This writing comes closest to American political analyses and it treats a range of issues about which most Soviet sources say little or nothing.

Again there are interesting ideas scattered throughout these in-cremental materials that are not systematized or pursued. Zolo-tukhin and Linnik remarked that the traditional role of these elections is to establish how the voters feel about the performance of government at all levels, a kind of checkup on the entire system (1978a, 30). This has not been noted by any other Soviet source. Anichkin identified a debilitating effect produced by the regularity of incumbent party losses in the midterm elections: following the 1976 election the Republicans were badly split, but they did little about it in 1977, expecting that the normal would happen—the Democrats would get into trouble with the voters and there would be a Republican comeback (1977). This regularity encouraged Pe-chatnov to argue that the results of the 1982 midterm elections were not so much an act of voter faith in the Democrats as they were a sign of growing distrust of the Republicans (1983, 32).

The incremental writings about the significance of elections also include some clusters of insights that do not appear elsewhere. Commenting on the last stages of the 1970 election, Anichkin (1970, 71) pointed out that Democratic control of the Senate had been the major roadblock to effecting President Nixon's policies, and Petrusenko (1970, 15) identified the battle to win control of the Senate as the major factor in that election. Writing after the 1970 election's conclusion, Zorin described the Republicans as having tried, and failed, to achieve the control of the Senate that had escaped them in 1968; thus they did not gain control of the committee chairmanships (Zorin 1970, 44). Here again one would wish a further analysis centered on the importance of these authors' insights into policymaking, but this has not yet been done.

There are also instances where basically important interrela-tionships are noted almost in passing. Zolotukhin and Linnik ob-served that since there would be a major redistricting in 1980, the 1978 state legislative elections assumed an unusual significance (1978a, 41–42). This relationship ought to have been noted much earlier in Soviet writing, but it was overlooked by Soviet analysts because ideology deflected attention from such seemingly minor details that did not touch the monopolies.

Incremental/factual writings devote considerable attention to identifying and analyzing the issues and strategies connected with campaigns.[5] In contrast, the ideological writers focus on demonstrating the demagogic nature of campaigns and treating issues and strategies as virtually nothing but tricks.

Factually oriented scholarly articles on elections published in the 1930s had presented a relatively realistic picture of the various campaigns. Roosevelt's victory in 1936 was attributed to the Republicans' basically having nothing to offer the voters, refusing to discuss substantive issues, and resting on their past laurels. The modest economic upturn helped Roosevelt, as did his attractive personality and James Farley's organizational talents (Noritskii 1936a). Once the incremental/factual writings had become established in the 1970s questions of strategies and their consequences were often discussed. For instance, George McGovern's shifts toward centrist positions as the 1972 campaign progressed were calculated to win the support of traditional Democratic constituencies (Berezhkov 1973, 5). But they actually alienated those Democrats who were very liberal while encouraging the alienation of those average voters who were, in the famous words of Scammon and Wattenberg that were quoted by Nikiforov, "neither young, nor poor, nor black" (1973, 101). He added, citing the *New York Times,* that McGovern did not possess an aura of competence and generally did not fit the image of president.

Writings of this kind enriched the Soviet analysis of the Goldwater presidential nomination of 1964, which was attributed (Fursenko and others 1974, 56) to his having formed an effective organization for achieving that end. Shamberg saw the nomination as partially attributable to the fact that Scranton became active too late while Lodge and Romney were not active at all (1965, 65). Moreover, note was taken of Goldwater's assessment that he had a more difficult opponent in Lyndon Johnson, who avoided a head-on confrontation of ideas, than he would have had in John Kennedy, who would have met him head-on (Fursenko and others 1974, 64). Factual analyses likewise took brief but serious account of the regroupings within the electorate caused by demographic changes and by shifts on issues. These resulted in adoption of both the Republican southern strategy and the law-and-order slogan (Zorin 1970, 47) as well as the Democratic strategy in 1980 of moving in a more conservative direction (Pechatnov 1980a, 197).

Perhaps the best treatment of strategy is Pechatnov's analysis of the 1980 election, which he felt Reagan won because of his promises of lower taxes, economic growth plus full employment without inflation, and the very active role of the right in organizing and funding the campaign (1980b). The Democrats lost because Carter went back on his promise to cut spending on arms and instead advocated an increase during the campaign. Contributing to the loss was the crisis within the party caused by Carter's rejection of the usual liberal–reformist domestic policies and by his growing toughness in foreign policy. These considerations serve as reminders that at some point the policies of incumbent presidents become intertwined with campaign strategies. This raises an interesting analytical issue on which Soviets have only rarely commented, as in the case of the 1940 election when Roosevelt lost much of the farm vote because his policies had not helped farmers on a broad enough scale (Zolotukhin 1968, 143–44). Gerald Ford made a number of personnel changes, most notably firing defense secretary James Schlesinger, in an attempt to take direct control of domestic and foreign policy so as to strengthen his hand before the election (Glagolev 1975).

Conventions and primaries are two features of campaigns that have warranted only rare comments apart from Lan's competent but dated treatment of conventions (1937, 516–26) and Gantman and Mikoyan's study of the 1968 conventions (1969, 169–81). Once IUSAC came into being its representatives attended four national conventions and produced firsthand reports on them in the institute's monthly.[6] Presidential primaries were also regularly reported. The Soviet embassy has followed these matters more closely. As early as the mid–1960s a senior Soviet KGB official at the embassy had a detailed familiarity not only with the major candidates in the New Hampshire primary but also with "the inner workings of New Hampshire politics" (Cox 1976, 50–51).

The standard Soviet attitude toward campaign funding had been that the sources of funds were numerous, but they were very rarely reported in their totality as required by law (Gromyko 1957, 77–82). The ostensibly democratic nature of elections was belied since large contributions were secretly made. As the years went by, skyrocketing campaign costs became the subject of articles in the American press like the one by Richard Harris in the August 7, 1971 issue of *The New Yorker*. IUSAC's monthly published it in Russian with a commentary that constituted a comprehensive and updated discussion of funding sources and campaign expenditures (Seregin 1972). The Federal Elections Campaign Act of 1974 was enacted to eliminate some of the problems connected with campaign financing. The major Soviet study of the act concluded, after examining the points made by its American supporters and critics, that the law was a typical example of bourgeois reformism calculated to strengthen the two-party system and weaken third parties (Seregin 1976). An analysis of the subsequent election concluded that either the personal wealth of millionaire candidates or political action committees funded by large corporations had been the chief sources of funding (Federov 1977). In the 1988 election the role of PACs was preponderant (Bratslavskii 1989). The incremental/factual studies confirm that, by virtue of their funding, elections remain controlled by the same institutions and people called monopolies and monopolists in ideological writings.

Although widely dispersed, the incremental/factual studies give Soviet readers a clearer picture of the role labor plays in elections. In particular, some statistics are given that were never cited in ideological writings. For example, the leadership of the AFL–CIO planned to forge a labor bloc at the 1972 Democratic convention composed of up to 600 "delegates representing the unions, i.e., 20% of all the delegates" (Popov 1972, 12). And in the 1980 campaign the unions spent $20 million, chiefly on behalf of Democrats, but somewhat in vain, at least so far as the presidential race was concerned, since 44% of the union members voting chose Reagan (Lapitskii 1981, 65).

But even when the unions win, they sometimes lose. Union support of the Democrats in 1976 did not result in adoption of the policies the unions favored—an old story, and not a chance result, because that's how the system operates (Lapitskii 1981, 66). Here is another conclusion, conforming to one in the ideological writings, that is indicative of the parameters of consensus within the Soviet academic community created by the operation of the mindset and the learning net.

Overall, the incremental/factual writings have helped advance the Soviet understanding of American elections, but their episodic and disconnected way of presenting information make this literature a poor vehicle for deepening Soviet perceptions significantly.

Clearly, innovative writings are the better way to accomplish this task.

The study of public opinion has produced innovative work. Under the sponsorship of IUSAC the late Mira M. Petrovskaia published just the kind of book whose absence I have deplored more than once in this chapter (1982). The early parts of the volume discuss how the study of public opinion is organized and operates in the United States. Large quantities of well-organized, informative data are communicated about the stages of development of the field, and major scholars, institutions, books, and methodologies are identified. The Soviet reader is given a rare treat: at last an important feature of American political life is presented in a very comprehensible and comprehensive way. In so doing, however, Petrovskaia felt it necessary to defend the very worth of studying public opinion against Soviet mindset attitudes by citing Chilean, Canadian, and French communist authors in support— as if those in the capitalist lion's den itself were the best witnesses to the validity of her effort (1982, 5–7).

Petrovskaia's wide-ranging analysis grew out of two previous studies. Her earlier volume on the subject (1977) essentially prefigured her 1982 book, as did her chapter in a book edited by Zamoshkin (1978, ch. 3). Some interesting comparisons and contrasts can be made between Petrovskaia's work and the materials in Zamoshkin. There is general agreement that public opinion polls in the United States have two functions: manipulation of public opinion by the ruling circles and intelligence gathering on their behalf the better to manipulate (Zamoshkin, ed. 1978, 16–18; Petrovskaia 1977, 5, 36, 1982, 5, 139). But Petrovskaia at once introduces the qualification, not found in Zamoshkin, that public opinion periodically has been at odds with the will of the dominating class, even though that class controls the means of communication, which have such a powerful effect on forming mass consciousness (1982, 6).

The Zamoshkin volume uses polling to measure the deepening level of crisis in America. This is illustrated by two chapter titles that reflect their contents well: "Public Opinion and the Deepening Crisis of the U.S. Political System" and "Reflection of the New Stage of the General Crisis of Capitalism in U.S. Public Opinion."

Nevertheless, the book contains enough advances (beyond the chapter by Petrovskaia) to place it in the category of ideological/ incremental writing. Petrovskaia (especially 1982) is notable for capturing the diffuseness and volatility of public opinion in addition to its tendency to cut across issues. Her 1982 study is much more detailed and technical than anything published before, and it communicates more concrete data about survey results than any one other Soviet source or combination of sources.

As would be expected, there are points of agreement. The Zamoshkin volume discusses the reformist orientation characteristic of the majority of American studies of public opinion (ed. 1978, 216–20). And Petrovskaia notes that there are many preconceptions or biases behind the questions asked in surveys (1982, 29). The reason is that only within-system, or reformist, alternatives are posed in the questions, and the "class approach" is avoided— that is, no questions are asked to elicit radical alternatives on matters that could involve making fundamental social transformations (Petrovskaia 1977, 84–87, 98). There is also a common recognition that splits within the ruling class are reflected in divisions in public opinion, but Petrovskaia pushes beyond that recognition to suggest that the pluralistic nature of American bourgeois society results in the creation of many different parties and groups whose interests often collide (Zamoshkin, ed. 1978, 113–44; Petrovskaia 1982, 6). Petrovskaia's important, if only implied, conclusion is that some aspects of public opinion are not merely the reflection of differences within the ruling class, as the analysis in Zamoshkin seems to suggest.

Of particular interest are the attempts in Zamoshkin to explain the role of the media in forming and reflecting public opinion on the Vietnam War, and in so doing to account for the battle between the media and the government that started in the mid–1960s. Although the media and public opinion originally supported the war, the opinion polls showed a marked shift against the war in 1968. The media thereupon became critical of the war out of fear of losing the public's trust and therefore their mass audience, their prestige, and their source of income (Zamoshkin, ed. 1978, 132–33, 139). However base their motives may have been, the media are complimented for having hastened the end of the war (137), and they get recognition for the positive role played by the ideological and moral sensibilities of thousands of people working in the media that contributed to the switch in the media's position (139).

The media's initial support of the government in the Vietnam War and their hushing up of the Watergate affair just after it had happened demonstrate the media's tendency voluntarily to reduce criticism once it begins to threaten the entire existing system (Zamoshkin, ed. 1978, 140). Still, the crises created by the war and by Nixon's unsuccessful attempts at muzzling the press, followed by the worsening problems facing Americans in everyday life, made it increasingly difficult to manipulate public opinion, and the crises forced the establishment to begin to pay attention to "the country's real public opinion" (143–44, 144 [quotation]).

Petrovskaia's contribution is to use American sources to show that disaffected public opinion is very fragmented and that it would be difficult to organize and unite it (1982, 152–55). But she also points out that disaffection may be mobilized by conservatives as, indeed, it was in the 1980 election (159–60). Yet precisely because of the fragmentation and the cross-cutting characteristic of public opinion, she did not feel that the Reagan victory was indicative of a massive shift to the right (166–74). On this point she agreed with other Soviet analysts of American political consciousness. The hope must be kept alive that the mass movements, so important in the Soviet mindset's analytical framework, will be revitalized.

Petrovskaia's chapter on elections discusses the positive and negative aspects of polling. On the plus side, it helps in working out campaign strategy and tactics by determining what is troubling people; it helps financial backers spend their money more effectively since nobody wants to back a loser; and it also helps to understand the limitations of the bandwagon effect through its identification of the complex cross-cutting factors involved when the voters make their choices (109–11, 116, 120–23). Negatively, the pollsters have in fact become political consultants who manipulate the voters and sometimes even the candidates, and there have been numerous abuses of polling by its practitioners and clients (112–13, 117–20). Patrick Caddell, a Democratic pollster, is quoted on the most negative effect of all: "We have created a system that does not reward making an attempt at solving fundamental problems" (124).

These studies of American public opinion created a new concern with what was ultimately called political consciousness. It is surprising that they did not call it class consciousness, and it was probably quite deliberately not called that to avoid a confining entanglement with troublesome ideological questions. The Soviets had traditionally studied class consciousness in the United States episodically and in very general terms. Their analyses were heavily skewed by ideological requirements and expectations. Since class consciousness was a research topic where the ideology did not fit the realities at all well, it abounded in complex and contradictory aspects. Using the term political consciousness was therefore the Soviet way of circumventing ideological oversimplifications and constraints and getting closer to the realities of the situation.

The IUSAC has been the prime vehicle for developing the study of political consciousness (Malcom 1984, 65–68). The institute's researchers draw heavily on American data banks and publications dealing with public opinion, voting behavior, political sociology, and political and social psychology. Their work is based on frequent research visits to the United States, especially stays at major American universities.[7] These studies are the best examples of the assimilation of American political science research and analytical techniques and they give Soviet readers an unusually comprehensive picture of the variety of views and perceptions in a pluralistic society. These, in turn, produce the political orientations of individuals and groups that have a direct impact on practical political activity, especially electoral behavior (Burlatskii and Galkin 1985, 248–67).

Over the decades, Soviet authors have compiled an imposing list of criticisms of American election practices. Shakhnazarov (1955, 63–67) complained that there were about fifty different requirements or limitations placed on voting, approximately three-fourths of the campaign funds came from the richest families, at the conventions the candidate was chosen through backstage deals, moral and physical force were used to affect voting (bribery, ballot box stuffing, miscounting, fists, and revolvers), many voters did not know who the candidates for the Senate and House were, and almost 50% of the voters stayed home in the 1952 and 1954 elections. Gromyko discussed legal barriers to voting by blacks and poor whites in the South as well as the universally limiting role of age and residence qualifications and literacy tests (1957, 54ff). Bel'son devoted his entire third chapter to demonstrating that elections failed to provide genuine representatives of and for the people (1960). Beglov analyzed the growing tendency since World War II for people of substantial wealth to hold elective office (1971, 400–415).

The changes made in the electoral system to overcome some of these flaws have been given mixed ratings. Aleksandr Nikiforov estimated that adoption of the Twenty-Fourth Amendment and legislation passed in 1971 and 1972 had expanded the electorate by over 32 million people, mainly college students who were, in words he puts in quotes, of "middle-class" origin (1973). But other Soviets evaluated the effects of the Federal Elections Campaign Act of 1974 very negatively (Seregin 1976; Federov 1977).

The basic criticism of elections in America flows from "the nature of bourgeois democracy, democracy in the interest of the exploiting minority" (Nikiforov, ed. 1976, 132). The election process is hopelessly flawed, particularly the manner in which nominations are made and campaigns are financed; and, given the nature of bourgeois democracy, these problems simply cannot be overcome (Kedrenovskaia 1978, 113). Besides, since both bourgeois democracy and American political institutions are in crisis, it does not much matter who wins this or that election (Vladimirov 1974, 45).

The President

Just as there are no Soviet books that survey elections, there are no one-volume works dealing comprehensively with the presidency. But many other kinds of studies have been written. There are biographies of Washington (Iakovlev 1973), Madison (Kalenskii 1981), Jefferson (Sevost'ianov and Utkin 1976), Lincoln (Ivanov 1964), Wilson (Gershov 1983), Franklin Roosevelt (Iakovlev 1965, 1969), Eisenhower (Ivanov 1984), Kennedy (Gromyko 1971, 1973; Iakovlev 1970), and Nixon (Gromyko and Kokoshin, 1985). George Bush's autobiography is due in 1990.

In addition, short, informative histories of twentieth-century presidents and their administrations appear in Ivanian (1975), and

similar treatment is accorded post–World War II presidents (Iakovlev 1983), although here the focus is more on foreign policy.

Like Gromyko (1971), these last two volumes are additionally
significant because at least 200,000 copies of each was published,
indicating that they were intended for a mass audience. The common theme in these books is criticism of widespread manipulation
in American politics. Needless to say, the Soviets neither discovered nor invented this facet of American politics. The examples
of hypocracy and demagogy given by the Soviet authors to substantiate their criticism are taken mainly from American publications normally cited in American scholarly literature through the
decades. As a by-product of this exercise Soviet readers are treated
to a wealth of information about the rough-and-tumble of American politics and are given illustrations of the possibilities existing
in the United States to criticize, unmask, or even unseat political
leaders.

A few books belong in the innovative category. Chetverikov
wrote an outstanding study of the president as policymaker and
of the complex relationships he enters into with his own executive
bureaucracy, Congress, and pressure groups when making policy
(1974). The comprehensiveness of his treatment in itself makes
the book innovative, as is the case with Nikiforov's (ed. 1976, 200–
254) pithier study of the office. Chetverikov's earlier book on
executive branch organization published under a pseudonym (Marinin 1967a) was an innovative precursor. Likhacheva's study of the
Council of Economic Advisers is in a category by itself as a narrowly focused analysis that goes into unusual detail and depth
pursuing its subject (1975). Similarly, the two books analyzing the
economic policies of the Roosevelt and Kennedy administrations
are in a category apart (Dalin 1936; Men'shikov, ed. 1964). Finally,
there is only one book on presidential–congressional relations, but
it considers only treaty making and executive agreements (Belonogov 1974).

Many specialized articles have been published on a broad range
of narrow topics relating to the presidency. There is only a handful
of general articles that could give Soviet readers a quick, intelligible
overview of the office (A. S. Nikiforov 1972 and Bel'son 1962, for
instance). Since there are no Soviet books dealing with this complex topic in a comprehensive fashion it is extremely difficult for

Soviet readers to develop a reasonably clear conception of the office, its powers, and its operation.

Thematically, studies of the presidency initially focused on the aggrandizement of its power at the expense of Congress since the time of Franklin Roosevelt and particularly following World War II. Soviet writers later became concerned with the limits on that power, leading them to examine more closely presidential–congressional relations and executive branch operations since the war. In the preceding sections of this chapter I noted some gaps and weaknesses in Soviet literature on parties and elections originating in the constraints imposed by the mindset. In the case of the presidency a similar statement by Burlatskii (1970, 110) remains partially valid: "It is known that in the party and state organs concerned with the foreign policy of the USSR the closest attention is given to the study of political leaders both within the ruling and opposition forces of the capitalist countries. Unfortunately, our theory is of little assistance to practice in this regard. At the same time it is difficult to overvalue the significance of that kind of research."

State–monopoly capitalism analyses in all their versions usually posited an undeviating growth in presidential power particularly at the expense of Congress and the states. These analyses had little or nothing to say about the Supreme Court in relation to the president and much to say about the president's being virtually a captive of the monopolies. Thus a specialist on elites in America could call Cleveland, Theodore Roosevelt, Wilson, Coolidge, and Hoover "the creatures" of Morgan and could consider McKinley, Taft, and Harding the "henchmen" of Rockefeller (Ashin 1966, 80). Later, when the monopolies' competition was viewed in a more complex way, presidents were considered beholden to broad, nationwide coalitions of monopoly groups, a phenomenon exemplified by Nixon (Zorin, ed. 1971, 371–81).

Some analysts found that Franklin Roosevelt and Lyndon Johnson managed to become independent of particular monopoly groups while simultaneously representing the interests of the entire bourgeoisie (Noritskii 1936b, 10; Tsagolov 1968, 170–72). Similarly, several authors interpreted John Kennedy's stern actions in his bout with U.S. Steel as playing referee in an intramonopoly battle (Men'shikov, ed. 1964, 126–29; Zorin 1964, 505–10; Gantman and Mikoyan 1969, 44). But Marinin viewed the episode as illustrating the relative independence of the state (1967a, 5), while N. Iaklovlev concluded, using a surprising formulation never before or since found in Soviet writing, that "the government won" (1970, 204).

These latter interpretations fit the contention of some Soviet analysts that the powers invested in the president by the Constitution were very imposing to begin with, that they were enlarged following the desire of either the monopolies or the entire ruling class to create a channel of influence within the government, which was more convenient than working through Congress, and that the president amassed more powers than even the Constitution had envisaged (Cherniak 1957, 24; Gromakov 1958, 12; Mishin 1954, 7, 17, 69). Just as economic power had become concentrated in the monopolies, political power was being concentrated in the executive, first as the accompaniment of state intervention in the economy, then as a consequence of expanding military and foreign policy involvements (Marinin 1967a, 10–13).

These general trends were first documented in Soviet writing by citing American authors (generally conservatives like Corwin 1941, West 1946, and Patterson 1947) who were alarmed at the real or possible concentration of power in the president. Since these Americans were not advocates of SMC analysis they had other explanations for the concentration of power, and occasionally Soviet writers added some of these (such as the president's numerous implied powers, many constitutional roles, and extraconstitutional functions) to their own SMC rationale (Boichenko 1959, 91–95; Nikiforov, ed. 1976, 233–38; Marinin 1967a, 233–39).

Some SMC analyses fleetingly noted that the president's power was in fact limited. The president was by SMC definition beholden to the monopolies, or at least to some of them, and these binding ties interfered with various presidents' attempts to effect their pet policies—including those calculated to aggrandize their power (Gantman and Mikoyan 1969, 78; Izakov 1972; Petrov 1978, 63; Anikin, ed. 1972, 282; Gromakov 1958, 15; Fedosov 1969). Within a week of his election victory, Jimmy Carter met with major businessmen at a posh Manhattan restaurant, an act interpreted as an expression of the monopolies' satisfaction with a president-elect who had run on an ostensibly populist platform and image (Shishkin 1976a, 54). The binding ties precluded embarking on any meaningful populist policies.

In a major study of presidential power based on the leadership theories and practices of Woodrow Wilson and John Kennedy, Nikolai Iakovlev concluded that the two presidents tried to overcome capitalism's crisis through drastically increasing presidential power and placing service to the state (with its attendant discipline and sacrifice) above the traditional capitalist values of the anarchy of production and the striving for gain (1970, 4–6, 338–42). In the words of the title of Iakovlev's book, *They Overstepped the Bounds* and suffered failure—and death in the case of Kennedy and his brother Robert, who shared John's ideas on leadership. The American bourgeois political system placed decided limits upon the appearance of *too* strong a leader. There was a lesson in this: to get too far ahead of the people in your own class in your thinking and actions can be fatal (Zorin 1964, 548–49).

Other analysts found constraints on the president in the fact that he must win an election, the constitutional limits on his incumbency, and the checking and balancing functions of Congress and the Supreme Court (Nikiforov, ed. 1976, 297; Kokoshin and others 1983, 114–15). The authors made these observations to dispute the prediction, periodically made by SMC authors, that the president would become a dictator. The separation of powers almost excludes personal arbitrariness on the part of the president, or at least makes it extremely difficult (Nikiforov, ed. 1976, 242). Some American observers felt that the president had become *too* dependent upon, and limited by, public opinion and the pollsters (Petrovskaia 1982, 94). The fact that the polls identified a new trend within the public—to neither trust nor give the benefit of the doubt to the president— helped explain the string of one-term presidents in the 1960s and 1970s (Petrovskaia 1982, 95; Kokoshin and others 1983, 117). And, last, episodic mention was made of the constraints put on the president by the autonomous role of the states in the federal system and by the importance of the states in the election system (Nikiforov, ed. 1976, 87; Krylov 1968, 59).

Other writers commented that the president's power is limited by his own cabinet appointees and by his large Executive Office staff (Novikov 1970, 129–32; Kokoshin and others 1983, 114). The latter factor is the basis of Chetverikov's innovative book on policymaking, which stresses the limitations placed on presidential power (especially the power to reorganize the executive branch) by the operation of the "triple alliance" composed of middle-level White House staffers, congressional staffers, and the representatives of monopoly interest groups (1974, 102, 150). Drawing on the copious American literature on this topic, Chetverikov was able to present the Soviet reader with an unusually comprehensive, realistic, and sophisticated analysis of how the decision-making system operates at the topmost levels, with the president portrayed as involved in a complex set of battles on various levels of government over a multitude of issues, chiefly regarding how much centralized control the president ought to have over the greatly expanded bureaucracy.

Behind this breakthrough was an earlier remark by Chetverikov, made in passing but full of ideological dynamite at the time, that the executive branch bureaucracy possesses "a measure of autonomy" as part of the superstructure, and that it also influences the economic basis of society (Marinin 1967a, 9). Gromyko, too, pointed to the president's being limited by the bureaucracy when, using quotation marks for irony's sake, he noted that it "informs" and "enlightens" him (1968, 276). A large group of analysts joined Gromyko in claiming that such autonomy and influence are possible because the financial oligarchy really controls the bureaucracy through staffing its higher reaches with its own members in the cabinet and other high appointive jobs.[8] But there was no agreement on precisely where the power resulting from this autonomy is concentrated in the executive branch—the cabinet, the Executive Office of the president, or the National Security Council (Bel'son 1960, 53; Marinin 1967a, 115).

Prior to Watergate it had been risky for Soviet writers to assert that Congress was anywhere near equal in power to the president, even though hints to that effect had been printed. Aleksandr Nikiforov (1972, 19) observed that presidential power constantly ran into obstacles such as "the state-legal and constitutional system of checks and balances and the political system of two-party government," and Chetverikov maintained that the Congress was relatively autonomous with respect to the president since it was totally controlled by the bourgeoisie and was useful as an arena for concluding political deals among the various bourgeois groupings (Marinin 1967b, 122).

Following President Nixon's resignation, it was easier to write about a decrease in presidential power and an increase in Congress's, but very different reasons were given for the shift. It was viewed as a consequence of a power struggle between two institutions (Nikiforov, ed. 1976, 195, 244–54) or as a negative reaction of powerful forces that could not forgive Nixon and Kissinger for attempting to improve relations with the Soviet Union (Iakovlev 1983, 24, 354–57). Zorin claimed that Wall Street concluded that Congress was now a better channel of influence than the president since the southwestern and far western monopoly groups had begun capturing the presidency in the persons of Johnson and Nixon (1978).

Chetverikov took the middle position. Even though a balance had been struck between president and Congress owing to the latter's relative autonomy and the stability of its role in the separation of powers, the objective process of strengthening presidential power could continue, although at a slower pace (1974, 28, 50–72). Indeed, toward the end of the 1970s it appeared that big business once again wanted to strengthen presidential power (Plekhanov 1979, 19). A Soviet symposium on the presidency in 1983 heard more comments to the same effect as well as the observation that, with domestic problems worsening and the resources needed to resolve them shrinking, a stronger president is essential (Kokoshin and others 1983, 112–16).

The inability of the allegedly irresistible presidential force to overcome the apparently immovable congressional object remains a problem. One reason is that two disparate Soviet perceptions— the pre-SMC notion that Congress was supreme and the later notion that the president was a dictator—were both wrong. The truth was somewhere in between (Nikiforov, ed. 1976, 194). In addition, the problem is unresolved because the Soviets failed to develop a methodology for measuring the shifting tendencies in the relative power positions of president and Congress.

There were only two instances where these problems were

recognized. Nikiforov cited a report in *Congressional Quarterly* on the 1941–1972 period that showed statistically how erroneous the usual Soviet contention was that congressional influence on formulating important laws is weak (ed. 1976, 240–41). Savel'ev suggested that a president's power could be measured by determining his effectiveness in incorporating his program into legislation (Kokoshin and others 1983, 117). The key variables were the effectiveness of his vetoes, the success rate of his legislative initiatives in surviving the legislative process and actually being voted on, and, finally, the extent of the president's victories in final votes. Adoption of these methods, which (it must be noted because Savel'ev did not) had originally been worked out by American political scientists, would help determine more accurately just where in the "in between" the truth lay at particular periods.

Some analysts concluded that the Nixon resignation initiated a crisis in the presidency (Kokoshin 1982, 76–117). Yet, as if to add a note of cautionary realism for the benefit of Soviet colleagues who might overestimate the seriousness and nature of that situation, Eduard Ivanian observed that it is more accurate to speak of a functional crisis than an institutional one (Kokoshin and others 1983, 113).

In summary, it is surprising how little publishing the Soviets have done on the presidency given its central role in SMC theory and in the actual workings of American politics. Without Chetverikov's two books (1974; Marinin 1967a) it would be difficult to conceive of how any Soviet reader dependent upon Soviet scholarly publications would imagine that institution to be structured and operate. Splendid though these two volumes are, they, along with the myriad other publications on the presidency, still leave too much untold. Meantime, more information is available on which many interesting and informative studies could be based, and a recent collection of translated American articles on how people become president shows what can be done (Plekhanov, ed. 1985). But the problem has also been that their theory has given Soviet authors little help in ordering and interpreting the available data. In the following chapter there will be an inventory of the progress made in developing that theory, particularly in the realms of the study of leadership and power. Since these advances should themselves produce studies that will fill some of the extensive gaps in the long run, we can end on a note of expectant optimism.

Congress

Congress has been the best studied branch of government. Two general books on Congress (Gromyko 1957; Mamaev 1962) appeared in the heyday of SMC analyses, even though the SMC approach posited Congress's decline. The most likely reasons are that pre-SMC theorizing had stressed the role of legislatures in capitalist countries, and in the American scholarly writings on which these two studies were based, more attention had been given to Congress than to the presidency prior to the 1960s. Dated though they now are, and heavily ideological though they may be, these two Soviet studies communicate a convenient understanding of how Congress works that is lacking with regard to the presidency. The chapters on the Congress in the five topical books on the American political system that have already been cited serve a similar function. A few articles fall into this category (Savel'ev 1973a; Silaeva 1977; Savel'ev and Silaeva 1977).

More than any Soviet book, Savel'ev's study of Congress enables the Soviet reader to make sense of an American political institution (1989). He discusses the concept of representation, the Constitution's role in establishing Congress, the history of Congress, its role in making foreign policy, and its relationship to the presidency, especially in the Reagan administration. Like his earlier analysis of the Senate (1976a), this volume mixes orthodox interpretations with breakthroughs.

Yet another reason for paying more attention to Congress is evident in the three books published on Congress's role in making foreign policy that fall into the factual, innovative, and topical categories (Belonogov 1974; Popova 1978; Ivanov 1982). The Soviets developed an interest in this topic in the early 1970s when they learned some painful lessons from the passage of the Trade Act of 1974, which denied most favored nation trading status to the Soviet Union, and from the failure to ratify the SALT II treaty. Soviet studies of Congress's foreign policy role are fully treated in a splendid analysis by Robert Huber (1988).

The one full biography of a senator is Vorontsov's book on J. William Fulbright (1971). Occasionally, biographical articles on senators have appeared, often because they were potential presidential candidates (Erokhin 1972; German 1972; Linnik and Savel'ev 1975). Members of the House of Representatives have not attracted such attention yet.

The most pervasive theme is that the bourgeoisie completely controls Congress. Shakhnazarov years ago included Congress among "the obedient tools of the dictatorship of the monopolistic circles" (1955, 80–81). Gromyko wrote of "the undivided domination in it [Congress] of the representatives of the monopoly bourgeoisie" (1957, 13). Dmitriev called Congress the most reactionary part of the entire political system (1963, 52).

Specifically, there are no members of Congress directly representing the workers in Congress. Most members are attorneys who interact with the army of lobbyists who are also mostly attorneys, which leads to corruption and malfeasance (Guliev and Kuz'min 1969, 92–94; Guliev 1970, 205–6). After the attorneys, the next largest group in Congress are the manufacturers, bankers, corporate leaders, and farmer-capitalists (Nikiforov, ed. 1976, 136). With many millionaires in the Senate, Congress as a whole is predominantly composed of wealthy males from the business world, and the minorities are poorly represented (Silaeva 1978).

The usual American rejoinder to these criticisms is that it is not necessary to be a worker to defend workers' interests. Savel'ev addressed that contention, saying that the real issue was the process of making partial concessions in order to preserve the capitalist system and that, however liberal Congress may be, the "henchmen" of the monopolies still predominated (1973b, 113–15). The neoliberals in the Senate have been notable partisans of concession making (Savel'ev 1976a, 49–50). But the self-interested willingness to make partial concessions that may somewhat benefit the workers is not at all the same as directly representing their interests fully.

For the Soviets, the important questions (and answers) are: how much of the loaf is demanded for the workers in the halls of Congress (it won't be much without direct representatives of labor), and how much is actually received (it will be a good deal less than it could have been were workers directly represented).

Congress directly represents the conflicting factions of the bourgeoisie, or the "interests of the local financial groups" (Savel'ev 1976a, 56; Beglov 1971, 521 [quotation]; Guliev 1970, 118). The top leadership in Congress represents the monopolies, while other members "to a certain degree" represent the interests of the nonmonopoly bourgeoisie, with a broader range of the interests of the bourgeoisie represented in the House than in the Senate (Mamaev 1962, 8, 30). The "certain degree" seems to express itself in the concessions that are made to the nonmonopoly bourgeoisie (Levin, ed. 1964a, 38). Thus "the class unity" of the Congress is demonstrated in its proceedings when bills that are antidemocratic or antilabor or that deal with military appropriations sail through, whereas bills on excess profits or civil rights matters experience difficulties (Mamaev 1962, 51–61).

In the Senate this unity is seen in the large number of bills that are passed unanimously, or nearly so, after private consultations among Senate leaders (Savel'ev 1976a, 168). Class unity is most important on major issues where compromises are worked out which must then be supported by individual senators who may well have accepted campaign contributions intended to encourage them to take a quite different position (Savel'ev 1976a, 20).

Another constant theme in Soviet analyses of Congress illustrates the durability of the belief that the institution has been in decline. The argument, a mainstay of SMC analysis, was that in the era of free-competition capitalism the legislature was supreme, but in the era of imperialism, and its resultant crisis of bourgeois democracy, the legislature was relegated to second place once the executive branch became the chief weapon of the ruling class's domination (Mishin 1954, 17; Marinin 1967a, 25). The legislature proved to be too unwieldy a tool and not an entirely dependable one, either, since there were too many people in it, there was too much publicity associated with its work, and its members were sometimes forced to take public opinion into account (Mishin 1954, 17; Bel'son 1960, 146–47).

The original strength of these feelings is powerfully illustrated in a volume published by the Soviet academic press specializing in books on legal matters:

> The American Congress has lost its former significance and has degenerated into an organ for sanctioning the unlimited arbitrariness of presidential power and for imparting an outward show of "lawfulness" to any of its lawless actions. The twaddle about "freedom," "democracy," and so on, serves only as a smokescreen for

covering up the acts of tyranny and violence that are being effected in the country by "the executive power" and as a mask for the reactionary activity of Congress itself, the powers of which are used by the monopolies in their selfish interests. (Mishin 1954, 136).

Initially there were only rare intimations that this Soviet position had been overstated. Anatolii Gromyko was first to contend that Congress was not as powerless as Soviet writers had maintained in the late 1940s and early 1950s (1957, 3–24). Congress retained more of its legislative functions than had legislatures in other capitalist nations because the two-party system made it easier to rule through Congress, and more functions could therefore be entrusted to it (Levin, ed. 1964a, 58). Chetverikov cited this source in making the same point (Marinin 1967a, 30) and later added that Congress's importance to the ruling class could and did remain high since the workers influenced Congress less than other parliaments because there was no worker party (1974, 52–53). Burlatskii questioned the validity of the assertion that legislatures were inevitably more progressive than executives, noting that the Senate is often more conservative than the executive precisely when it is exercising its powers most fully (1970, 221).

The revivification of Congress inaugurated by Watergate emboldened some analysts to go further—although still gingerly—in modifying the old SMC position. Chetverikov wrote that Watergate demonstrated the durability of Congress's political role and showed that it possessed "a measure of autonomy" (1974, 71).

In a study sponsored by IUSAC, Popova cautiously interpreted the reassertion of congressional prerogatives as an indication that there were some limits, although indefinite, on the tendency for presidential power to expand at the expense of Congress (1978, 21). On the other hand, in a major attack on a fundamental proposition of SMC theory, statistical evidence originally published in American sources was adduced to show that Congress had played a key role in determining policy in this century with only very few exceptions (Savel'ev 1976a, 150–52; Nikiforov, ed. 1976, 240–41). A spate of points in a similar vein was scattered throughout these last two volumes (Savel'ev 1976a, 114–15, 152, 175–76; Nikiforov, ed. 1976, 123–24, 180, 186, 191–99, 241). Finally, a revival of Soviet studies of Congress's role in making foreign policy produced four volumes (Belonogov 1974; Savel'ev 1976a; Popova 1978; Ivanov 1982).

Much attention has been devoted to the question of how the congressional committee system has operated in the past and in more recent times (Gromyko 1957, 97–151; Mamaev 1962, 150–73; Belonogov 1974, 46–62; Ivanov 1982, 107–36). Soviet academic specialists have developed an appreciation for the complexities involved and for the periodic surprises that occur, but it is highly unlikely that the nonspecialists (particularly the Soviet political leaders) would have been able to cope with this brand of organized chaos until they were forced to experience a similar kind of relatively freewheeling politicking in the Gorbachev era. Almost the same could be said about some facts well known to Soviet writers: although Congress is organized on the basis of the two parties' relative strength, it often operates on the basis of constant, shifting, or temporary coalitions rooted in the members' ideological orientation or the economic interests of the states or districts they represent (Kislov 1961; Popova 1978, 36–46; Savel'ev 1976a, 44–56; Nikiforov, ed. 1976, 142–48; Ivanov 1982, 136–46).

The rapid growth of the congressional staff has further complicated the questions of influence and control in the congressional setting. But as in the case of the committees and coalitions, for the Soviets the complexities resolve into what could be called their "bottom line": the monopolies control the staff through the close ties the staffers maintain with them (Savel'ev 1976b, 127).

The Soviet position remains unchanged in its basics: Like all bourgeois legislatures, Congress is potentially a very democratic institution, but up to now it has been owned and operated by the ruling class.

The Supreme Court

The Court had been the least studied of the three main national political institutions until it suddenly became a major research topic in the 1980s, most likely as a consequence of Watergate. A historical study of the Court's development (Chernilovskii 1982) was quickly followed by a book describing the Court's organization and procedures and its relation to the legal and political systems (Zhidkov 1985).

There was also a concern with the Court's treatment of issues involving freedoms, rights, and equality that was connected with growing Soviet criticism of the human rights situation in America. A translation of Ann F. Ginger's *The Law, the Supreme Court, and the People's Rights* (Dzhindzher 1981) was published, as was a Soviet study of the Court's record of decisions in civil liberties cases connected with the Bill of Rights (Kalenskii 1983).

Before these books appeared, the Court had been treated only as a small part of broader studies (Boichenko 1959, 51–67; Niki-forov, ed. 1976, 279–94) or in a few articles (e.g., Chervonnaia 1978; Nikiforov 1978). The four books devoted to the Court are in the factual and innovative categories, but the other publications do not fit neatly into any of them.

Expressing well a point long made by many Soviet authors, Nikiforov remarked that the American Constitution had been for-mulated according to the spirit of its times in grandiloquent, gen-eral, and vague language (1971, 44). The consequent lack of clarity created a need for constitutional interpretation, which gave the ruling circles the opportunity to introduce changes into the Con-stitution as needed (Marinin 1967a, 23). But since insufficient changes were made to adequately reflect the many social and eco-nomic changes in American life, "alongside the old Philadelphia charter a new constitution has arisen consisting of a whole series of Supreme Court decisions, customs, and acts of Congress" (Mishin 1954, 8). If originally the Constitution was praised and idealized in the United States, Americans later saw it as a dead letter but then came to think of it as archaic and requiring prag-matic changes (Bel'son 1962, 66). Half of the changes through amendments adopted over the past hundred years dealt with voting rights (Savel'ev 1976a, 21).

Soviet legal specialists in the tradition of state and law have been highly critical of judicial interpretation of the Constitution by the Supreme Court because that became "a normative force creating new laws and establishing new legal norms" (Boichenko 1959, 52–53). Along with some American conservatives whom she cited, Boichenko contended that the Court had gone so far in placing itself above the Constitution that it had become a Constitutional Convention in perpetual session and also a third house of nonelect-ed legislators (1959, 51–67). Other Soviets were critical of judicial review, noting that American jurists, political scientists, and pol-iticians commented on the paradox of elective bodies and officials being regulated by "a body operating on manifestly undemocratic principles" (Vlasikhin and Savel'ev 1982, 36 [quotation]; Levin, ed. 1964a, 72ff).

The court is viewed both as legislator (Nikiforov, ed. 1976, 285–87) and in its reverse role as interpreter of the Constitution in the light of legislative acts as, for instance, when the Court upheld the constitutionality of the Smith Act, the McCarran–Wood Act, and the Taft–Hartley Act in the 1950s (Boichenko 1959, 50). On the other hand, an American attorney was quoted to show that in its *Brown v. Board of Education* decision the Court had brought about changes in the law that could not have been made through either a constitutional amendment or federal legislation (Guliev and Kuz'min 1969, 131).

The need to be cautious in making such statements arose from the mindset's prescriptions regarding the rule of law and the functions of the bourgeois legal system. One article was devoted to showing that the rule of law had indeed advanced the forward march of democracy centuries ago, but it now was being used to mask the lawless power of the monopolies (Tumanov 1963). The legal system's purposes are to manipulate the population ideologically and to defend capitalist property, the economic system, and also law and order in ways benefiting the dominant political forces (Puchinskii 1979, 186). The concrete meaning of the rule of law is determined not by abstract legal ideas or theories but by the will of the dominating class and the correlation of class and political forces at any given time (Zhidkov 1961, esp. 79, 81).

The Supreme Court acts as "guardian of the capitalist system," and it is a myth, used to manipulate the population ideologically, that the "bourgeois court" is "above class" and acts with "political impartiality" (Vlasikhin and Savel'ev 1982, 33, 41). The fact that, for the first time in history, the 1980 Republican party platform designated a specific direction the Supreme Court ought to follow in interpreting the law was a sign that the politicians were counting on the Court to become more active in serving the interests that the politicians were representing (Vlasikhin and Savel'ev 1982, 31). More important, the justices and the Court's staff members had been associated with the monopolies before assuming their positions on the Court (Gromakov 1958, 35–36; Zhidkov 1985, 28–38).

These are potent negative considerations in the Soviet mindset. As counterpoint it is important to examine the ways Soviet writers treated the Court's decisions with which they agreed.

The Soviets have recognized the Court's importance in favorably affecting the following issues: racial integration of schools, black voting rights, the Vietnam War's legality, the death penalty, the publication of secret government documents, access to college education, and the legality of presidential actions (Vlasikhin and Savel'ev 1982, 35). Buried in a footnote dealing with the last issue, the authors revealed the consequences of the Court's decision on the Nixon White House tapes, "the end political result of which was the forced resignation of R. Nixon from the post of president" (35).

The most systematic and detailed treatment of some of these issues is, quite expectedly, in Ginger's translated volume (Dzhindzher 1981). Typical of Soviet practice until the 1980s, various decisions were discussed sporadically, but not systematically, in Soviet writings (e.g., Zorin, ed. 1971, 201–8; Nikiforov 1971, 1978; Geevskii 1973, 105–10).

The liberal trend in the Court's decisions was welcomed but criticized as producing only limited and fragmented gains for various minorities (Chervonnaia 1978, 59–62), which was typical of the "limitations and inconsistencies" characteristic of "bourgeois-liberal constitutionalism" (Vlasikhin and Savel'ev 1982, 34). It was also considered typical that parts of the *Brown* v. *Board of Education* decision either were not executed or were implemented in such a way as to be harmless to the ruling class (Zhidkov 1961, 81). Sometimes the stress in Soviet writing was reversed so as to criticize more than to welcome, as in one analysis of the Court's decisions on laws dealing with subversion. Six pages of outrage and anger denouncing the early decisions in favor of those laws are eventually followed by two very low-key pages on how the Court finally declared those laws unconstitutional (Chernilovskii 1982, 179–84, 190–92). The author's sense of travesty was apparently not matched by his feeling for triumph. At other times attempts at balance were made, although with some distortion, as when Vlasikhin and Savel'ev enumerated the Court's accomplishments but then attacked its record on human rights, finding that it consisted of guaranteeing the freedom of expression of the Ku

Klux Klan as well as that of pornographers, and, in the realm of the inviolability of the person, permitting the use of contraceptives (1982, 34–35). But no other human rights decisions were registered.

Another way of treating the Court's positive decisions was to note the growing conservatism of the Court following the 1960s, which meant that either no further progress has been made on various issues or that the Court has retreated from its earlier positions (Vlasikhin and Savel'ev 1982, 39–41; Nikiforov 1978, 111–12; Chervonnaia 1978, 62; Zhidkov 1985, 143–220). As for the Court's future, Chernilovskii doubted that the conservative trend would mean a return to the formal legalism of yesteryear. And conservative trend or not, he asserted that the Court would never be able to end discrimination since "access to power belongs to a minority," and the Court cannot change the minority rule that is at the very basis of the political system (1982, 207–8). This is a sobering statement of the fundamental and unyielding Soviet attitude that the entire political system is discriminatory since it belongs to the bourgeoisie and serves the interests of that minority class. Once again, the class approach is basic to Soviet analyses.

Within the confines of these considerations, the Soviets perceive the Court as swinging moderately from left to right following a policy of self-limitation (Chernilovskii 1982, 210–11). In addition to being influenced by the entire bourgeoisie's stake in either modifying the system or maintaining it, the Court is also swayed by various parts of the class at different times, or by public opinion in general, or by democratically inclined public opinion in the country and throughout the world—that is, by the domestic and international level and intensity of the ideological struggle between capitalism and socialism (Geevskii 1973, 105–10; Gutsenko 1961, 55; Gromakov 1958, 37, 227; Levin and Tumanov, eds. 1974, 22–24, 41; Bel'son 1960, 173; Guliev and Kuz'min 1969, 131).

Reversals are one form that the Court's own swaying takes. Early Soviet comments on this phenomenon were not favorable: "The Court interprets the Constitution willy-nilly, not rarely changing its interpretations and decisions in connection with changed conditions" (Levin, ed. 1964a, 77). A more recent study commented favorably upon an American source that viewed reversals as an indication that the Court learned from experience and that it operated somewhat on the basis of trial and error (Nikiforov 1978, 110). Perhaps the most interesting explanation of all was in the SMC vein: since the Court could no longer support the bourgeoisie as straightforwardly as it had in the past, and to avoid loss of prestige in the eyes of the people, "it is forced to maneuver, adopting directly contradictory decisions on matters affecting the important institutions of bourgeois-democratic legality" (Gutsenko 1961, 47). If that had been the case up to 1961, later evidence showed that the Court's imputed strategy continued to succeed since opinion polls showed a less negative public attitude toward the Court than toward the president, Congress, or the political parties (Vlasikhin and Savel'ev 1982, 41).

Whatever one's reaction to any particular Soviet perspective on the Supreme Court may be, and given the many gaps in Soviet treatments of the Court, it appears that the overall range of views expressed in Soviet writing exhibits some commonalities with American attempts to explain the elusive, confounding, and sometimes breathtaking behavior of the most aristocratic part of the American government.

Policymaking

A discussion of the quintessentially political activity of how decisions are made and implemented would be a fitting conclusion to any analysis of how a political system's institutions and processes operate. Unfortunately, in Soviet scholarly writing the serious study of policymaking has hardly begun. This creates built-in limitations both on the kinds of analyses Soviet writers can produce and on any treatment based upon these analyses. Generally, Soviet policy analysis is somewhere back where American analyses were in the 1940s and earlier. The Soviet academics have been at their weakest when it comes to the study of the political process.

The book most closely approximating a general treatment of policymaking is Chetverikov's *Who Makes Policy in the U.S.A. and How It Is Made* (in Russian), a broad-ranging overview of the process in the executive branch (1974). Together with his earlier study of the executive branch (Marinin 1967a), this was a giant step forward in published Soviet policy studies. It was followed by another in the form of a one-page interactive flow chart of the policymaking process taken from an American source (Mel'nikov 1987, 232).

The earliest Soviet policy study was Dalin's book on Franklin Roosevelt's economic policy (1936). The next book on policy dealt with Kennedy's economic policy (Men'shikov, ed. 1964), and the latest book on domestic economic policy is Likhacheva's study of the Council of Economic Advisers as a policymaking body (1975). The first two volumes focus on the content of policy decisions and also discuss the inputs of various social forces. Likhacheva's book is qualitatively different, being a case study of the establishment and development of the council, stressing the professional commitments of its successive chairmen, their differing leadership styles, the formal and informal relations of the council with the president and Congress, and the transformation of the council's role from that of analytical specialist to policy advocacy and implementation. The role of changing administrations is also considered, as are the policies, in some detail, of fighting inflation and recessions.

A similarly exceptional study is Geevskii's book on racial policies (1973). Nowhere in Soviet writing is there so much information about the dynamics of American politics revolving around a social movement, the nature of the arguments made before the Supreme Court on behalf of the movement's aims, and the Court's resultant decisions. The focus is on presidential–congressional relations, particularly on the powerful role of committee chairmen and the filibuster as only southern senators could practice that art. Three books deal with social policies, primarily as system output (Kassirova 1978; Shkundin 1980; Plekhanov, ed. 1988). Two volumes are in the state and law tradition, stressing the content of decisions as adopted but not yet implemented; the last looks at alternatives and strategies to achieve them.

There is an interest in the making of foreign policy (Belonogov 1974; Popova 1978; Ivanov 1982). These volumes resumed a tendency of analysis initiated, but then dropped, in a collectively authored book whose translated title is *Motive Forces of the USA's Foreign Policy* (Lemin, ed., 1965). Robert Huber has thoroughly analyzed Soviet studies on how American foreign policy is made (1988, esp. 18–85).

The most pervasive theme in Soviet writing on American political institutions is monopoly control of their policies. The best Soviet books on policy stress this point, as indeed they must (Chetverikov 1974, 16–17, 47–48, 177; Geevskii 1973, 195–281; Likhacheva 1975, 10–27). It might seem as though nothing has changed in Soviet views since the heyday of primitive SMC. Yet the data on policymaking in the books on policy and the materials on policy scattered throughout Soviet studies of American politics present it as such a multifaceted and fragmented process that the seemingly obvious interests of the monopolies become much less definite in the complex institutional battles that precede the making of final decisions. Soviet authors have been unable to state this conclusion in print in so many words, but it is an important subliminal message in their writings.

The problem is first to determine each participant's interests. The Soviets consider the ruling class as a whole to have general interests that are opposed to the workers', and the monopolies as a whole have general interests opposed to those of the petty bourgeoisie and the workers. As a result of their economic competition, every single subunit of the bourgeoisie as a whole, the petty bourgeoisie, and the monopoly bourgeoisie has interests that sometimes conflict with all the other subunits, most of them, or simply some of them. The partial monopoly domination SMC version of American politics is replete with conflict.

The next problem is to establish, in concrete cases or specific policy problems, how all these factors interact in the pervasive conflicts accompanying the making of policy in capitalist countries. The question is: If the monopolies are in such effective control of the political system, why all these conflicts?

The answer would be unpalatable to the Soviets because it means recognizing that there are reasons other than the class struggle and monopoly control which explain conflict and fragmentation. Power itself is fragmented. And, except to closed minds, whether this is as basic as any other factors (including the class struggle and monopoly control) in the origin and management of conflicts, and whether they are resolved, partially resolved, or left in abeyance by the system, remains moot. This has to do with the way political institutions are organized and operate and with what the Soviets call the relative autonomy of the state. But Soviet writing rarely addresses the relative autonomy of *parts* of the state owing to functional separations of power not only at the level of the executive, legislative, and judicial branches but also within each of these, not to mention the division of power created by federalism. In its American variant, federalism, when combined with the way political parties are (dis)organized and operate, creates some troublesome analytical problems in explaining national politics and policymaking.

Soviet authors have minimized the significance of the *kinds* of conflicts being discussed here. They consider the conflicts to be of secondary importance, if that. So innovative an analyst as Chetverikov attacked conflict theory as an inadequate and misleading means for interpreting decisionmaking in the executive branch (1974, 115–19). Gromyko (1957, 14–16), no great partisan of innovation, excoriated Levin (1951) for having stressed the high level of conflict between president and Congress and also attacked Mishin (1954) for not taking a consistent position on this question.

However they may have chosen *not* to interpret it, the Soviets have nevertheless given due attention to conflict within the presidential and congressional domains and between president and Congress, most often in commenting on the complexity of the organizations and processes involved in making policy.

The growing bureaucratization of the presidential office and Congress through expanding staffs has been viewed as eroding the president's control of his own realm as well as complicating his relations with Congress. A "triple alliance," composed of presidential and congressional staff members and representatives of the monopoly interest groups, was gaining control of the policymaking process (Chetverikov 1974, 24, 30, 60, 72, 96, 99, 135–36, 141, 150, 158–59). Various presidents attempted to reassert control through instituting a program of "bureaucratic centralization" based on strengthening and expanding the Executive Office and the National Security Council and establishing a series of coordinating committees (Marinin 1967a, 41–45; Chetverikov 1974, 10, 35, 179–95). Conflicts abounded, showing the older SMC assertion that "the entire bureaucracy is at the undivided disposal of the president" (Bel'son 1960, 170) to have been patently wrong. Whether through a triple alliance or a centralizing mechanism the monopolies would be in control. The question could have been which monopolies (or for that matter, even which nonmonopoly interests) would control, or at least be in a better position, as a result of these moves, but the Soviet writings do not pose that bothersome question.

The complexity and frustrations in executive branch policymaking have been documented quite well in Chetverikov's books. No one author has done the same for Congress. The most detailed studies have been on the Senate, especially in its foreign policy role.

Historically, Soviet authors have lodged the following criticisms against Congress: its leaders were despotic; most of its work was done by committees and subcommittees that were not provided for by the Constitution; the committees did not as much supervise agencies in the executive branch as they assisted them; committee sessions were sometimes held in secret; the legislative process was fragmented; and filibusters prevented the possibility of voting on some issues (Guliev and Kuz'min 1969, 102–3).

In the past, most attention was given to proving that monopoly capital controlled congressional committees (Gromakov 1958, 30–33; Mamaev 1962, 51–61). Recently the focus has been the complexity of the legislative process as it affects the fate of policies (Guseva 1978; Ivanov 1982, 107–36; Belonogov 1974). The Soviets have also recognized that committee hearings, far from being meaningless exercises, served to complicate the work of executive agencies, to publicize shortcomings and malfeasance, and to focus attention on backstage activities in government (Marinin 1967a, 32–33).

In the later writings either monopoly control is simply assumed or its existence is implied when authors remain silent about the inputs of the various nonmonopoly political forces in the course of committee hearings and in the lobbying process. Conforming to the theory of class struggle, they make only fleeting reference, if any, to these other forces. Alternatively, they may treat these forces as playing a role through the effects of mass movements upon the policy process (e.g., Popova 1978, 19). Later writing has also taken into account the growing role of the congressional staff in readying legislation (Novikov 1974, 55–71), and some of these studies have made the point that the monopolies are well represented among the staff members (Savel'ev 1976a, 84, 1976b, 127; Nikiforov, ed. 1976, 163).

The later publications reproduce American arguments over the relative merits and demerits of various policies and are also informative about the concrete ways in which policy proposals have been modified. Despite their limitations, these sources yield a more fleshed-out picture of both congressional procedure and policy substance (and the ways they can be modified) than it had been possible to create prior to the 1970s. For example, the Soviet study of the lawmaking process became sophisticated enough to identify fifteen steps in passing a bill and to suggest that more steps could be added (Mishin 1976, 112–13; Ivanov 1982, 129).

Presidential–congressional relations are a major aspect of policymaking. In SMC analyses Congress was seen either as subordinated to the president or as working hand-in-glove with him in executing the will of the monopolies. Policy differences either tended to disappear or were thought to be insignificant. The focus was on the ways the president influenced the legislative process (Bel'son 1960, 170). Eventually the Soviets did realize that Congress could controvert the president: presidential programs often encounter serious opposition in Congress; the committee system produces real oversight of the executive branch and also creates blockages in decisionmaking; the power of the purse is great; hearings are an effective tool of influence; the Senate's power in confirming executive branch appointees is considerable (Marinin 1967a, 124–25; Nikiforov, ed., 1976, 241–42, 252–53).

In Soviet scholarly writing after World War II the first significant recognition that Congress could be troublesome for the president appeared in Igor' Geevskii's study of racial policy (1973, 178–87). Knowing that negative sentiment among powerful circles in Congress against enacting civil rights legislation was running strong, President Kennedy thought better of submitting a bill. But the Birmingham, Alabama, racial disorders produced a rash of submissions of civil rights bills originating in Congress itself. Kennedy then introduced a bill that was broader yet, but he did not press very hard for adoption. He feared a northern backlash and loss of the support of southern congressmen for other parts of his program.

The next recognition of Congress's power came in analyses of the events leading up to Richard Nixon's resignation (Chetverikov 1974, 55–72) and of the battles between president and Senate over treaty obligations going as far back as the Bricker Amendment (Belonogov 1974; Popova 1978, 8–22, 154–82). It was also noted that the Democratic majority in Congress created additional difficulties for Nixon (Nikiforov, ed. 1976, 246).

The significance of the resignation was played down on the grounds that Nixon and Congress on the whole cooperated in policy matters even during the Watergate hearings (Nikiforov ed. 1976, 250–52; Ivanov 1982, 189–93). Nevertheless, brief note was made that checks and balances actually did serve to check the president (Nikiforov, ed. 1976, 239). Moreover, the Senate now considered its oversight function to be as important as lawmaking, and Congress was in no mood to give up its reestablished powers vis-à-vis the president (Savel'ev 1976a, 173; 1977a, 73; 1977b, 81).

The policymaking battle takes place within the limits of a unique sort of bipartisanship exercised in creating *domestic* policy: the monopolies control the policymaking process through their domination of the political parties, elections, and the political institutions. The ruling class continues to rule.

Conclusion

While retaining the basic tenets of their interpretive framework, the class approach to the study of politics, Soviet analysts have clearly modified their understanding of how American political institutions and processes work. In welcoming this progress, the many important gaps in Soviet studies must be kept in mind, as must the question of how much has been effectively communicated to the politically powerful people in the Soviet Union and how much they have absorbed. As Huber suggests, much of the leadership's understanding has improved, but on questions like the separation of powers or Congress's oversight responsibilities their comprehension seems to be at "a surface level" (1988, 145–50, 161–62, 161 [quotation]).

That situation may change. Vladimir A. Kryuchkov, chief of the KGB, commented favorably on the suggestion that the Soviet legislature create a commission to oversee Soviet intelligence operations: "I think that we'll borrow some of the experience of the Americans" (Kryuchkov 1989).

Some of the gaps that do exist are attributable to the relatively small number of Soviet specialists available to analyze the intricacies of American politics, especially the twists and turns in the policymaking process. Others originate in the underdeveloped state of the Soviet study of politics, which made it difficult for Soviet scholars to make maximum use of the work done by American political scientists. Still other gaps result from restrictions built into the ideology: only the ruling class can participate in institutional politics and their associated political processes. With the exception of voting, which the Soviets consider to have minimal significance because they see no real choice in the candidates, everybody else must be relegated to the politics of social movements.

PART IV

Interpretation

7 EXPLAINING AMERICAN POLITICS: THEORIES OF CLASS, PLURALISM, AND ELITISM

Soviet approaches to American politics highlight two of the most fundamental questions in political analysis: Who rules and how do they rule?

The Soviets have answered these questions in their own way. We in turn can evaluate the quality or tenability of their replies by considering where they fall within the range of possible answers. Among the options some are more relevant to the American political experience than are others. The most relevant at first sight seem to be mutually exclusive, but further examination shows that the vitality of any alternative, the Soviet one included, depends upon its capacity for absorbing modifications, some of which may actually originate in another option.

Each possible answer functions as an information-patterning system. The concept "mindset" has served here as shorthand for the Soviet information-patterning system. "Theory" or "cognitive mapping" could have been used to roughly the same effect. This chapter's primary purpose is to investigate how information-patterning systems change. The most serviceable way of discussing the processes of modification is to use the concept of paradigm as the most nearly universal way of patterning information.

Options

The classic options for answering the question "Who rules?" were established in Chapter 3 of Aristotle's *Politics,* which observed that the one, or the few, or the many may rule. Aristotle's insistence that it makes a significant difference whether the rich or the poor rule is particularly important to the present discussion.

Applying these considerations to American politics, we can exclude the option that only one rules, even though some Soviet SMC analysts, and later some American writers on the imperial presidency in the 1970s, seemed to feel that a rule by one was being approximated. Otherwise, the argument among American political scientists over whether the few or the many rule has been heated, and Soviet analysts have for all practical purposes unanimously maintained that the few (the *rich* few) rule America.

The basic issue is how power is distributed, or how power is structured, in the United States. The range of present-day options for analyzing this matter has been delimited by Knoke (1981) in five models: radical-democracy, democratic-pluralism, multiple-elites, power elite, and class conflict. Alternatively, Hamilton has discussed the options in the light of five theories of modern democratic politics, which he calls the Marxist view, the modifications of Marxism, pluralism, mass society, and group-based politics (1972).

From the discussions of these two lists by their respective authors it is clear that, by and large, Knoke's class conflict model and what Hamilton calls the Marxist view and the modifications of Marxism have a good deal in common with Soviet perspectives. To the degree that they do, this approach can be called the class analysis paradigm. Its adherents maintain that in the United States the few rule and that they get just about everything important that can be gotten out of the political system. Both Knoke and Hamilton also treat the pluralist paradigm, whose supporters hold that the many rule in the United States and that just about everybody gets something of value out of the political system. Finally, although only Knoke discusses the elitist paradigm fully (Hamilton treats elements of it in passing), its importance in scholarly debates over the distribution of power warrants considering it well. Like the partisans of the class analysis paradigm, elitists maintain that the few rule in the United States but that they get the most, rather than essentially all, of what is to be gotten from the political system.

In the sense that I am using it here, a paradigm is a specific way of approaching, analyzing, understanding, and explaining a research topic. Advocates of this particular "way" are normally convinced that it is the exemplary way to investigate a problem and answer any questions that arise. In the process, information is fitted into a pattern. As Karl Deutsch wrote, "Information . . . is not events as such, but a patterned relationship between events" (1966, 84).

A paradigm patterns information. It is based on a theory and is the source of a model or models that are fashioned to illustrate how relationships are patterned. A typical vocabulary or terminology is associated with a paradigm. Finally, a paradigm focuses the attention of its advocates on certain preferred topics, often to the exclusion of others, and treats them according to definitely preferred analytical methods.

The three paradigms identified in the preceding paragraphs are the research and analytical options most widely discussed by students of American politics. Their relative merits and weaknesses have been hotly debated, usually in the context of trying to answer the question of which *one* is right. Rarely are attempts made to determine how much of American politics each explains, or which aspects of American politics each explains most fully.

The usual way of discussing these matters is to outline the essential or unique aspects of the paradigms and then contrast either two, or all three, of them (Knoke 1981; Hamilton 1972; Manley 1983; Prewitt and Stone 1973; Garson 1977). Since that has been done so often and so well, the most efficient way to initiate this discussion of the relevant issues is by noting that some of these contrasts have stressed the incompatibility of all three major paradigms (Knoke, 1981) and in particular of the pluralist and class paradigms (Manley 1983; Chilcote 1981; Garson 1977). After all, class analysis is concerned with a fundamentally antagonistic dichotomous division of society and also with the domination of one of the classes by the other. Pluralism is concerned with achieving consensus through compromise, thereby overcoming to a significant degree the large number of only moderately antagonistic divisions perceived by adherents to this paradigm.

Some analysts have drawn attention to certain compatibilities between at least the elitist and pluralist approaches (Prewitt and Stone 1973; Knoke, 1981). Some advocates of class analysis (e.g., Garson 1977) have suggested that there is a high degree of compatibility between pluralism and the particular version of the elite theory known as democratic elitism (Bachrach 1967). Parenti similarly maintains that, if pluralism exists at all, it is pluralism for the few, and not the many (1977). Hamilton agrees (1972).

Two conclusions can be drawn from these discussions. First, the authors identify the most basic incompatibilities, and their greatest number, when they describe or contrast ideal or pure paradigms. Second, the most significant and numerous compatibilities emerge when paradigms are developed from within by some of their advocates through critical refinement.

In doing ideal or pure paradigmatic analyses writers normally stress the unique insights, qualities, and terminology characteristic of each paradigm. The analyst is interested in applying *the* one exemplary analytical approach in order to explain how politics in general, and American politics in particular, works. This enterprise is often fundamentalist in tone, with its concern for uncompromising purity and defense of the fundamental truth-perceptions of the paradigm. There is a heavy stress on the dichotomous (right and wrong, we and they) and on the exclusiveness of the paradigmatic vision. Because of the strength of belief and commitment, passion, orthodoxy, dogmatism, and a penchant for the categorical appear frequently.

When contrasting ideal paradigms analysts generally use one paradigm to criticize the fundamental aspects of another. Here authors have an investment in stressing incompatibility.

At these two levels, there is not much hope for cross-fertilization between or among paradigms. Knoke maintains that it is generally impossible to resolve the basic conflicts in analytical approach among his five models; moreover, owing to their low level of formalization, it is not at all easy even to compare and contrast these models, or to design critical empirical tests for establishing their relative validity (Knoke 1981; Hamilton 1972). The totality of available empirical evidence (or even most of it) has never produced enough unconditional substantiation to make any of the paradigms convincing beyond a doubt. On the other hand, each of the three paradigms has sufficient empirical validity (however limited that may be) not to be declared unequivocally false. We are in the realm of theory, not law. Moreover, to the extent that these three paradigms are theories, there is an additional dual problem stated elegantly by Waltz: "Facts do not determine theories; more than one theory may fit any set of facts. Theories do not explain facts conclusively; we can never be sure that a good theory will not be replaced by a better one" (1979, 9).

For these reasons, the arguments among proponents of the paradigms most often generate more heat than light. Too frequently one encounters maneuvers such as the liberal use of the Procrustean bed to make the evidence "fit" better, the suppression of contrary and contradictory evidence, or various forms of evasion ranging from the creation of narrowly confining definitions to flights into the most abstract ethereal realms where making any kind of meaningful distinctions becomes impossible. The methods try to make reality conform to a set of truth-perceptions. Other analysts reverse the process and try to bring their paradigmatic perceptions into greater conformity with reality. The level of critical refinement within paradigms is significant because the changes that have transpired have resulted in some telling movement in the direction of cross-fertilization. The agents of change at this level have been in-house critics working within a paradigm who succeed at the delicate tasks of first pointing out some of the paradigm's shortcomings and then suggesting ways of remedying them without challenging, or seeming to challenge, paradigmatic fundamentals. Critics of this kind either may be reacting directly to criticisms coming from proponents of other paradigms or they may more or less independently generate refinements of their own paradigms. In either case, the effect is to move that paradigm incrementally closer to another, and at times even substantially closer.

Generally these critics initiated their publishing careers by professing adherence to the unique aspects of their chosen paradigm. But in the course of thinking and writing, the intellectual process of criticism prompted them to move in the direction of one or another of the other two paradigms. This process provides some interesting and well-known case studies in intellectual biography. Robert Dahl and Charles Lindblom were originally partisans of the theory of pluralist democracy but became so critical of its inadequacies that they developed the concept of polyarchy. Ultimately they incorporated substantial elements of class analysis into their work (Dahl 1982; Lindblom 1977). A roughly similar outcome can be identified in the writings of John Kenneth Galbraith and Theodore Lowi in the 1970s. Like Dahl and Lindblom, they incorporated varying amounts of class analysis. One question can be posed, but it is not easily answered: Did one or another of these writers effectively abandon one paradigm for another or create a midway position?

Critical refinement has also occurred within the elite paradigm. In its fundamental division of society into elite and masses this theory approximates the basic dichotomous division of classes characteristic of class analysis, granted all the substantial differences between the two approaches. Yet, once elite theory is refined to include multiple elites rather than just one it *begins* to approximate pluralism since it then stresses the relative autonomy of elites rather than their cohesion. It also stresses the diversity of the elites' social origins and that job performance is more important than inherited social status in establishing and maintaining membership in the elite (Knoke 1981).

On the other hand, in his power elite version of the theory, which stressed elite cohesion, C. Wright Mills (1956) moved elite theory closer to class analysis. Once class analysis has been refined to take account of some elements of elite theory it *begins* to approximate that theory.

For all practical purposes, the three paradigms seem incompatible at the level of the ideal. But at the level of critical refinement within paradigms many potential insights are missed if analysts continue to focus on the incompatibility issue. Since practicing critics of the respective paradigms have themselves seen the need to incorporate various refinements, and have found this feasible, it makes more heuristic sense to concentrate on the possibilities for modifying the paradigms that have already been actualized by their internal critics. I would in particular point to the possibilities opened up by the modifications of the elite paradigm that have been made at the critical refinement level. These seem to bridge apparently unbridgeable differences between the pluralist and class analysis paradigms, and this process deserves far more attention than it has received.

If in the past most attention has been focused on incompatibility, more consideration ought to be given to the question of modifiability. This is not to suggest that at some point in the future these paradigms will converge. Convergence in essentials is not possible because the paradigms owe their origin to a fundamental theoretical and analytical problem that is not likely ever to be resolved: How does one at the same time distinguish between the social and the political, society and government, and yet show how they are connected? Part of the answer lies in the formal constitutional, official institutions or power structures. But then another question arises: Is there anything basic to the political organization and operation of a polity outside of the constitutional or institutional structures? All three paradigms answer yes, with the pluralists specifying that groups are basic, class analysts maintaining that classes are, and elitists insisting that an elite is or that multiple elites are. Indeed, so basic is each of these elements to its respective paradigm that different answers to the question "Who rules?" emerge.

At bottom, it is misleading to ask the question in that form. If politics is defined as the process through which binding decisions are reached and implemented, then there are more revealing questions: Who, if anybody, rules always, most of the time, sometimes, rarely, never, on which issues, under which conditions? Who is politically active, concerned, and participates in which ways? Who is politically inactive, does not wish to participate or cannot participate and why? And with regard to participation it is critical to establish the level at which the participation occurs, its frequency, the method by which it is exercised, and also its perceived or subjective significance to the person or persons participating. The latter factor is particularly important in establishing the level and degree of relative satisfaction with the political system's operation in its input and feedback functions.

All these factors have combined to produce some limited convergence (I have called it modification). In practical terms this serves to make the paradigms less exclusive, to narrow the distance between them, and to create a greater number of commonalities and shared perspectives. Most important, this process helps to add correctives to what each paradigm does not consider in its normal purview, or consciously censors from awareness. Censorship of this kind is common to those highly committed to a given paradigm and is expressed both in the outright refusal to consider alternatives from outside as well as in the great difficulty of finally contemplating alternatives. In the Soviet context these normal processes very often have been carried to extremes.

Some basic questions arise here. Are the two social classes the best basic units of analysis, or do the multitudinous groups serve that function better? Is the distribution of political power as clear-cut as class analysis would seem to have it, or is it as convoluted as the pluralists would see it? Or is it some of both—and if so, how does one determine where each paradigm is particularly productive of valid insights? Harold Lasswell asked: Who gets what, when, how? Perhaps the most interesting question of all is how does the elite paradigm bridge the gaps between the other two?

American and Soviet Intellectual Contexts

These queries lead to the second fundamental question: How do they rule?

In broadest terms, the answers take the form of the typologies of political regimes or systems that have long filled textbooks on comparative politics. American proponents of the three paradigms provide their own answers.

Pluralists typically maintain that the many rule through creating a broad social consensus about basic community values (especially the open nature of political decision-making processes) and then arranging political compromises among competing interest groups (Solomon, ed. 1983; Skilling and Griffiths, eds. 1971). The policymaking process itself is the agent that legitimates the compromises while adopting binding decisions—laws, or administrative regulations in execution of laws (Anderson 1979; Jones 1977).

Elitists maintain that the few rule in America through democratic elitism. Elites committed to observing democratic procedural norms act to ensure that the rest of the population, ostensibly not thus committed, observes them as well (Bachrach 1967; Walker 1966; Dye and Zeigler 1970–1987; Burch 1980).

In class analysis the few are said to rule because they control the economy through their ownership of productive property (Garson 1977, Greenberg 1989). The ruling class legitimates its rule by either justifying the privileges of the ruling class or denying that they exist; by allowing others to participate in politics, but without meaningful power; by making a virtue out of gradualism so as to discourage people from raising demands for fundamental change; and by coopting protest (Parenti 1978).

Soviet analysts have taken an expectedly negative attitude toward the two perspectives, pluralism and elitism, which they find in conflict with their own. The negativism on pluralism has been almost total, but there has been ambivalence toward elitism. Both paradigms initially attracted Soviet interest only as objects of criticism. But lately some Soviets have looked at them more favorably because they grapple with a question that Soviet writings have treated often and ritualistically but not satisfactorily: In what ways do all classes and social groups, and not just the ruling class, connect with the government? What are the mechanics, the mechanisms? And in particular, what are the mechanisms involved in wresting concessions from the ruling class?

Soviet criticisms of American pluralism begin by fixing its location in "bourgeois" political theory. It is viewed as a variety of pluralist democratic theory reminiscent of turn-of-the-century French institutionalism, whose main trait was the fragmentation of state sovereignty (Tumanov, ed. 1967; Kalenskii 1969; Guliev 1970). Beyond this critique rooted in Soviet state and law theory, American pluralist theory is attacked for creating a "market model" of the political process that depoliticizes politics (Burlatskii and Galkin 1985, 111–14). Soviet criticism also takes into account the challenge to American pluralist theory posed by the American neo-elitists. The Soviets admire the challenge but disparage the neo-elitist attempt to preserve the essence of the pluralist position by developing the theory of democratic elitism. The more critical variant of the ruling elite theory in the writings of C. Wright Mills and, later, Alan Wolfe meets with greater approval (Kalenskii 1969; Ozhiganov 1979).

Burlatskii recalled that group theory "arose as a direct attempt to present an alternative to the Marxist theory of classes," and rightly noted that Arthur F. Bentley, the father of American interest group analysis, admitted as much (1970, 191). A related basic criticism was that, in pluralist analysis, group aims and interests were "artificially juxtaposed to general national and general class interests" (Bobotov 1969, 115).

Just as basically, Guliev contended that pluralist theory seeks "to represent the state power of the capitalist class in the form of the collective rule of a multitude of social organizations, both bourgeois and worker" (1970, 97). Or, as Kalenskii put it, group theory is an attempt to conceal the class character of the state; it ignores the relative autonomy of the state (i.e., the state's semi-independent institutional power), turning it into a weak adjunct of the most influential groups of the ruling class (1969). Similarly, pluralism was attacked for suggesting a division or separation of power between the state and various interest groups (Guliev 1961). And, in consonance with SMC theory, pluralists were criticized for diminishing the role of the state, while its role is actually expanding (Tumanov, ed. 1967).

Finally, Ashin criticized the pluralist model as an idealization and romanticization of bourgeois democracy from the days of free-competition capitalism that is hardly applicable to the conditions of SMC. He approvingly quoted G. William Domhoff's observation that, to the extent pluralism exists at all, it is the pluralism of the upper and upper middle classes (1975b).

The Soviets have identified various negative motivations behind pluralist theory. The theory is used as an ideological weapon to manipulate the mass consciousness (Il'in 1983). Pluralism's purpose is to attract the support of the middle strata of the workers and the worker aristocracy and thereby strengthen the bourgeoisie's class domination (Guliev 1970). Pluralist theory is also used to attempt to compensate for the breakdown of the separation of powers that accelerated after World War II by suggesting the existence of a balance of power between governmental and extra-governmental agencies and organizations (Guliev 1970; Kalenskii 1969).

Worst of all, the aim of pluralist theory is to convince the workers that their ultimate aim of controlling the political system has already been achieved by asserting that workers' organizations actually have been participating in the management of public affairs. All that remains is to achieve the "correct coordination of the efforts of all organized social groups and to expedite their co-operation" (Guliev 1961, 83). Soviet theory rejects both this sort of participation and also the placing of bourgeois and proletarian groups in the same category. Consequently, the pluralist assertion that all organizations are equal whether they are, to use Soviet terminology, either bourgeois or proletarian in their social nature is firmly rejected since "no pressure group can compare in might and limitless power with the alliances of capitalists" such as the National Association of Manufacturers (Guliev 1970, 108). Soviet writers, irrespective of how sophisticated they may or may not be in other matters, are quick to stress the nonparticipation of the workers in both the government and governing, and they highlight the struggle between the workers and the bourgeoisie in politics (Burlatskii 1970; Guliev 1970; Boichenko, 1970).

On only one occasion, it seems, did a Soviet writer suggest that pluralist theory originated as an attempt to account for new political realities. If in early nineteenth-century political theory the fundamental political relationship was conceived of as "the citizen– the state," it later came to be "the citizen—the organization–the state" once political parties became a permanent fixture, as the role or the church grew, as the mechanism of state control over society became more complex, and as worker organizations became more active (Guliev 1970, 88).

This is a rather short list of the factors that ultimately produced the kind of fragmentation in twentieth-century American politics that other Soviet writers have been commenting upon since the 1960s. The fragmentation could be viewed as the beginning stage of the mass society phenomenon. Yet even partisans of mass society theory recognize that there are countertendencies: Ashin cited the contention of some American theoreticians of mass society that, in connection with the decline of private associations produced by the bureaucratization of the functions they formerly performed, democratic structures have given way to elite structures (1975b).

In the United States itself pluralist theory had a very short heyday in the 1950s. Soon after its publication in 1956 C. Wright Mills's *The Power Elite* initiated a process of criticism and posing of alternative explanations. In the 1960s variants of elite theory (especially in the form of widespread criticism of the Establishment) contended with pluralist perspectives, and elements of the two were even joined in the theory of democratic elitism. Although pluralism seemed to be under siege, it retained, and continues to retain, a very strong attraction among American mainstream analysts even today.

We can expect some modifications in Soviet views on pluralism that will come from their concern with establishing "socialist pluralism," one of Gorbachev's favorite terms. A start has already been made. Readers of *Pravda* consulted standard Soviet reference sources to learn what pluralism is and were confronted with definitions beginning with the likes of "pluralism—a false, idealistic world outlook." Their letters to the editor sought enlightenment, and V. Kerimov was asked to specify what it involves positively. It means that "a diversity of opinions exists on the basis of a common socialist platform. . . . Pluralism therefore does not signify imposing a single point of view. It is the way toward a synthesis of everything valuable" (*Pravda*, January 13, 1989).

Soviet attitudes toward the elite paradigm are more complex. I will first consider some basic Soviet criticisms, then their criticisms of multiple or plural elite perspectives and of C. Wright Mills in particular, and finally their incorporation of aspects of elite theory into their own intellectual framework.

As the Soviets see it, the main problem with elite theories is that they ignore the socioeconomic basis of the division of society into classes. Elite theories posit that the fundamental conflict in society is not between classes but that it takes place among elites— the minority of the population (Ashin 1966, 1975b). Alternatively, in Western analyses the ruling elite is considered to be either outside of or above classes (Burlatskii and Galkin 1974). To the degree that elite theories treat classes, they attribute the formation of classes to power and not to property ownership (Beglov 1971). Thus another basic flaw is that elite theory puts politics before economics, a reversal of the scientifically correct order (Ashin 1966). Finally, "bourgeois sociologists" have been attacked for maintaining that an elite is a necessity for every normally functioning society (Ashin 1966).

As in the case of pluralist theory, the Soviets find negative motivations behind elite theories. They originated to explain away the growth of the state apparatus and executive power and to explain away the class antagonisms of capitalism as just another example of the division of society into the elite and the crowd (Ashin 1975a). Since pluralist explanations did not succeed in concealing the power of the elite, the task of elite theories was to whitewash that power (Ashin 1975b). "The aim of these theories is to declare present-day monopoly capitalism a natural and per-petual system and to substantiate the necessity and utility of the existence of an elite" (Ashin 1966, 16). In addition to that, the theory provides a justification for social inequality (Dmitriev 1971).

Most disturbing to Soviet analysts is the theory of democratic elitism. In their eyes, Pareto's and Mosca's essentially flawed elite theories at least had the virtue of having been consciously opposed to the conventional nineteenth-century theory of bourgeois de-mocracy; Mannheim and Schumpeter, however, were wrong in melding the two into a theory of elitist democracy (Ashin 1975b). In its more recent American manifestations this theory has con-tinued to posit that the elite is the defender of the democratic political system, whereas the masses are a potential threat to it. The Soviets are highly critical of this version of democracy, which requires an elite in order to make it work (Savel'ev 1971) and which is based on fear of the people (Ashin 1975a, 1975b; Ashin and Shafir 1971) and because it was (according the Soviet preface to a translated American book) the working class, the farmers, and the petty bourgeoisie who defended democratic values while the "elite top leadership was always the initiator of antidemocratic acts" (Dai and Zigler 1984, 23).

Ashin's point about fear of the people is linked to his earlier noted remark that pluralism was an idealization of the past. There is an issue here that has been basic to the discussion of politics since eighteenth-century radical democratic theory turned the in-dividual citizen into at least a potential god whose innate capacities could be developed through participation in political affairs. The theory was challenged by the early elite theorists, who felt that politics was a province of the elite and that the great mass of individuals was politically inert. It was also contested by the latter day democratic elitists who felt that the great mass of citizens was antidemocratic. In the context of this theoretical argument, it is interesting that some American critics of the theory of democratic elitism came close to making the same point as Ashin (Walker 1966). Here pluralist theory functions as a middle ground between radical democracy and elitism.

For the Soviets, the theory of elite pluralism or multiple elites is only somewhat less disturbing than democratic elitism. Elite pluralism makes democratic freedoms contingent upon disputes among the elites and upon the balance struck among those elites, yet it says nothing about the main function of all those elites—to make possible the bourgeoisie's continued exploitation (Ashin 1975b). The pluralist elitists are wrong in maintaining that the ruling class has disappeared and has been replaced by competing elites (Kalenskii 1969). Consequently, David Riesman's theory that elite veto groups balance each other out fails, as do all theories of countervailing power, because the monopolies dominate the system (Ashin 1975b, 1966). It is true that the bourgeoisie consists of various strata and elements, but "they are identical by virtue of their exploitative nature" (Ashin 1966, 78), and they have a common interest in maintaining the existing capitalist system (Kalenskii 1969).

From the tone and direction of these critiques the Soviets should have little or no use for elite theory. Yet in certain ways it has had an ineluctable attraction for them. The first intimation of this came in 1959 when they translated C. Wright Mills's *The Power Elite* into Russian a short three years after its original publication. As a matter of previous policy, the Soviets had translated works of which they approved, but from the avalanche of criticism directed at this book it was clear that they had serious reservations about it that emerged only after publication.

To begin with, Mills was not a Marxist, although he fell somewhere on the left, either among the "left liberal researchers" (Burlatskii and Galkin 1974, 131) or on the "left flank" of bourgeois sociology, which criticized capitalism, but inconsistently, from the vantage point of bourgeois liberalism (Ashin 1966, 24). He was a petty bourgeois democrat influenced by southern populism and by the social reformist ideology of the 1930s and 1940s (Zubok 1984). His methodology was criticized for replacing the clash of dichotomous economic interests with the rivalry of three functional elite components—the economic actors, the politicians, and the military—and for underrating the power of the banks and of monopoly capital in general (Beglov 1971; Dmitriev 1971). Kalenskii agreed with Robert Dahl's criticism that Mills failed to spell out the mechanism of the power relationships which he had identified (1969). Similar criticisms have been leveled at Mills's followers, notably G. William Domhoff and his school of power structure research (Dmitriev 1971; Zubok 1984).

However, Mills was viewed positively as a critic of elitism and elitist theories—he was an anti-elitist, and he had come "close to understanding the real structure of power in the USA" (Ashin 1975a, 1975b). This was Mills's real attraction, and it is suggestive of the reasons why some aspects of elite theory proved so seductive to Soviet analysts that they moved from simply attacking elitist theory toward incorporating elements of it into the Soviet analysis of politics in general and American politics especially. This process is one of the better examples of critical refinement between paradigms, illustrating how the Soviets sharpened their understanding of the structure of power once they perceived some shortcomings in their own theoretical perspectives.

Burlatskii hinted at the basic problem in noting that while the methodology basic to the Soviet class paradigm (historical materialism) led to an understanding of the laws governing the development of society, Western structural-functional and systems analyses broadened the possibilities for understanding the functioning of society (1970). What was behind this hint? In explaining the structure of power, historical materialism focused on the ruling class and the state together with their dominating role, but it was not at all clear how power at the very top of the power pyramid was organized and exercised. In addressing this question SMC analysts spoke only of the financial oligarchy, its political "henchmen," and of the *verkhushka*. This last term, which Soviet writers use even now to designate the top leadership is, interestingly enough, a Russian slang expression, and not yet an established analytical term (Evgen'eva, ed. 1981–1984, vol. 1).

The Soviet hesitancy in discussing power at the top is partly attributable to Marxism's radical democratic origins. The expectation was that, come the revolution, there would be no need to worry about power at the top—there would *be* no top. The revolution having come in Russia, and the Soviet political system along with its scholarly and academic subsystems having been created, there was a notable reluctance to conduct scholarly investigations of power even as a general political concept until well after Stalin had departed the scene. As Archie Brown pointed out, it is only since the late 1960s that some cautious spadework has been done on this question by Soviet researchers (1983).

Polish Marxist sociologists and political scientists were not sub-

jected to such handicaps for so long a time, and in 1966 Wlodzi-
mierz Wesolowski published an outstanding study (translated into
English only in 1979) treating classes, strata, and power. Chapter
2 is entitled "Dominant Class and Power Elite: The Dimensions
of Analysis and Their Interconnections" (1979). The difference
between the dominant class and the power elite is that the elite
actively participates "in the process of shaping and making decisions, i.e., fulfilling the functions of politician" (1979, 54). In a
daring departure, Wesolowski made it clear that he was using
"power elite" in place of the traditional Marxist term, the state
(1979).

My purpose is not to present a detailed treatment of Wesolowski's pathbreaking ideas but to sketch briefly the lengthy process through which Soviet analysts incorporated these and similar
ideas into their paradigm. Galkin (1969) took the first steps by
breaking down "the ruling elite of present-day capitalism" into a
number of elites, as Wesolowski and Mills had done. In particular,
Galkin distinguished the economic and political elites, the former
acting as "the decisive pressure group" with respect to the latter
(1969, 77). Although the economic powers that be ultimately dominate in this fashion, their primary interest lies in ensuring that the
political elite rule effectively on their behalf, so that in selecting
members for the political elite the question of whether they will
be successful at politics is important (1969).

Burlatskii almost simultaneously took the next step in coining
the term "politocracy" to describe "the higher political bureaucracy which, in bourgeois society, is connected with the technoc-
racy. This is the political elite directly connected with managing
the state and with working out and formulating policy" (1970, 107).

Chetverikov then took up and discussed politocracy at length,
breaking it into three groups and estimating the size of each (1974).
The top (*verkhushka*), which is a part of the financial oligarchy,
is composed of several dozen persons holding the highest governmental posts. Next come the 400 to 500 persons holding less important "political" posts (the quotation marks are Chetverikov's).
Finally, there are the leading staff members of the permanent
bureaucracy totaling about 8,000 persons. The minimum number
in the politocracy is therefore 8,600.

Burlatskii and Galkin (1974, 123–71) returned to Galkin's 1969 terminology and wrote a section "Present-Day Capitalism's Ruling Elite" in a chapter entitled "Sociopolitical Leadership," another topic only rarely treated before in Soviet political analyses. The ruling elite consists of the tops of the various strata in the exploiting class and also of the groups reflecting the interests of that class through managing the economic, social, and political life of society on behalf of that class (Burlatskii and Galkin 1974). Two groups make up the political elite—the decisionmakers and the group that effectively puts pressure on them. The economic elite, the elite's "backbone," consists of the owners of the monopolies and the directors and managers of private and government-owned companies (134). The authors then single out and discuss very briefly the bureaucratic, the military, and the ideological or media elites in a way suggestive of the multiple elites approach.

Although they came close to doing so, these writers did not go so far as to adopt that approach in the face of the longstanding Soviet objections to it. Kalenskii noted that, wrong though he thought it was, the approach was useful in that it reflected some of the basic changes in the structure of the ruling class in the twentieth century occasioned by the appearance and development of SMC, the sharpening of the class struggle, and the transformations associated with the scientific and technical revolution (1969). But such positive evaluations present an analytical problem for the Soviets. It makes empirical sense to disaggregate the ruling class, and the Soviets have been doing so in their own time-hallowed way.[1] Yet it is ideologically dissatisfying to go much beyond that lest the ruling class seem so disunited that it appears less formidable than its only too well-know nefarious deeds warrant. Dmitriev typified this orientation in perceiving the ruling elite to be synonymous with the standard Soviet ideological formula—it is the "top (*verkhushka*) of the financial oligarchy plus its henchmen in the most important posts of the state apparatus" (1971, 49–50). It would be subversive of the class paradigm to adopt the multiple-elites approach.

Soviet analyses of these phenomena's political consequences were disjointed because they were scattered throughout a vast literature and because they were expressed in a narrowly formulaic way that tended to suppress further creative development. The incorporation of some elite perspectives created the possibility of breaking through the old intellectual logjam and served to detail and clarify both the structure of power at the top and its operation. Indeed, Burlatskii and Galkin mentioned the need to clarify the processes through which the ruling class's domination is exercised and the concrete forms which that domination involves (1974). Years later they addressed the issue more comprehensively in discussing the variations on the ruling elite concept and the structure of ruling elites in various capitalist countries with a focus on the elite's effectiveness in governing (Burlatskii and Galkin 1985).

The best illustration of the impact made by the selective adoption of elite perspectives is Gennadii Ashin, who had practically made a career of criticizing elite theory. In his latest writings he finally recognized its usefulness and not only criticized his earlier attitude but even identified some positive features in the elitist approach. Elite studies reveal the mechanism of power in capitalist countries, showing how the elite integrates and subordinates clashing interests within the ruling class, while the theory of democratic elitism demonstrates that the Marxists are correct in maintaining that bourgeois democracy serves the interests of privileged minority (Ashin 1985).

It bears repeating that the Soviet study of policymaking remains weakly developed. Despite the incorporation of various elite approaches into Soviet analyses in the early 1970s by some top Soviet writers, there has been no notable increase in the number of published studies specifically on the American elite, or the political elite, or even the American ruling class. Rather, experience has shown that now and then fleeting reference has been made to either the American ruling or political elite (Nikiforov, ed. 1976; Zamoshkin, ed. 1978; Plekhanov 1979). Burlatskii and Galkin's recent study is the major exception (1985). This does not necessarily mean that no confidential studies have been done on this very important matter.

The difficulty in winning acceptance for these insights originating from outside the Soviet paradigm highlights several universal problems involved in critical development between paradigms. It also illustrates some problems in the class analysis paradigm that are reflected in ways peculiar to Soviet academic writing.

Knoke maintains that the class analysis paradigm is notable for utilizing "higher order abstractions" than the other paradigms as well as some "global" categories such as classes and the state (1981, 299). In Soviet writing this produced a tendency toward overgeneralization and lack of clarity regarding the structure of power in the United States. Some of their own within-paradigm critics complained about that and attempted to rectify it.

Soviet criticisms of their own paradigm have been made at two levels. At the level of SMC analysis the total monopoly domination approach was criticized by advocates of the partial monopoly version. One notable attempt by Vladimir Shubin utilized within-paradigm criticism to restructure SMC analysis by joining it with aspects of systems analysis.

Shubin's merger of SMC and systems theory makes several advances in methodology and terminology (1978). Avoiding the usual formulaic repetitions normal to SMC analyses, he works out a system for identifying the variety of regimes that can exist under SMC. He boldly and directly, yet somewhat briefly (for political reasons), balances the weaknesses of SMC as a system with its "reserves." The weaknesses are the same ones that have often been noted by Soviet analysts; the "reserves" are SMC's strengths, which typically were assumed but seldom noted by Soviet writers, and then only in unsystematic fashion. No less importantly, he develops some concepts for analyzing the phenomenon of crisis— a term that is quite simply overused and underspecified in Soviet writing. Of particular interest is Shubin's contrast of the system's "instability" and its "effectiveness," or its "capacity to keep political power exclusively in the hands of the ruling class" and "not share with anybody the adoption of the most important state decisions" and "to effect the management of society in the interests of the dominating class" (89–90).

Since Shubin uses his new methodological and terminological departures to produce some familiar conclusions, this may be either a case of old wine in new bottles, or, as I am suggesting, an example of the complexities connected with critical development within paradigms. In any event, the one very palpable shortcoming in Shubin's innovative attempt is its schematic nature, a common difficulty in systems analysis.

At another level, criticism of Marxist theory, schematism is not the problem, but the degree of analytical specificity is. Burlatskii observed that since historical materialism is a "global approach" that yields a "cosmogonic" picture of political life, it needs as a corrective "a system of concepts and categories derived from a concrete sociological analysis of each given system and each given situation" (1970, 37). Taking an Aesopian swipe at Soviet ideological conservatives, he charged that it was the Maoists who insisted on using only the rather abstract "global" approach in analyzing politics in capitalist countries. He drew attention to the resultant counterproductive misreading of concrete political situations that were of significance to Soviet policymakers and gave the example of underrating the differences between a John Kennedy/Lyndon Johnson "moderate-sober" approach in world politics and a Goldwater "military-aggressive" approach (111).

Burlatskii opted for creating a more concretely sociological "materialist theory of politics," "a middle-range theory uniting the most general categories of Marxist–Leninist sociology with concrete investigations of politics and the political process" (1970, 39). He maintained that "it stands to reason that many facts, phenomena, and conditions generally do not come into the field of vision if the researcher uses the most general sociological laws as his measuring instrument" (43). He concluded that "one must not limit oneself to the analysis of political institutions, for it is necessary to go further to the study of the political process, political interrelations, and political behavior—in a word, the whole picture of political life" (148).

In Soviet circumstances this was a tall order, requiring something so basic as the greater "differentiation or concretization" of analytical concepts and categories (Burlatskii and Galkin 1974, 74). It really had to do with the thorny question, raised by Burlatskii in 1965, of establishing political science in the Soviet Union. The specifics of the most forward-looking research agenda were finally published by Shakhnazarov and Burlatskii (1980) just as, unfortunately, the general intellectual environment in the Soviet Union took a turn toward a conservatism that lasted for five years or so.

Criticism

Since Marxism is often called a critical theory, any critique of Soviet perspectives on American politics is to some extent a criticism of criticism. As a starting point, one can criticize the primary purpose of Soviet studies of American politics, which is to subject the political system to criticism—this is what "adherence to the class principle" and "the party approach" (*partiinost'*) mean.

Many adjectives can be used to qualify the word "criticism": measured, misplaced, on-target, constructive, carping, and devastating are among them. Most Soviet criticism of American politics is at least strongly negative, much of it is dedicatedly negative, and some of it is unremittingly negative—for example, the assertion that the workers do not participate in the political system and cannot be "included" in it (to keep those evidently all-important quotation marks).

The inevitable question this version of criticism raises in the mind of the reader is: How could a political system that is so bad and has so many problems survive for so long? The Soviet answers are in the partial monopoly version of the SMC model and in the collateral discussion of bourgeois democracy's manipulative aspects. But more basically, the answers are rooted in the deficiencies of the Soviet Marxist–Leninist critical paradigm, especially in its terminology and methodology.

On the level of paradigm, using class as the basic unit of political analysis has its drawbacks and problems. With respect to the Soviet case, the many shortcomings in Soviet studies of class in America that I assessed in earlier chapters create a shaky basis for analyzing politics in the United States adequately, much less convincingly. A comparison of the Soviet efforts up to the present with Hamilton (1972) would effectively show how far the Soviets have yet to go, particularly in using survey research and in studying the increasingly important case of the South.

Hamilton advocates a revisionist version of Marxism, which is, like Eduard Bernstein's original revisionism, itself a criticism of the original Marxian criticism. He maintains that "this version has become the basic 'centrist' position in contemporary social science" (1972, 29). It is the version that "stresses the upgrading of the workers rather than the downgrading of the middle class. In this view, the sources of conflict or strain are gradually being eliminated" (29). The studies he did on this basis suggested two significant conclusions: "From the beginnings, the main lines of cleavage in the United States tended to be vertical rather than horizontal. The division was along ethnic and religious lines rather than being primarily along class lines" (191). And no less important is the conclusion regarding the five theories or paradigms in terms of which American politics can be studied: "In fact, the evidence to be presented [in his book] does not accord very precisely with any of the five theoretical 'programs' outlined" (62). From the Soviet vantage point Hamilton's perspectives are not Marxist or scientific in the sense that the Soviets use these terms.

To the extent that the Soviets have remained committed to what they stoutly maintain is a nonrevisionist Marxism, they create an unresolvable dilemma: in principle, capitalism cannot be reformed, yet the struggle to expand democracy and wrest concessions from the dominating class has produced successes (read: reforms), and the further development of SMC continues to introduce elements of socialism (read: ameliorative reforms) into American life.

DiTomaso raised a number of crucial questions that class analysis, whether revisionist or not, has yet to address convincingly (1980, 257). She suggests that "the meaning of fragmentation and conflict within the dominant class" needs to be clarified, especially in relation to the apparent success that its competitive members have had in retaining "control, coordination, and loyalty from the many." And, finally: "How can one explain the 'successful' opposition at times by subordinate classes to the control of a dominant class?"

Some terminological and definitional criticisms may be added to these paradigmatic ones. The class approach is like the systems approach in that its categories are so broad that they implicitly encompass any and all political phenomena, but they lack the kind of specificity about particulars that is spelled out more clearly and explicitly by other approaches. With regard to the state, to focus on the classic example, even at this late date it is not at all clear just who or what comprises that semi-abstract entity. On the other hand, its function is crystal clear—and, consequently, it might well be that anybody, or any body, performing the function of suppression is in fact part of the state. However, another function of the state that is to some degree at odds with its definition as the agent of suppression is to make reluctant partial concessions in order to keep itself in power. Among the largest gaps in Soviet analyses is the total absence of a systematic study of the extent and nature of the concessions made by the state. An equally serious gap is the failure to consider comprehensively the process through which the social movements achieve the adoption of those concessions by the state, whose "essence" is suppression. A start was finally made in Rogova's recent study of the labor unions' many links with the government, but it has not been followed up yet, and it is not likely to be for quite some time if past practice be any guide (1983, 46–63).

In the realm of what would be considered thinking about the unthinkable in the Soviet Union, one could fault the Soviets for failing to disaggregate the state or to explain disunity and strife within the state. A very weak start was made toward correcting these flaws to the degree that Soviet analysts have treated the relative autonomy of the state and the policymaking process. The concept of relative autonomy freed Soviet analysts from the formerly prescribed vision of total subordination of the state to the ruling class, a vision that was itself part of the larger process of ruling class domination. Translated into less obscure terminology, relative autonomy means that politicians holding office are not automatically and directly programmed by members of the ruling class who are not presently holding office or who may never have held office or may never do so in the future.

If officeholding politicians can be autonomous in this sense, why should they not also be autonomous of each other in some degree? Yet the Soviets have been unable to reach the point of discussing the relative autonomy of the Congress, or the Supreme Court, or the several states, or even of cities and towns. In only one instance have Soviet authors barely hinted at the possibility of the relative autonomy of the bureaucracy (Burlatskii and Galkin 1974). Chetverikov's (1974) discovery of the triple alliance (iron triangles) ought to have been a natural point of departure for studying a complex instance where several relative autonomies are in action— or interaction. But this avenue has not been pursued.

To express it figuratively, the Soviet preference is to view the state as one gigantic consensus on the part of that proverbial handful of people who favor, achieve, and maintain economic exploitation and political domination. As an exercise in analysis, it would make sense to give systematic consideration to dissension within the state, however one conceives that entity. The Soviets have been reluctant to do this, even though they do not hesitate to discuss at length (though not in a very organized way) the sometimes ferocious disagreements within the dominating class. The state evidently reflects what the Soviets perceive to be the singular will of that class rather than the class's competitive strife. But why neglect half the picture?

Disaggregating the state would not necessarily result in abandoning these perspectives, but it would result in modifying them more or less.

It would be rewarding for the Soviets to produce a full-scale treatment of the concept of power and how it is exercised that goes beyond the usual formulaic, stereotyped discussions. The changes in Soviet attitude toward the separation of powers issue are just a beginning. Moreover, a tantalizing remark made in passing may someday serve to expand theoretical perspectives: "The concentration of economic power is not accompanied by a directly proportional concentration of political power—there is a more complex dependence existing between them" (Nikiforov, ed. 1976, 194). Another example would be Burlatskii and Galkin's observation that there is a simultaneous concentration and diffusion of power in capitalist countries since larger numbers of people are becoming involved in the exercise of power (1974). These considerations point to the conclusion that the exercise of power does not always correspond to its formal or perceived structure and organization. Studies of the exceptional cases would be of substantial importance to the development of political theory in the Soviet Union and the more adequate understanding of American politics.

Something similar could be said of Soviet treatments of crisis. The American political, social, and economic systems have been depicted as in a state of crisis for decades now, yet the collapse of these systems recedes further and further into the future. The Soviets regularly use the word crisis to describe economic depressions and recessions without differentiating them. In all the writing about the crisis of the presidency, only once did an analyst note that the crisis was more a functional than an institutional one—his way of saying that it was not as severe as most other writers had portrayed it (Kokoshin and others 1983).

Addressing the commission preparing a new version of the Soviet

Communist party's official program the party's leader, Konstantin Chernenko, spoke about the proper way to treat the rivalry between capitalism and socialism: "We do not in the least doubt that socialism will win this competition in the final analysis. At the same time, while stressing the eventual historical doom of present-day capitalism, it is necessary to take into consideration that, even under the conditions of its general crisis, it still possesses not inconsiderable and far from exhausted reserves for development" (*Pravda*, April 26, 1984). The theme was reiterated by Anatolii Dobrynin while serving as a top adviser to Gorbachv when he mentioned some "new aspects in the development of capitalism, which has shown a considerably larger reserve of durability than was previously imagined" (*Pravda*, April 12, 1988). Perhaps somebody in the Soviet Union has done a study of capitalism's reserves, its strengths. But because of the Soviet mindset's strength, publishing such an "uncritical" study in that country remains impossible, and the closest any author has come to initiating an analysis of this kind is Shubin (1978).

Enough has already been said about methodological problems to warrant simply mentioning them as another point justifying criticism. But a particularly important example deserves brief consideration. Here is a quote from the advance publication notice of a book by A. A. Poduzov on the development of the American economy whose translated title is *Factors and Rates of Economic Growth in the USA (An Analysis of Long-Term Tendencies)*: "The monograph is the first investigation in Soviet literature of the long-term tendencies of economic growth in the USA" (*Novye knigi SSSR 1984*, no. 16, p. 20). It is astonishing that a tradition of scholarly analysis based upon predictions of long-term economic decline should have done without a book of this sort for so many decades. The long-held expectation of impending collapse of the very object of research discouraged producing a volume that all too evidently would soon be put in the category of ancient history.[2]

Soviet studies of American politics also merit criticism for the serious omissions produced by adherence to class analysis. The following list is by no means inclusive. Analyses of concessions, especially as parts of broader studies of the policymaking process, are in effect missing. Theoretical studies of sociopolitical movements are lacking, as are analytical studies of the reasons for disunity within them and interpretive studies of the concrete results they have achieved in the form of concessions. The study of political participation was practically ignored until publication of a general survey of the topic (Kovler and Smirnov 1986), as was analysis of apolitical behavior, though the rapidly developing study of political consciousness may lead Soviet researchers in that direction as well. The Soviets need to give much more attention to the significance of the variegated activities and programs sponsored by civic, church, and youth organizations to the extent that these provide vehicles for inculcating, experiencing, and putting political values into effect, particularly at the local level. The study of political leadership has barely begun, even though Burlatskii and Galkin recently addressed the matter in a substantial way (1985). Past practice suggests that their initiative will not be followed up soon. The study of upward social mobility has been avoided. And, finally, on the basis of the totality of Soviet writing on American politics one would never even think of wondering about how much and what kinds of patriotism exist in the United States or considering their various political effects.

Most, if not all, of the items just listed are closely connected with the sources of the political system's legitimacy. It bears repeating that only Burlatskii has so far considered this issue at all directly in his comments on the system's base of mass support (1970). Indirectly, the rapidly developing Soviet studies of political consciousness and public opinion also address the question. It would clearly be useful for Soviet policymakers to learn more about this particular "reserve" of the capitalist system. Naturally, legitimacy is subject to erosion for many political, social, economic, and ideological reasons. But it can also be strengthened, and, as the good dialecticians that they claim to be, the Soviets ought to take this more seriously.

Conclusion

What have the Soviets accomplished? What overall estimate can be made of their efforts? Answers can be found by weighing the continuities and changes in Soviet studies of American politics. Soviet analysts continue to adhere to the fundamentals of class analysis, but they have moved away from the narrower, more constricting perspectives of SMC analysis and toward incorporating terminology and insights from other paradigms that they feel actually support various aspects of class analysis. To the degree that these incorporations have been made successfully, the Soviets have now gone even further than did the earlier analysts of the Varga type in the days before SMC became orthodoxy.

The question could be answered by asking another: How full is the glass? Harsher Western critics of Soviet interpretations of American politics would maintain that the glass is entirely empty and that the Soviet interpretations create an unrecognizably distorted caricature of American politics unworthy of serious attention. The Soviets would argue that the glass has always been full as far as the analytical essentials are concerned but that some modifications have been made and some gaps plugged in the nonessentials. A more balanced judgment would be that the glass is half full precisely because these modifications have been made, and that it is half empty since the Soviets have a great distance to go before the totality of whatever future modifications may be made creates an unquestionably marked change in Soviet interpretations.

The latter judgment could be made more confidently if the modifications that are articulated in the scholarly literature were to find greater reflection both in statements by the political leadership as well as in the mass media. The manner in which American politics and society are treated in those three contexts becomes a touchstone for evaluating the limits on improved U.S.–USSR relations at any given point. It becomes a yardstick for measuring the limits of peaceful coexistence and detente, and it remains an illustration of what the Soviets mean when they say that there is no such thing as peaceful coexistence in the ideological struggle, the battle of ideas.

Soviet excesses and blind spots in their treatment of American politics and society would naturally tend to encourage American readers to overlook the strengths in these analyses, many of which intersect with points raised by various individual American critics of the political and social systems as well as entire critical schools. To cite just one example, the Soviets are not alone in realizing that widespread dissatisfaction in America with the failure of the system to respond to various needs, frustrations, and dislocations has created social movements (Walker 1966). But along with such intersections there are partings of the ways, as when the Soviets prefer not to indicate systematically how, in which areas, and to what extent these movements have produced changes in the way the political system operates and in the quality of the decisions it produces. In essence, the Soviet position is that the changes are always too little, and they will be enough only when the system is revolutionized away by either peaceful or violent means.

The issue here is the capacity of the system to respond satisfactorily to old and new demands made upon it. The Soviets have contended, with rare exceptions, that the class that exploits, dominates, and rules would ultimately not be able to satisfy the traditional demands that the other class has continually made upon the system for over a century now. Nevertheless, time and experience have shown thus far that the concessions and compromises made by the first class or—to put it the other way around—the victories won by the second class have served to keep a large enough number of people in both classes semisatisfied enough to ensure that the thus modified system survive and in some ways even thrive despite its many problems.

The key to the situation seems to lie in the word "enough," if it is taken to indicate both the degree and the extent to which large sectors of both classes, or weighty and influential parts of them, experience a sense of sufficiency with what they get out of the political and social systems. The use of sufficiency rather than satisfaction is quite deliberate, since these terms distinguish two very different attitudes: "I get enough out of the system," as opposed to "I get everything I want out of the system." Naturally, there are those in both classes who are even totally satisfied—or say they are. But the most important thing is that few in either class seem to expect to get the whole loaf. This explains the relatively limited attraction of those versions of Marxism, including the Soviet one, that do promise the workers the whole loaf, and the relatively limited attraction of extremist theories of laissez-faire that promise the capitalists the same thing. Moreover, in the United States there has been abroad in the land for quite some time an abiding skepticism about any kind of total or final solution for life's basic problems. After all, "campaign promises," that consummate expression of skepticism in modern politics, wears a "Made in the U.S.A." label.

Criticism is a universal component of political attitudes, but there is a peculiarly American version of it that provides stiff competition for the Soviet versions of criticism together with their proffered solutions. Skeptical criticism is not unique to America. But there is a decidedly American variety of it that is distinguishable from others, and the subtleties make quite a difference in the conduct of politics. Some analysts would call this a manifestation of the national character. For the Soviets, it is the problem of American exceptionality which, it must be stressed, manifests itself in many, many more ways than the Soviets have ever even thought of entertaining.

Another line of criticism begins with the observation that all paradigms have their strengths and weaknesses, and in the final analysis it may be necessary to choose from among them the one that seems either to describe or to explain American politics best. Hamilton maintains that a revised version of Marxism, which is sometimes at great variance with the Soviet one, serves these purposes (1972). Knoke, however, concludes that the multiple-elites approach is the most adequate one (1981). Alternatively, Domhoff opts for integrating elements of pluralist, elitist, and Marxist paradigms as at least components of the best way (1983).

The Soviets appeared to have made their choice long ago. But their recently accelerated tendency to incorporate perspectives from outside their paradigm amounts to highly incremental criticism of the paradigm's insufficiencies. In fact, they have made two choices that are often in conflict. One is to retain the essentials of the paradigm. The other is to go through a tortuous process of introducing changes that do not affect the essentials of the paradigmatic vision. The long and complex nature of this very process leads one to suspect that there is a gnawing feeling of unease among many Soviets that perhaps some essential matters are in fact being affected. Or perhaps many find it difficult to separate the essential from the accretions in the ideology. Ostensibly, they are doing this with respect to the way they use the ideology to interpret their own politics, and that partially involves adopting and modifying terms like pluralism.

It has been hardest for the Soviets to understand and incorporate pluralist perspectives in their explanations of American politics, yet some progress has been made. A recent major study of the American Constitution displays an unusual grasp of, and sensitivity toward, the theoretical basis and institutional setting of American pluralism (Mishin and Vlasikhin 1985). Likewise, a book that devotes much attention to the usual forms of checks and balances also discusses some unusual "centers of power" that in practice also play a role in the overall process of checking and balancing—the federal bureaucracy, the two-party system, pressure groups, and the media (Mishin 1984).

The Soviets will also find it necessary to come to further grips with pluralism obliquely while incorporating elements of elite theory for the purpose of improving their analysis of decisionmaking. They will find a broader range of actors in that process than they ever allowed themselves to imagine.

The burgeoning Soviet studies of American political consciousness and public opinion could lead to further consideration of pluralist perspectives, especially if the Soviets begin to study how differing political perspectives impact differentially upon the policymaking process. To further enrich their understanding, they could correlate all that with the increasingly significant political activities of the intermediate strata about which they have been commenting with increasing frequency.

Now that Mikhail Gorbachev has begun speaking about the desirability of encouraging "socialist pluralism" in the Soviet Union (Brown 1988, 3–4) it becomes ideologically easier for Soviet analysts to view pluralism in a more favorable light, even though its "bourgeois" versions must continue to be criticized. The status of this incorporation of pluralism is, at this point, somewhat tenuous. But the use and utility of the term seem to be connected with the need to recognize and link the various interests in society to the purposes of primarily economic and secondarily political reform.

These are a few of the many pressures pushing toward breaking new ground in the Soviet study of American politics and society. But the mindset, the class analysis paradigm, and the mainstream remain formidable obstacles to breakthroughs (and follow-ups to breakthroughs), not to mention major changes in Soviet perceptions. On the fundamental issue of how to define democracy, for example, Gorbachev exemplifies the mindset in stressing that the Western countries will become democratic in his view only when the media switch from criticizing the politicians to criticizing the corporations and their owners and managers. A further requirement (reflecting Gorbachev's ideas on further democratization in the Soviet Union itself) is that production and office workers start electing their owners and managers (Gorbachev 1987). Liberal democracy is still found wanting.

The Soviets are not likely to remain where they have been in evaluating American politics and society. This book shows how difficult it will be for them to move forward. But it also identifies the many routes through which they have made progress in the past and it indicates possible or likely paths for future development. We know what to look for and where to look for it. We should now be in a much better position to understand and evaluate.

8 CONCLUSIONS

Three conclusions emerge from the foregoing analysis. First, with respect to the study of American politics and society the Soviet mindset has doggedly persisted in its essentials. Second, the changes that have occurred have been incremental. Third, the mindset has recently become potentially susceptible to substantial modification—but within the limits permitted by Gorbachev's vision of socialism, or within whatever other parameters the rough-and-tumble of Soviet politics may create in the future. Just how far and in what directions will these changes go at the level of practice, theory, and foreign policy, especially Soviet–American relations?

The mindset is composed of at least seven elements: individuals, groups, institutions, processes, values, traditions or practices, and the vast body of patterned information that incorporates or reflects all these and is the data base for this book. In each of these areas, and in varying combinations of them, change takes place at different times, in different ways, at different speeds, and to different degrees.

Various elements of this complex mindset have been under cautious, though accelerating, attack by Soviet scholars for almost thirty years. Lately the scholars have been joined by Soviet candidates for elective office, fledgling officeholders, reporters, and even average citizens, all of whom are participating in the new political processes associated with the extensive political reform initiated in 1988. They were all, in one of Gorbachev's favorite expressions, "learning democracy." An expanding market for information about American politics was created that could only serve to increase the quantity and improve the quality of the knowledge that more and more Soviets functionally need.

Under their own conditions, the Soviets were practicing a refinement and development of socialist democracy that is reminiscent of what they called the expansion of bourgeois democracy under American conditions. It meant expanding freedom of speech (socialist pluralism), limiting official arbitrariness (socialist checks and balances), and adopting American election techniques.

Strangely enough, the Soviets are borrowing from a system that they criticize vigorously and perhaps even find abhorrent. This seems to be the case with Aleksandr Yakovlev. Of course, the continued attacks on the American system may be a smokescreen for incorporating useful elements from the object of criticism. This may be Gorbachev's tactic.

The Soviets are less critical of West European, and even Asian, democratic systems, but they are borrowing more from the American than from the others. The European and Asian variants are multiparty systems and the Soviet leadership is squeamish about anything more than one party. The Soviets could more easily borrow from the United States the idea of a second party (and only one more). Their concept of the American bi-unitary party of big capital could be translated into a bi-unitary party of socialism.

A bi-unitary party of socialism (especially in its exalted version) would allow the Soviets to retain their strong sense of unity. But rather than the monolithic uniformity of the past, it would provide for diversity within a larger consensus—another Western word that has been creeping into the Soviet political vocabulary. Yet despite the utility of a bi-unitary party and a Soviet preference for it, the severe ethnic cleavages within the country render consensus unlikely, as would any growing or sharp social differentiation that results from economic reforms incorporating market mechanisms. These factors would encourage a European-type multiparty system.

In the Soviet Union political practice has outrun theory. The practical borrowings from American politics have outstripped the theoretical arguments that could be made in their favor. The Americanists' political activities as candidates and advisers to candidates have far outstripped their published analyses. Perhaps one day

Americanists will be able to say in print what they say when visiting the United States or in private consultations with members of the burgeoning new Soviet elite—the candidates for and holders of elective office. As a member of the reorganized Supreme Soviet, the Americanist Sergei B. Stankevich has been a moving force among the more radically oriented legislators, especially as an advocate of creating alternative political parties (*Washington Post,* May 24, 1989; *New York Times,* September 24, 1989).

Even if there were to be more openness in treating American politics than there has been so far in the Gorbachev era, the Soviets would undoubtedly still be expected to be, and could well want to be, critical of American politics and society. However, their criticism would be less distinctively Soviet and more like that of Western Marxists, partisans of elite theory, and practitioners of investigative reporting. A number of paradigms and versions of paradigms would interpenetrate.

Finally, what effect has the Soviet study of American politics and society had upon Soviet–American relations? Since the basic direction of Soviet policy toward the United States is established by the leadership in the Politburo, the hardest evidence we have for answering that question is in Huber (1988). His conclusion that the Soviet leaders' knowledge of American domestic politics is weak suggests that the impact of Soviet studies of American politics has not been significant. But as I argued in the Introduction and Chapter 5, substantial expertise was added with the promotion of Yakovlev to the Politburo and Dobrynin (temporarily) to the party's Secretariat and the proximity of Shakhnazarov and Burlatskii to Gorbachev.

The leaders can now expand their knowledge about American politics and society, but this does not dispose them too much more favorably toward the United States. The recent book edited by Alexander Yakovlev to which he and Shakhnazarov contributed demonstrates that convincingly (1988). Rather, a new group, including Gorbachev, Shevardnadze, and Yakovlev assumed primary responsibility for directing Soviet foreign policy in general and relations with the United States in particular.

In conjunction with adopting new thinking about world politics generally, the Soviets could now stress what many of them had . known since the 1970s—that the United States was beset with very serious domestic problems and was not much of a threat to the Soviet Union (Zorin, ed. 1971). Under the pre-Gorbachev old thinking on foreign policy this knowledge had been submerged by the predominant feature in the Soviet image of the United States as imperialist country number one, *the* major threat.

Put another way, if the Soviets could still envisage American intentions as imperialistic, they also could perceive more clearly than before a marked deterioration in American capabilities starting in the 1970s because of domestic weaknesses—and also, of course, because of foreign policy problems of a political and economic nature.

A final, paradoxical, conclusion can be drawn. The Soviet leaders have recently transplanted into their own body politic some ideas, operating principles, and processes from American political experience that they had long condemned. That is, the leadership ultimately came to agree with the positive evaluation of those phenomena that some Americanists had been cautiously advocating. But Soviet studies of American domestic politics have had some negative effects on Soviet policy toward the United States.

To the extent that such studies were driven by ideology, by the striving to unmask, and by a primitive mindset, the effect was to substantiate an aggressively "anti-imperialist" Soviet policy directed primarily against the United States. American foreign policy was seen as either exclusively or largely the creature of the ruling class, the same small class that, according to Soviet analyses published at various times, wielded a dictatorship over all other Americans, shamelessly manipulated and hoodwinked them, influenced their political consciousness in more subtle ways, and directly or indirectly bought politicians off.

The positive advances the Soviets have made in studying American politics and society made it easier for them to enter into a broad range of cooperative, collaborative relationships. But the improved knowledge has also made it possible for the Soviets to engage more subtly than ever before in manipulating the American media, influencing mass political consciousness, and swaying politicians more effectively—exactly the things they condemn the monopolies for doing. Alternatively, this mix may be viewed as characteristic of the expected give and take in any working relationship, even one between two countries.

We are at a fascinating turning point in the development of Soviet studies of the United States. My hope is that this book will help us understand more clearly where the Soviets can go from here.

We will be able to determine where they are going by monitoring whether the limits on publishing documented here are expanded or eliminated and whether the topics that need the most attention actually get it. We will have a clearer view of the process by which the Soviets incorporate elements of the American political experience into their own system. Only in the Gorbachev era could we better discern the role of the former diplomats and the top academic specialists in this dynamic.

The learning process could be facilitated and buttressed by making higher quality published information on American politics more widely available in the Soviet Union. Under very difficult conditions, the Americanists have made notable progress in analyzing American politics and, somewhat less, American society. This book shows how much more remains to be done. Though much still remains clouded with uncertainty, there is currently greater hope than before that considerable progress can be made in a short time.

Will it happen?

NOTES

Introduction

1. *New York Times*, September 9, 1987, C24. Mr. Golenpolsky made this statement to a Western reporter to explain why the Soviets did not allow some Western books that they disliked to be displayed at the book fair.

2. See also the books and articles cited in Mills 1972, and for the pre-Soviet period the bibliography in Hasty and Fusso, eds. 1988, and Allen 1988.

3. A good overview of the problems involving perceptions is in White 1984. Using arms control as a focus, Frei 1986 contains an unusually comprehensive treatment of the roles played by differing perceptions. His bibliography of Soviet and Western writings is outstanding. On a more general level, the *New York Times Magazine* devoted its November 10, 1985, issue to the topic "How We See Each Other," had an article on culture shock by the Soviet émigré writer Vassily Aksyonov (1987), then carried a study of Aleksandr Yakovlev by Bill Keller (1989).

4. Given their training and life experiences, a particular form of "schematic" political cognition has been characteristic of Soviet leaders. "Schema-based understanding . . . is holistic, category-based, or theory-driven. When a person responds schematically, the person draws on organized prior knowledge to aid the understanding of new information. A new person, event, or issue is treated as an instance of an already familiar category or schema." Fiske 1986, 41–42. It remains to be seen how much of this changes under the impact of *glasnost*, new thinking, and the new experiences produced by democratization.

5. Both books deal with American foreign policy. When the authors discuss the domestic motive forces behind that policy they use the language and analytical techniques that I consider in Chapters 1 through 4.

6. *New York Times*, December 7, 1987, A1.

7. The fundamentals are explained in 662 pages by V. F. Konstantinov and others 1974. Moscow's rationale for following the party's current interpretation of the fundamentals is presented in the article entitled "Partiinost'" in the *Great Soviet Encyclopedia* 1973–1983 (a translation of the 3rd Russian-language edition), vol. 19.

8. Jewish émigrés experienced similar problems communicating with their relatives in the Soviet Union. See Rothchild 1985. The experience of David Shipler 1984, the *New York Times* correspondent in Moscow in the late 1970s and early 1980s, confirms these and Costa's observations.

9. In his second chapter, "The Monopolies and the State," Malcom is chiefly concerned with American social structure in terms of elite activity at the very apex of economic, social, and political power. In this he follows Griffiths 1972.

10. Arbatov is near the top, Yakovlev is at the top, and Dobrynin was at the top at a critical period from March 1986 to September 1988. See Mills 1981 and also Chapter 5 below for an explication of the difference between near the top and at the top.

11. Approximately 300,000 copies of the text's first six editions were sold in the United States. The Soviet translation of the fifth edition (Dai and Zigler 1984) was published as *Demokratiia dlia elity: vvedenie v amerikanskuiu politiku*, which, translated into English, is *Democracy for the Elite: An Introduction to American Politics.*

12. The announcement of this book's publication specifically states that the book is intended for research libraries. See *Knizhnaia letopis'*, no. 7, 1985.

Chapter 1

1. The first book on the general crisis was published in 1933 (Varga and Mendel'son, eds.) and was followed by several other major studies: Dragilev 1957; Dokunin and Trepelkov 1963; Varga 1974; Vygodskii and others, eds. 1961; Inozemtsev and others, eds. 1976; Trepelkov 1983; Iaz'kov, ed. 1988. Day 1981 traces the origins and development of this and related concepts through 1939.

2. The fullest studies of the personal union, accompanied by concrete examples from American politics, are in Kuz'minov 1955; Dalin 1961; Rubinshtein and others, eds. 1958. Examples of the personal union in various administrations are in Novikova 1961 (Eisenhower); Zorin 1978 (Carter); Abramov and Kokoshin 1982 (Reagan).

3. A good example is the article "State–Monopoly Capitalism" in the first edition of the standard encyclopedia: *Bol'shaia sovetskaia entsiklopediia* 1926–1947, vol. 18. Day 1981 reviewed Soviet studies published in the 1920s and 1930s.

4. Franklin, ed. 1972, 478. Some interesting materials on how the new formula came to be included in Stalin's work are in Griffiths 1972. A detailed treatment of the internal Soviet politics behind the development of this version of the model is in Nordahl 1972.

5. Anatolii Gromyko 1968, 8 maintained that in the United States "monopoly capitalism undividedly dominates in all spheres of state and social life." The last and strongest defense of this position is Kovaleva 1969.

6. Kulikov 1969. Boichenko 1970 produced an analysis memorable for reaching three different conclusions—first that the entrepreneurial organizations control the state, then that the state's coercive power controls those organizations, and, finally, that in any event the monopolies control both the state and those organizations. The latest analysis (Sakharov 1980) takes the unusually balanced view that these

organizations play a very important role in politics and the economy but says nothing about their being *the* dominating factor.

7. For an elaboration of Soviet views see Malcom 1984.

8. Krylov 1968, 4. Later in the book he qualifies this perception to show that there is conflict within the ruling circles, thereby having the best of both worlds. In Chapter 5 I shall explain this phenomenon, which is characteristic of Soviet writing.

9. Kovaleva 1969. Since the brunt of her attack was on Varga 1968 and Dalin 1961, and because she at this astonishingly late date declared Stalin to have been a better Marxist than they, it seems safe to assume that she was speaking on behalf of the by now less visible and voluble community of unreconstructed Stalinist analysts.

10. Chetverikov 1974. These points had been noted individually by various Soviet analysts twenty years earlier, but I cite Chetverikov because he finally drew the elements together. The earlier analysts are treated later.

11. See *The New York Times*: November 7, 1985, A7; November 14, 1985, A1; and December 2, 1987 A1. Armand Hammer was told the same directly by Gorbachev (see *Time*, January 4, 1988, 30).

Chapter 2

1. Sevost'ianov and others, eds. 1960, vol. 1 discusses some of the exceptions.

2. Levin, ed. 1964a; Cherniak 1957. Boichenko 1959 treats these processes in detail. Originally, Soviet writers viewed Congress as keeping the executive somewhat in check, and in the early 1950s a few analysts saw Congress as assimilating the powers of the states. But Mishin 1954 considered that Congress had been relegated to a secondary position by the ever-expanding executive power. This view became, and remained, the standard Soviet interpretation until the late 1970s.

3. This was a serious misperception of at least the committee's position. It was formally responsible to the House of Representatives, and I would argue that it was responsive to the House as well—and vice-versa. During most of the committee's existence it most likely reflected the views and attitudes of most House members. Until the final years of the committee's existence House members disapproving of the committee were in a very weak political position to do much about it. But once the composition of the House and the country's political climate both changed, the fact that the committee was formally responsible to the House was the reason for its demise.

4. By 1967 it was possible for Soviet authors to note without irony and sarcasm that real though limited planning on a national scale had been introduced by the New Deal, quite the reverse of Soviet attitudes during the 1930s. An example of the latter is the volume edited by Lev Eventov in 1936 entitled *"Planning" Maneuvers in Capitalist Countries*. In Eventov's day the full SMC analytical framework containing an explanation for the existence of planning in capitalist countries had not yet been developed, and Soviet authors very much resented the bourgeoisie's stealing their planning thunder.

5. I have been considering the Soviet treatment of the New Deal only from the

perspective of this chapter's concerns. Sivachev 1966 treats the overall politics of the New Deal in detail.

6. Fursenko and others 1974; Androsov 1971. Full treatments of the Great Society are in Iakovlev, ed. 1969; Gusev 1974; Liven' 1975. Zorin, ed. 1971 contains much material on social policies in the 1960s.

7. Androsov 1971; Levin and Tumanov, eds. 1974. In the Soviet view, there is a danger stemming from the workers' achieving considerable purchasing power in that it causes them to make a fetish of material goods and creates of cult of property ownership (Zorin, ed. 1971). Both are inimical to creating the one and only appropriate class consciousness that is critical of the capitalist system.

8. Gusev 1974 often makes the point. In addition to being costly, private implementation sometimes serves to hamper policy effectiveness, as in the case of the housing construction policies analyzed by Mikhailov 1973.

9. Both authors make the link indirectly only, especially through including consumer credit and the large federal debt in the list of factors contributing to inflation. The point has also been made that the social programs are paid for by the taxpayers and not by business (Gusev 1974). Stated in this bald form the false implication is that business pays no taxes.

10. The most comprehensive study of the media in capitalist countries seeks to document monopoly control (Beglov 1972). Of course, the variously denominated worker, democratic, and progressive press is another matter, although Soviet analyses are ambiguous about the impact these publications have had in the United States.

11. Some recent major studies of the crisis have focused on the numerous institutional and policy problems connected with the Congress and the presidency in the Nixon, Carter, and early Reagan administrations (Savel'ev 1986; Kokoshin 1982). The role of money in politics as a means of control by the monopolies has been treated comprehensively for the first time (Danilenko 1985), and special attention has been given to the growing tax burden on the ordinary taxpayer (Vetrova 1983) as well as to the resultant taxpayer revolt and its negative social and political consequences created by cutbacks in social programs (Kokoshin 1982). Some studies have also identified structural-functional problems such as the growing independence of the armed forces and the intelligence agencies from the legislature to which they are nominally subordinate. The conflicts that result undermine the effectiveness of the political system as a whole (Burlatskii and Galkin 1985). The relation of SMC's failed policies to the crisis of bourgeois democracy in the 1980s is treated extensively in Iaz'kov, ed. 1988 and in Yakovlev, ed. 1988.

Chapter 3

1. The best attempts to systematize Marx's perspectives on class are Ossowski 1963 and Wesolowski 1979. A sympathetic consideration of Marx's views on class is in Draper 1978; a critical one is in Cohen 1982. The best pithy treatment of the concept of class is in Kernig, ed. 1972, vol. 2. More comprehensive treatments of the general concept are in Calvert 1982 and Szymanski 1983.

2. Mel'nikov 1974 is the best example of the more popular approach. He quotes

Lenin's three-class enumeration and states his agreement with it but then seems to oscillate between attempting to keep the petty bourgeoisie a class and effectively placing it within the intermediate strata. Semenov 1969 outright refuses to call the petty bourgeoisie a class and consigns it to the category of a middle or intermediate stratum. Arzumanian and others, eds. 1963 is unique in identifying four classes, apparently in an attempt to overcome the disparity between Marx–Engels's two-class interpretation and Lenin's.

3. Mel'nikov 1974 made this point, which remains valid even today. It is astonishing yet symptomatic that Soviet encyclopedias, social science dictionaries, and glossaries are of little if any help in clarifying the meaning of the analytical categories being considered in the discussion at this point. The best clarified concept is class.

4. Semenov 1969 treats these matters in typical fashion. See also Arzumanian and others, eds. 1963; Mostovets and others, eds. 1972; Iakovlev, ed. 1969.

5. The earliest mention of social mobility as a significant factor was by Kalenskii 1969, who attributed upward mobility to the broad development of secondary and university education and to the increased need for highly skilled and highly paid specialists. There is still no major Soviet study of upward social mobility in the United States, and the two most detailed treatments of it are more circumspect in their conclusions than Kalenskii. In his study of the psychology of American workers, Vainshtein 1977 concludes that there has been very little upward mobility for people whose initial job classified them as workers—but, he continues, the "stereotype" that there is a high degree of such mobility remains widespread and firmly held. In her study of university students, Novinskaia 1977 grants that higher education does serve as an avenue for upward job mobility, although it does not guarantee it. Moreover, she notes, specialists having university educations are becoming functionally more like workers.

6. Compare Mel'nikov 1974 with Gauzner 1968, Kats 1962, and Goncharova 1973.

7. Analyses of the general class structure in the United States are in Urlanis 1964; Semenov 1969; Mostovets and others, eds. 1972; Vozchikov and others, eds. 1974; Anikin, ed. 1972; Mel'nikov 1974; Burlatskii and Galkin 1985.

8. Here is another case of a topic that is mentioned time and again in a multitude of Soviet writings, yet there is no major study of it. The best systematic treatment is in Guliev 1965, and there are materials in the sources I cite in the discussion of liberalism and conservatism in Chapter 6.

9. Lest we be too harsh in judging Zorin let us note that years later Henry Kissinger commented after his incumbency as Secretary of State: "Business has no perception of its long-range interests." *New York Times*, June 30, 1977, D1.

10. The famous photograph of Sewell Avery, the unyielding but not quite indomitable president of Montgomery Ward Co., being carried bodily out of his corporate office during World War II by two soldiers representing the U.S. government is a particularly stark illustration of the problems involved in the process.

11. The middle strata are analyzed in various contexts in Shishkin 1972; Mel'nikov 1974; Semenov 1969; Boichenko 1970; Arzumanian and others, eds. 1963. Diligenskii and others 1985 discuss the new middle strata.

12. On the role of the military-industrial complex in these conflicts see Piadyshev 1974, Kuz'min 1974, and Tsagolov 1985.

13. Kalenskii 1969 and Dmitriev, 1971 are the best examples of attacks upon the elite concept. The differences between the political elite and ruling class explanations of politics will be considered in Chapter 7.

14. Dalin 1972. Shishkin 1972, 53 sharply disagrees with Dalin on the general proportion in 1900, but not with the general tendency, in stating that 70% of the gainfully employed population worked for hire in 1900, while fully 90% worked for hire in 1968.

15. See Gauzner 1968; Androsov 1971; Shishkin 1972; Mel'nikov 1974; Bochkova 1976; Bushmarin 1977. These sources place a greater stress on the distinctions which I have called "major" than on the "other divisions."

16. Having made these dangerous observations that went against some fundamental precepts of the Soviet mindset, Lapitskii immediately referred to Lenin to show that it was necessary to look at labor the way it really is rather than construe it as some sort of fantastic ideal. Moreover, Lapitskii's use of the term "conservative" rather than "reactionary" to describe the union leaders was an additional sign of the Soviet times. Writers in the 1940s through the 1960s would have preferred the more ideological term.

17. Anikin, ed. 1972, 235. Vozchikov and others, eds. 1974, 35 calculated that the proportion of "industrial workers" among the working class was 52.8% in 1947 and 47.0% in 1970. Mel'nikov 1974, 70, Table 8, calculates the proportion of "workers" (*rabochie*) in the sphere of material production among the total employed population at 25.9% in 1971. Androsov 1971, 145 calculated the proportion of "industrial workers" among all those working for hire at 47.7% in 1950 and 40.8% in 1968.

18. Grechukhin and others, eds. 1970. As used in this source the blue collars do not include service sector personnel or agricultural workers. The white collars are identified as employees (*sluzhashchie*), engineers and technical personnel, and those in retailing and the service sector. The confusion here lies in the disparities between American and Soviet sociological terminology. In trying to explain what "white collar" means in Soviet terms Soviet authors end up using overlapping categories.

19. The most important studies on that party are Timofeev 1967; Boichenko 1970; Mostovets and others, eds. 1972; Mikhailov, ed. 1970, 1971; Vozchikov and others, eds. 1974; Grechukhin 1975.

Chapter 4

1. The best comprehensive view of the subject is still Furaev's 1967 bibliographical article.

2. The chief attempts at calculating the rate of exploitation are Kovaleva 1969; Vygodskii 1975; Goncharova 1973; Varga 1968; Veber 1986. Gauzner 1968 and Kats 1962 discuss real wages in detail. Rubinshtein, ed. 1953 addresses the worsening condition of the American workers and of the farmer. Kats 1962 and Kuz'minov 1960 treat impoverishment in terms of housing, food, working condi-

tions, and the like. Guttsait 1961 outlines the history of unemployment in the twentieth century; Gauzner 1968 carries the analysis to the mid-1960s; and Goncharova 1973 is the latest study. Ershov 1972 traces the changes in the ways and means by which exploitation has been accomplished.

3. Varga 1968 attacked Kats 1962 and Kuz'minov 1960 strongly on this score. Varga in turn was stoutly attacked by Kovaleva 1969.

4. Vygodskii 1975, 187. I am here reproducing the figures he considers most likely and not the alternative maximum (145% and 412%, respectively) or minimum figures (106% and 213%), which he also gives. A major non-Soviet study of the theoretical issues involved is in Roemer 1982.

5. Kuz'minov 1960 and Kats 1962; Varga 1968.

6. These views are deeply ingrained in the mindset, paralleling Lenin. Ershov 1972 discusses the physical and nervous expenditure problem in detail.

7. Gerasimov 1984 is a good example of these works. It is a mass market second edition with a printing of 100,000 copies that is unrelievedly negative. Gerasimov is at this writing the major spokesman for the Soviet Ministry of Foreign Affairs and often appears in American television news broadcasts. He is author of the "Sinatra Doctrine" in Soviet foreign policy. See *New York Times*, October 26, 1989.

8. Keremetskii 1970. This book is the major Soviet study of collective bargaining and contains the only detailed Soviet treatment of fringe benefits.

9. Mikhailov, ed. 1970, 1971, vol. 1 came closer to American perspectives in attributing the oscillation of strike activity following World War II to the effects of the business cycle.

10. Baglai 1960 discusses the matter in a section entitled "The Meaning of the Right to Strike in the USA and the Forms of Its Limitation." He illustrates crosscutting mindset attitudes in maintaining that "the strike movement in the USA is growing every year" (5) and that "the general tendency of the development of legal regulation of labor in the USA is thus observable in the legal regulation of strikes as well. The real possibility for the toilers to use their right to strike is, increasingly, more limited" (101).

11. Androsov 1971. Business unionism's origins are traced in Askol'dova 1976.

12. Geevskii 1962. Even after all the problems the American unions experienced with both major parties in the 1970s there is still no mass worker party, and Geevskii's perception remains valid in Soviet eyes. Political parties are especially important to the Soviets since they are the highest form of organization that a social class can achieve (Arzumanian and others, eds. 1960). In the United States, so far only the bourgeoisie has its own parties.

13. The fullest analysis of the noninclusion of the working class and its organizations in the political system is in Boichenko 1970.

14. The authors did not use the terms "owner" and "overseer" here as Liven' did, but it is plain that this was essentially what they had in mind. They did not address the issue of how their innovative statement squares with the SMC personal union concept, which suggests just the opposite.

15. The political role of the labor unions is treated extensively and informatively (at last!) in Rogova 1983. She discusses the interaction of the unions with the legislative and executive branches, the Democratic party, political campaigns, and

big business. Since the book was printed in 2,000 copies, reader access is very limited, and the mindset has not yet been much affected by this information.

16. In a book entitled *The Class Struggle in the USA* one would have expected Shishkin 1972 to discuss revolution at some length. He did not, confining himself to a few brief remarks on violence (not revolution) in racial incidents.

17. Kalenskii 1969; Boichenko 1970; Mishin 1972. A recent Soviet study of revolution attempting to balance general laws at work and particular exceptions to them is Zagladin and others 1981. A statement of these perspectives in the English language is in Krasin 1985.

18. See Arzumanian and others, eds. 1963 for the appeal to Marx, Engels, and Lenin as ideological justification for this position and for the appeal to the practice of seeking temporary allies in the Comintern years.

19. Since heavy industry is the major material base of the working class, this source argues that the leading role in the class struggle will always be played by factory workers and miners. These primary components are joined by construction and transportation workers. Finally there are the "less developed" sections of the proletariat in agriculture, retailing, and crafts.

20. This is not to say that the Soviets had forgotten about the turbulent battles already fought and lost by American "revolutionary and democratic forces" since the last quarter of the nineteenth century. Gromakov 1958 treats these earlier episodes.

21. This drama is fully illustrated in Arzumanian and others, eds. 1963, where Chapter 5 discusses the middle strata as allies of the bourgeoisie and Chapter 6 treats them as allies of the proletariat. An important recent analysis is in Diligenskii and others 1985.

22. Were Soviet writers generally to admit that upward social mobility occurs, they would surely count this right wing propensity on the part of many of the recently upward mobiles to be one of its chief negative characteristics.

23. The third, and most recent, edition of *The Great Soviet Encyclopedia* has no article on mass movements, political movements, or social movements. Specialized social science dictionaries and reference sources did not have entries either until the publication of Gvishiani and Lapina, eds. 1988. I know of no books or journal articles analyzing the general topic conceptually or theoretically at any length.

24. There are detailed studies of these problems in Chirkin 1958; Luzik 1960; Nitoburg 1971; Luzik 1976; and Petrovskii 1967. Prior to 1956 Soviet writers were more concerned with how and to what degree the Negroes were being persecuted than with what they were doing to combat the persecution. Geevskii 1952 and 1954 are the best examples of that preoccupation. The Soviets used the designation Negroes into the early 1970s and thereafter used the word Blacks.

25. Geevskii cautioned against either overestimating or underestimating the significance of these differences. Tumanov, ed. 1967 contains the best Soviet consideration of the conceptual issues involved in American discussions of civil rights problems.

26. The statement on membership loss is an obvious last-minute addition to the text in correction of an earlier carefully hedged prediction that the evolution of the Panthers from a separatist organization to one willing to ally with other forces

showed that the ongoing regrouping of social forces might in the final analysis result in an alliance of all mass movements. Contrary to this expectation, at least Newton took the capitalist route. Mitrokhin 1974 argues that nobody could have predicted the course along which the Panthers evolved, a very unusual admission for a Soviet writer to make so bluntly. Normally this is either done very circumspectly or a pretense of certitude is maintained.

27. See also the biography of Dr. King by Kondrashov 1981. Practically no Soviet writers have addressed the black clergy's central role in the movement. Mostovets and others, eds. 1972, briefly note it.

28. Contrast Shishkin 1972, a writer on the class struggle, with Geevskii 1974 and Vozchikov and others, eds. 1974.

29. The relationship between objective and subjective factors is addressed in the few books cited in the article "The Subjective Factor in History," in Konstantinov and others, eds. 1960–1970, vol. 5.

30. They are listed here in the order of greater to lesser attention given them in Soviet writing on movements. Vozchikov and others, eds. 1974 has a discussion of the four largest farmer organizations, and Zolotukhin 1968 does a study of farm policy starting in the 1930s. See also Boichenko 1970. Novikova 1975 treats the women's movement most comprehensively. See also Vozchikov and others, eds. 1974 and Geevskii and Salycheva, eds. 1978. These last two sources treat the Spanish-speaking agricultural worker movement.

31. Gurvich 1937 is a case in point. A more recent major study of the general crisis of capitalism considered the severe political and economic problems besetting the advanced capitalist countries both internally and in their international aspects in the 1960s and 1970s and was notably restrained in its conclusions. The volume's editors raised the question of revolution only to suggest somewhat archly that its study and discussion is not the business of specialists on the general crisis of capitalism but is the province of other, unidentified, specialists in the Soviet scholarly community (Inozemtsev and others, eds. 1976). The distancing here is very telling.

Chapter 5

1. Some representative articles on politics in the monthly are V. Lan, "The Republicans and Democrats in the Presidential Elections," no. 8, 1928; V. Lan, "Hoover's Victory," no. 1, 1929; V. Lan, "Roosevelt's Victory," no. 11–12, 1932; A. Noritskii, "The Presidential Election in the United States," no. 8, 1936; and A. Noritskii, "Roosevelt's Victory," no. 12, 1936.

2. See Mills 1972 on the thirteen-volume study and Eran 1979 on the return to topicality.

3. Lan 1932 and a much enlarged revision in 1937. This book was the only one of the projected thirteen volumes to be published. Lan was the mainstay of topical analysis of American elections in the late 1920s and the 1930s. He combined in himself the two primary tendencies in the institute's work—the party's preference for topical research and writing and the more scholarly concern with basic research. There is much on these and related matters in Day 1981.

4. The issues that arose when the needs made themselves felt, the political

interactions involved, and the debates among various scholarly factions are discussed in detail in Simirenko, ed. 1969, especially the chapters by Mandel, "Soviet Marxism and Social Science," and Bociurkiw, "The Study of Politics in the U.S.S.R.: Birth Throes of a Soviet Political Science." My remarks in this and the following paragraphs draw heavily on these sources and Eran 1979.

5. *Vestnik Akademii Nauk SSSR*, no. 2, February 1968, 114. The decision was apparently taken in November 1967. See Central Intelligence Agency 1976. In this CIA report, as in all other biographical sources, Arbatov is identified as a doctor of historical sciences rather than of philosophical science as in the announcement by the Academy of Sciences.

6. In those days Soviet historians produced the largest number of studies on the United States. An exhaustive annotated bibliography of these works is in Okinshevich 1976. An example of this kind of historical analysis in English translation is Sivachyov and Yazkov 1976.

7. Varying estimates of Arbatov's and IUSAC's roles are in Schwartz 1978; Beloff 1980; Levchenko 1982; Grant 1980; Malcom 1984; Shevchenko 1985; Corson and Crowley 1985; Huber 1988.

8. These training programs have not been studied by Sovietologists to the extent that their importance warrants. The key aspect is the extent and the content of the ideological portion at various levels of training.

9. The primary vehicle for publishing negative books is a series initiated in the late 1970s entitled "Imperialism: Events, Facts, Documents." Various publishing houses issue these books in editions of 60,000 to 70,000 copies if they are not very negative (e.g., Kokoshin 1982; Nikonov 1984) or of 100,000 copies if they are very negative (e.g., Ashin and Midler 1986; Kondratenko 1986; Tsagolov 1986; Vetrova 1983). Even the prestigious Soviet academic press Mysl' has published several of these, doubtless an example of the publishing insurance policy noted.

10. Announcement of the respective establishments appears in *SShA: ekonomika, politika, ideologiia*, no. 11, 1974 and no. 3, 1976.

11. On the general problem of how governments and organizations learn and incorporate new ideas and approaches into their organizational culture, see Etheredge 1981; see Hedberg 1981 for how organizations learn and *un*learn. Gustafson 1981 considers the many factors, relationships, and strategies involved in Soviet circumstances, especially in Chapter 6, "Bringing New Ideas into Soviet Politics." Brown 1984 and Hough 1986 have additional insights. The difficulties in assessing the influence of experts in these processes are amply discussed in Remnek, ed. 1977 and Hill 1980.

12. For even more relevant factors see Griffiths 1972.

13. Zorin's 1978 long, two-part article published in IUSAC's monthly heralded the return to modified SMC modes of analysis in the 1980s that was discussed in Chapter 1.

14. The importance of the critical attitude in Marx is discussed by the editor in Tucker, ed. 1978, and by Marx in the same volume. This intellectual stance subsequently characterized the writings of most Marxist schools, the Soviet one in particular.

15. This proposition is illustrated cosmically in English in Konstantinov and others 1974. It is worth pursuing these questions in the *Great Soviet Encyclopedia*

1973–1983 in the following articles: "Science," vol. 19; "Objectivism," vol. 18; and "Partiinost'," vol. 19. There is no article on objectivity, but the topic of objective reality is treated in the article "Matter," vol. 15.

16. Two examples of this stance are Burlatskii 1978 and the article "Politics" in the *Great Soviet Encyclopedia* 1973–1983, vol. 20.

17. The article "The State" in the *Great Soviet Encyclopedia* 1973–1983, vol. 7 contains the standard interpretations on these points, to which the sharpest Soviet challenge is in Kalenskii 1977.

18. Advances in incorporating Western methods and means of analysis are documented in Brown 1984 for politics as a whole and by Malcom 1984 for American politics in particular. Kerimov, ed. 1984 contains numerous examples of such incorporation.

19. These remarks do not pertain to general Soviet studies of politics such as Burlatskii's many publications, especially those written with Galkin, which make extensive use of American politics for illustrative purpose but do not focus on those politics.

20. This problem, as well as the possible effects that institutional personality may have on the analysis of American politics, is treated in an interestingly differentiated way in Griffiths 1972.

21. Their rarity makes them important enough to warrant noting their full translated title, the number of pages, and number of copies printed. Gurvich 1930, *The Political Structure of Contemporary States—The USA*, 183 pp., 4,000 copies; Mishin 1954, *The Central Organs of Power of the USA—Tool of the Dictatorship of Monopoly Capita*, 175 pp., 10,000 copies; Mishin, 1958a, *The State System of the USA*,, 99 pp., 50,000 copies; Cherniak 1957, *The State Structure and Political Parties of the USA*, 241 pp., 15,000 copies; and Nikiforov, ed. 1976, *The State Structure of the USA*, 326 pp., 10,000 copies. The total number of copies is 89,000, assuming that there were no additional printings of these volumes. We must add to this list the Russian translation of the American textbook by Dye and Zeigler (Dai and Zigler 1984), with 4,210 copies printed.

22. Some early examples of these approaches are in Shabad's "An Apology for the Political System of Capitalism (On So-Called 'Political Science' in Bourgeois Sociology)," *Kommunist*, no. 2, January 1960. Since political science did not exist as a separate discipline in the Soviet Union it had to be placed within some familiar academic context, and that was within sociology. Until the 1980s American political scientists were most often identified as sociologists, and up to the 1970s they were always so identified.

23. Examples are Kalenskii 1969; Nikiforov, ed. 1976; Shakhnazarov, ed. 1982, 1985. Malcom 1984 and Brown 1984 have documented and analyzed these processes. A breakthrough was made in October 1987 when the first Symposium on Theoretical and Methodological Questions of Political Science was held by representatives of the American Political Science Association and the Soviet Political Science Association.

24. Boichenko 1959. She manages to discuss the process of adopting the Constitution and the basic principles contained in it without considering the separation of powers. In true state and law fashion, since the principle is not mentioned as such directly in the Constitution, she does not mention it either. Of course, at the

time it was also *safer* not to say anything. And her neglect is also doubtless partly the result of the fact that until the early 1960s very little had been published in the Soviet Union on the political theories underlying the American Revolution and the adoption of the Constitution. A bibliography of the studies published in the 1970s is in Sevost'ianov 1981.

25. In a discussion of political philosophy Kalenskii 1977 found the concept really meaningful on the level of principle and then provided the richest treatment of the concept in all Soviet writing in his biography of James Madison (1981). The actual operation of the principle through the mechanism of checks and balances is discussed in Mishin 1984. Savel'ev 1976a noted earlier that the mechanism made personal arbitrariness on the part of the president almost impossible. See also Chetverikov 1974 and Prozorova 1974.

26. Gutsenko 1961 citing Lunts 1948; Gromyko 1957. Another Soviet writer later called this idea "primitive" (Lan and others eds., 1966, 55). The concept of checks and balances has been misunderstood in other ways as well: Shakhnazarov 1955 obviously thought that the Supreme Court was not involved and that only the president, the Senate, and the House of Representatives were.

27. Levin 1951 noted that the president's power over Congress was very limited when his party was in the minority and that he had serious rivals in the caucus leaders, the Speaker, and the chairman of the Rules Committee. Later qualifications of the standard interpretation are in Marinin 1967a; Gantman and Mikoyan 1969; Chetverikov 1974; Zorin, ed. 1971; Savel'ev 1976a.

28. Shakhnazarov 1955; Gromyko 1957; Cherniak 1957; Gromakov 1958; Boichenko 1959; Bel'son 1960; Gantman and Mikoyan 1969. The most detailed treatment of lobbying as bribery is in Iur'ev 1961.

29. See Tumanov, ed. 1967. Other fleeting uses of the term to include labor are Kulikov 1969; Grechukhin and others, eds. 1970; Burlatskii 1970; Shishkin 1972; Chetverikov 1974; Kuz'min 1977.

30. Less than a handful of works on policymaking can be cited if we exclude books on foreign policy and those that simply describe policy output and deal only with those devoted to the policy process, particularly decisionmaking. For examples, see Zolotukhin 1968; Geevskii 1973; Chetverikov 1974; Savel'ev 1976a.

31. The most recent concise statement of these attitudes is in the *Great Soviet Encyclopedia*, "Ideology," vol. 10; "Marxism–Leninism," vol. 15; "Science," vol. 17. There are no entries for either "the social sciences" or "political science," an indication of the low level of their acceptance even in the late 1970s.

32. Examples of these changes in various time periods are in Wetter 1958; Graham 1966, 1987; Joravsky 1970, 1983.

33. Thomas Kuhn's 1979 book (together with his pithier 1977 analysis) is a classic statement of the issues involved. Imre Lakatos has developed some very challenging general perspectives on pluralism in scientific endeavor that illustrate how far the Soviets have yet to go (Lakatos and Musgrave, eds. 1964).

34. It is impossible to ascertain with even a low degree of accuracy just who in the Soviet Union believes how much of the ideology in general. Shlapentokh 1986 considers this question in some detail. The impressionistic judgments of Soviet dissenters and recent émigrés on this point go in two directions—nobody

believes the ideology, or, amazingly and depressingly, many do believe it. At the more general level the problem of how belief systems affect political cognition, judgment, and action receives detailed and complex treatment in Axelrod, ed. 1976. Though the book focuses on decisionmaking in foreign affairs, the conceptual and analytical materials are highly relevant to this chapter's subject matter. Robert Jervis's (1976) chapter, "Cognitive Consistency and the Interaction Between Theory and Data," is especially important. Griffiths 1972, ch. 3 considers the role played by foreign policy advocacy on the part of Soviet students of American domestic politics in changing Soviet perceptions of those politics. Overall, the problem is encapsulated in the title of Berger and Luckman 1967, *The Social Construction of Reality*, in which two chapters, "Society as Objective Reality" and "Society as Subjective Reality," are particularly valuable. A person's perception of reality is socially conditioned in many important ways.

35. Only rarely in Soviet writing was *The Federalist* mentioned in passing, a typical form of the mindset's inattention to fundamental matters. Kalenskii 1981 remains the fullest Soviet study of the topic.

36. *SShA: ekonomika, politika, ideologiia*, no. 5, 1971. Similarly, Guliev called *Government by the People: The Dynamics of American National Government* by James MacGregor Burns and Jack Peltason "a fundamental investigation" of the topic without realizing that it was a textbook—and a splendid one at that (1970, 90).

Chapter 6

1. The monthly's editors and writers eventually began to refer to earlier articles in their journal on a given topic. This bespeaks their awareness of the need to build cumulatively, but they still limit their theorizing.

2. This is an interesting reversal of the American theory that it was the Republicans, especially in the Eisenhower administration, who legitimized New Deal policies.

3. It may, of course, be too early to expect an application. But the real issue here may prove to be the difficulty the Soviets typically experience in applying theoretical advances, a problem in virtually every area of Soviet political, social, and economic life.

4. Schwartz 1966 comprehensively treats Soviet ideological analyses of the 1964 election.

5. Examples are Barsukov 1972; Shishkin 1976a and 1976b on presidential campaigns; Savel'ev 1976a, 70–73 on Senator Fulbright's defeat, a shocking and lamentable event for the Soviets.

6. See Zorin 1972a and 1972b; Shishkin 1976a and 1976b.

7. Examples are Zamoshkin, ed. 1978; Vainshtein 1977; Petrovskaia, 1977, 1982; Popov 1981; Emel'ianov 1986.

8. Mishin 1954, 103; Shakhnazarov 1955, 102–7; Zorin 1964, 183–202; Gromyko 1968, 136–39; Beglov 1971, 506–38; Ashin 1966, 88; Levin, ed. 1964a, 88–89; Fedosov 1969; Novikov 1970; Zorin, ed. 1971, 381–90.

Chapter 7

1. See the section on the bourgeoisie in Chapter 3 and Burlatskii and Galkin 1985, 117–23.

2. Iziumov and Popov 1988, 7 cite other roughly similar studies that came out later.

REFERENCES

In these references *SShA* is the abbreviation for the periodical *SShA: ekonomika, politika, ideologiia*, the monthly publication of the Institute of United States and Canadian Studies—IUSAC.

Abramov, Iu. K., and A. A. Kokoshin (1982). "The Composition of the Upper Echelons of the Reagan Administration." *SShA*, no. 11, 117–27.

Aksyonov, Vassily (1987). "A Soviet Emigre Takes the 'A' Train." *New York Times Magazine*, May 3.

Allen, Robert V. (1988). *Russia Looks at America: The View to 1917*. Washington, D.C.: Library of Congress.

Anderson, James E. (1979). *Public Policy-Making*. 2nd ed. New York: Holt, Rinehart and Winston.

Androsov, Vladimir P. (1971). *Profsoiuzy SShA v usloviiakh gosudarstvenno-monopolisticheskogo kapitalizma*. Moscow: Nauka.

——— (1964). "The Role of the U.S. Government in Relations Between Labor and Capital." *Mirovaia ekonomika i mezhdunarodnye otnosheniia*, no. 5, 36–46.

Anichkin, O. N. (1980). "The Election Campaign of 1980: Before the Decisive Stage." *SShA*, no. 8, 49–52.

——— (1977). "The Republicans Heal Their Wounds." *SShA*, no. 5, 62–67.

——— (1974). "Results of the Congressional Elections." *SShA*, no. 12, 55–59.

——— (1972). "The Democrats Before the Election." *SShA*, no. 4, 15–23.

——— (1970). "What the Primaries Showed." *SShA*, no. 9, 71–74.

Anikin, Andrei V. (ed.) (1980). *Soedinennye Shtaty Ameriki.* Moscow: Mysl'.

——— (ed.) (1972). *Soedinennye Shtaty Ameriki.* Moscow: Mysl'.

Arbatov, Georgii A. (1972). "The 'Political Year' and the Problem of Political Priorities." *SShA*, no. 7, 3–15.

———, and others (eds.) (1988). *Sovremennye Soedinennye Shtaty Ameriki. Entsiklopedicheskii Spravochnik.* Moscow: Izdatel'stvo politicheskoi literatury.

Arzumanian, Anushavan A., and others (eds.) (1963). *Gorodskie srednie sloi sovremennogo kapitalisticheskogo obshchestva.* Moscow: Izdatel'stvo AN SSSR.

———, and others (eds.) (1960). *Soedinennye Shtaty Ameriki: slovar'-spravochnik.* Moscow: Gosudarstvennoe izdatel'stvo politicheskoi literatury.

Ashin, Gennadii K. (1985). *Sovremennye teorii elity: kriticheskii ocherk.* Moscow: Mezhdunarodnye otnosheniia.

——— (1983). "The Elite and the Dominating Exploiting Class." *Voprosy filosofii*, no. 2, 74–84.

——— (1975a). "Elitism: American Variants." *SShA*, no. 2, 43–56.

——— (1975b). "Political Pluralism or 'Elitist Democracy'?" *Mirovaia ekonomika i mezhdunarodnye otnosheniia*, no. 3, 99–106.

——— (1966). *Mif ob elite i "massovom obshchestve."* Moscow: Izdatel'stvo "Mezhdunarodnye otnosheniia."

———, and Aleksandr P. Midler (1986). *V tiskakh dukhovnogo gneta: Chto populiariziruiut sredstva massovoi informatsii SShA.* Moscow: Mysl'.

———, and M. A. Shafir (1971). "Elitism and Democracy." *Sovetskoe gosudarstvo i pravo*, no. 2, 137–42.

Askol'dova, Svetlana M. (1976). *Formirovanie ideologii amerikanskogo trediunionizma.* Moscow: Nauka.

Axelrod, Robert (ed.) (1976). *Structure of Decision: The Cognitive Maps of Political Elites.* Princeton: Princeton University Press.

Bachrach, Peter (1967). *The Theory of Democratic Elitism.* Boston: Little, Brown.

Baglai, Marat V. (1960). *Zakonodatel'stvo SShA v bor'be s zabastovochnym dvizheniem.* Moscow: Gosiurizdat.

Baichorov, Aleksandr M. (1982). *Ot "razbitogo" pokoleniia k kontrkul'ture (Paradoksy molodezhnogo protesta v SShA).* Minsk: Izdatel'stvo Belorusskogo gosudarstvennogo universiteta.

——— (1975). *Problemy konsolidatsii demokraticheskikh sil SShA v sovremennykh usloviiakh.* Minsk: Izdatel'stvo Belorusskogo universiteta.

Barghoorn, Frederick C. (1950). *The Soviet Image of the United States: A Study in Distortion*. New York: Harcourt, Brace.

———— (1948). "The Varga Discussion and Its Significance." *American Slavic and East European Review*, 7, no. 3 (October), 214–36.

Barsukov, Iu. V. (1972). "The Republican Party on the Eve of the Elections." *SShA*, no. 6, 16–25.

Batalov, Eduard Ia. (1989). "American Experience and Our Perestroika: Sociological Reflections." *SShA*, no. 1, 3–12.

Beglov, Ivan A. (1971). *SShA: sobstvennost' i vlast'*. Moscow: Nauka.

Beglov, Spartak (1972). *Monopolii slova*. 2nd ed. Moscow: Mysl'.

Beloff, V. Nora (1980). "Escape from Boredom: A Defector's Story." *Atlantic Monthly* (November), 42–50.

Belonogov, Aleksandr M. (1974). *Belyi dom i kapitolii. Partnery i soperniki. Priniatie Soedinennymi Shtatami Ameriki mezhdunarodnykh obiazatel'stv*. Moscow: Izdatel'stvo "Mezhdunarodnye otnosheniia."

Bel'son, Iakov (1962). "Old Phenomena and New Concepts in State–Legal Ideology in the USA." *Sovetskoe gosudarstvo i pravo*, no. 11, 64–73.

———— (1960). *Sovremennoe burzhuaznoe gosudarstvo i narodnoe predstavitel'stvo*. Moscow: Gosudarstvennoe izdatel'stvo iuridicheskoi literatury.

————, and Konstantin E. Livantsev (1982). *Istoriia gosudarstva i prava SShA*. Leningrad: Izdatel'stvo Leningradskogo universiteta.

Berezhkov, V. M. (1973). "The Political Situation after the Elections." *SShA*, no. 1, 3–17.

Berger, Peter L., and Thomas Luckman (1967). *The Social Construction of Reality: A Treatise in the Sociology of Knowledge*. Garden City, N.Y.: Doubleday.

Bertram, Christoph (ed.) (1980). *Prospects of Soviet Power in the 1980s*. Hamden, Conn.: Archon Books.

Bialer, Seweryn (1985). "The Psychology of U.S.–Soviet Relations." *Political Psychology*, 6, no. 1 (June), 263–73.

Bobotov, S. V. (1969). "The Influence of Pressure Groups on the Apparatus of Power in the USA." *Sovetskoe gosudarstvo i pravo*, no. 8, 114–20.

Bobrakov, Iurii I. (1981). "On the Reagan Administration's Economic Program." *SShA*, no. 5, 46–51.

————, and V. A. Fedorovich (eds.) (1976). *SShA: gosudartsvo i ekonomika. Mekhanizm gosudarstvennomonopolisticheskogo regulirovaniia ekonomiki*. Moscow: Nauka.

Bochkova, A. (1976). *SShA: kvalifitsirovannye promyshlennye rabochie (izmenenie kvalifikatsii, mesta v organizatsii truda, form klassovoi bor'by)*. Moscow: Nauka.

Bogdanov, Radomir (1986). *The U.S. War Machine and Politics*. Moscow: Progress Publishers.

Boichenko, Galina G. (1970). *Politicheskaia organizatsiia SShA. Obshchestvennye instituty i ikh vzaimodeistvie s gosudarstvom*. Minsk: Izdatel'stvo Belorusskogo universiteta.

———— (1959). *Konstitutsiia Soedinennykh Shtatov Ameriki. Tolkovanie i primenenie v epokhu imperializma*. Moscow: Izdatel'stvo "Mezhdunarodnye otnosheniia."

Boiko, K., and V. Shamberg (1973). "The USA: The Two Party System and the Political Course." *Mirovaia ekonomika i mezhdunarodnye otnosheniia*, no. 5, 83–89.

Bol'shaia sovetskaia entsiklopediia (1926–1947). Moscow: Sovetskaia entsiklopediia.

Borisiuk, Viktor I. (1988). "The Language of Cultural Contact." *SShA*, no. 5, 45–51.

————, and others (1988). *Politicheskie instituty SShA: istoriia i sovremennost'*. Moscow: Nauka.

Borisov, S. (1966). "The White House Apparatus: Its Role in the U. S. Government." *Mirovaia ekonomika i mezhdunarodnye otnosheniia*, no. 8, 127–34.

Bratslavskii, Devis Ia. (1989). "The Financing of Elections by Business Circles in the USA." *SShA*, no. 3, 108–14.

Brown, Archie (1988). "The Soviet Leadership and the Struggle for Political Reform." *Harriman Institute Forum*, 1, no. 4, 1–8.

———— (1984). "Political Science in the Soviet Union: A New Stage of Development?" *Soviet Studies*, 36, no. 3, 317–44.

———— (1983). "Pluralism, Power, and the Soviet Political System: A Comparative Perspective." In Solomon (ed.) (1983), 61–107.

Bugrov, E. (1970). "The Military–Industrial Complex." *Mirovaia ekonomika i mezhdunarodnye otnosheniia*, no. 3, 29–40.

Burch, Jr., Philip H. (1980). *Elites in American History*, vol. III. *The New Deal to the Carter Administration*. New York: Holmes & Meier.

Burlatskii, Fedor M. (1978). *The Modern State and Politics*. Moscow: Progress Publishers.

———— (1970). *Lenin, gosudarstvo, politika*. Moscow: Nauka.

————, and Aleksandr A. Galkin (1985). *Sovremennyi Leviafan. Ocherki politicheskoi sotsiologii kapitalizma*. Moscow: Mysl'.

————, and Aleksandr A. Galkin (1974). *Sotsiologiia, politika, mezhdunarodnye otnosheniia*. Moscow: Izdatel'stvo "Mezhdunarodnye otnosheniia."

Bushmarin, Igor V. (1977). "Changes in the Composition of Unskilled Workers." *SShA*, no. 7, 84–94.

Caldwell, Lawrence T., and Robert Legvold (1983). "Reagan Through Soviet Eyes." *Foreign Policy*, no. 52 (Fall), 3–21.

Calvert, Peter (1982). *The Concept of Class: An Historical Introduction*. New York: St. Martin's.

Central Intelligence Agency (1976). *Biographic Report: USSR Institute of the USA and Canada*. April.

Cheprakov, Sergei V. (1984). *Monopolisticheskie ob"edineniia v promyshlennosti SShA*. Moscow: Nauka.

Cheprakov, Viktor A. (1964). *Gosudarstvenno-monopolisticheskii kapitalizm*. Moscow: Mysl'.

Cherniak, Efim B. (1957). *Gosudarstvennyi stroi i politicheskie partii SShA*. Moscow: Izdatel'stvo Akademii Nauk SSSR.

Chernilovskii, Zinovii M. (1982). *Ot Marshalla do Uorena. Ocherki istorii Verkhovnogo suda SShA*. Moscow: "Iuridicheskaia literatura."

Chervonnaia, S. A. (1978). "The Supreme Court and Civil Rights." *SShA*, no. 4, 58–64.

Chetverikov, Sergei B. (1974). *Kto i kak delaet politiku SShA*. Moscow: Izdatel'stvo "Mezhdunarodnye otnosheniia."

Chilcote, Ronald H. (1981). *Theories of Comparative Politics: The Search for a Paradigm*. Boulder, Colo.: Westview Press.

Chirkin, Veniamin (1958). *Diskriminatsiia natsional'nykh men'shinstv v SShA*. Moscow: Gosiurizdat.

Cohen, Jean L. (1982). *Class and Civil Society*. Amherst: University of Massachusetts Press.

Corson, William R., and Robert T. Crowley (1985). *The New KGB: Engine of Soviet Power*. New York: William Morrow.

Corwin, Edward S. (1941). *The President: Office and Powers*. New York: New York University Press.

Costa, Alexandra (1986). *Stepping Down from the Star. A Soviet Defector's Story*. New York: G. P. Putnam's Sons.

Cox, Arthur Macy (1976). *The Dynamics of Detente*. New York: W. W. Norton.

Crozier, Michael, Samuel P. Huntington, and Joji Watanuki (1975). *The Crisis of Democracy: Report on the Governability of Democracies to the Trilateral Commission*. New York: New York University Press.

Dahl, Robert A. (1982). *Dilemmas of Pluralist Democracy: Autonomy vs. Control*. New Haven: Yale University Press.

Dai, T., and Kh. Zigler (1984). *Demokratiia dlia elity: vvedenie v amerikanskuiu politiku*. Moscow: Iuridicheskaia literatura.

Dalin, Sergei A. (1972). *SShA: Poslevoennyi gosudarstvennomonopolis-ticheskii kapitalizm.* Moscow: Nauka.

—— (1961). *Voenno-gosudarstvennyi monopolisticheskii kapitalizm.* Moscow: Izdatel'stvo AN SSSR.

—— (1936). *Ekonomicheskaia politika Ruzvel'ta.* Moscow: Gos. sots.-ek. Izdatel'stvo.

Dallin, Alexander (1980). "The United States in Soviet Perspective." In Bertram (ed.) (1980), 31–39.

Danilenko, Viktor N. (1985). *Den'gi i politika: vozdeistvie krupnogo kapitala na politicheskuiu zhizn' v kapitalisticheskikh stranakh.* Moscow: Mezhdunarodnye otnosheniia.

Darchiev, Aleksandr, and Elena Ia. Kortunova (1989). "America Through the Prism of the Elections." *SShA,* no. 3, 12–20.

Day, Richard B. (1981). *The "Crisis" and the "Crash": Soviet Studies of the West (1917–1939).* London: NLB.

Deutsch, Karl (1966). *The Nerves of Government: Models of Political Communication and Control.* New York: Free Press.

Dewhirst, Martin, and Robert Farrell (eds.) (1973). *The Soviet Censorship.* Metuchen, N.J.: Scarecrow Press.

Diligenskii, German G., and others (1985). *Sotsial'naia psikhologiia klassov. Problemy klassovoi psikhologii v sovremennom kapitalisticheskom obshchestve.* Moscow: Mysl'.

DiTomaso, Nancy (1980). "Organizational Analysis and Power Structure Research." In Domhoff (ed.) (1980), 255–68.

Dmitriev, Anatolii V. (1971). *Politicheskaia sotsiologiia SShA. Ocherki.* Leningrad: Izdatel'stvo Leningradskogo universiteta.

Dmitriev, Boris (1963). *SShA: opasnost' sprava.* Moscow: Izdatel'stvo Instituta mezhdunarodnykh otnoshenii.

Dokunin, Vladimir I., and Vasilii P. Trepelkov (1963). *Obshchii krizis kapitalizma.* Moscow: Sotsekgiz.

Domhoff, G. William (1983). *Who Rules America Now? A View for the Eighties.* Englewood Cliffs, N.J.: Prentice-Hall.

—— (ed.) (1980). *Power Structure Research.* Beverly Hills, Calif.: Sage.

Dragilev, Mikhail S. (1957). *Obshchii krizis kapitalizma: ocherk razvitiia kapitalisticheskoi sistemy za 40 let.* Moscow: Gosudarstvennoe izdatel'stvo politicheskoi literatury.

——, and others (eds.) (1975). *Gosudarstvenno-monopolisticheskii kapitalizm: obshchie cherty i osobennosti.* Moscow: Politizdat.

Draper, Hal (1978). *Karl Marx's Theory of Revolution,* vol. II. *The Politics of Social Classes.* New York: Monthly Review Press.

—— (1977). *Karl Marx's Theory of Revolution,* vol. I. *State and Bureaucracy.* New York: Monthly Review Press.

Dye, Thomas R., and L. Harmon Zeigler (1970–1987, various editions). *The Irony of Democracy: An Uncommon Introduction to American Politics.* Monterey, Calif.: Brooks/Cole.

XXII S"ezd KPSS. Stenograficheskii otchet. (1962). Moscow: Gospolitizdat.

Dzhindzher, Enn F. (1981). *Verkhovnyi sud i prava cheloveka v SShA.* Moscow: "Iuridicheskaia literatura."

Efimov, Aleksei V. (1934). *K istorii kapitalizma v SShA.* Moscow: Gos. sots.-ek. izdatel'stvo.

—— (1969). *SShA: Puti razvitiia kapitalizma (Doimperialisticheskaia epokha).* Moscow: AN Otdel istorii.

Emel'ianov, Iurii V. (1986). *Obostrenie sotsial'no-politicheskikh protivorechii v SShA i molodezh.* Moscow: Nauka.

Engver, Nikolai (1989). Quoted in *New York Times,* May 27, A6.

Eran, Oded (1979). *Mezhdunarodniki: An Assessment of Professional Expertise in the Making of Soviet Foreign Policy.* Ramat Gan, Israel: Turtledove Publishing.

Erokhin, A. V. (1972). "Senator Edward Kennedy." *SShA,* no. 6, 108–15.

Ershov, Stal' A. (1974). *SShA: razvitie form i metodov kapitalisticheskoi ekspluatatsii.* Moscow: Nauka.

—— (1972). *SShA: kapitalisticheskoe proizvodstvo i zdorov'e trudiashchikhsia.* Moscow: Nauka.

Etheredge, Lloyd S. (1981). "Government and Learning: An Overview." In Long (ed.) (1981), 73–161.

Evenko, L. I. (ed.) (1985). *Gosudarstvo i upravlenie v SShA.* Moscow: Mysl'.

Eventov, Lev Ia. (ed.) (1936). *"Planovye" manevry v kapitalisticheskikh stranakh. Sbornik materialov pod redaktsiei L. Eventova.* Moscow: Gos. sots.-ek. izdatel'stvo.

Evgen'eva, A. P. (ed.) (1981–1984). *Slovar' russkogo iazyka v chetyrekh tomakh.* 4 vols. Moscow: Izdatel'stvo "Russkii iazyk."

Federov, V. I. (1977). "Who Paid for the 1976 Election." *SShA,* no. 4, 59–64.

Fedoseev, Anatolii A. (1989). *Sovremennaia amerikanskaia burzhuaznaia politologiia: istoki, traditsii, novatsii.* Leningrad: Izdatel'stvo Leningradskogo universiteta.

Fedosov, G. (1969). "The Limits and the People of the New Administration of the USA." *Mirovaia ekonomika i mezhdunarodnye otnosheniia,* no. 3, 66–71.

—— (1968). "The Democratic and Republican Party Apparatus." *Mirovaia ekonomika i mezhdunarodnye otnosheniia,* no. 10, 110–14.

Fiske, Susan T. (1986). "Schema-Based Versus Piecemeal Politics: A Patchwork Quilt, but Not a Blanket, of Evidence." In Lau and Sears (eds.) (1986), 41–53.

Franklin, Bruce (ed.) (1972). *The Essential Stalin: Major Theoretical Writings*. Garden City, N.Y.: Doubleday.

Frei, Daniel (1986). *Perceived Images: U.S. and Soviet Assumptions and Perceptions in Disarmament*. Totowa, N.J.: Rowan and Alanheld.

Furaev, Viktor K. (1967). "Soviet Historiography of the Class Struggle in the USA in Recent Times." In Revunenkov (ed.) (1967), 148–79.

Furman, Dmitrii E. (1984). *Religion and Social Conflict in the U.S.A.* Moscow: Progress Publishers.

——— (1981). *Religiia i sotsial'nye konflikty v SShA*. Moscow: Nauka.

Fursenko, Aleksandr A. (1971). *Kriticheskoe desiatiletie Ameriki. 60-e gody*. Leningrad: Nauka.

———, and others (1974). *Amerikanskaia istoriografiia vnutripoliticheskikh problem SShA v poslevoennyi period*. Moscow: Nauka.

Gadzhiev, K. C. (1983). Review of J. D. Barber, "The Pulse of Politics"; E. Costikyan, "How to Win Votes"; S. Eldersfeld, "Political Parties in American Society". *Novaia i noveishaia istoriia*, no. 4, 195–99.

Galkin, A. (1969). "Contemporary Capitalism's Ruling Elite." *Mirovaia ekonomika i mezhdunarodnye otnosheniia*, no. 3, 74–86.

Galkin, A. A., and G. G. Diligenskii (eds.) (1971). *Sotsial'no-politicheskie sdvigi v stranakh razvitogo kapitalizma*. Moscow: Nauka.

Galkin, I. V. (1982). "Activities of the Democratic Party's National Committee." In Sivachev (ed.) (1982), 155–73.

Gantman, Vladimir I., and Sergo A. Mikoyan (1969). *SShA: gosudarstvo, politika, vybory*. Moscow: Iuridicheskaia literatura.

Garment, Suzanne (1987). "Oddly, Israelis Misunderstand Us." *New York Times*. March 25, op-ed page.

Garson, G. David (1977). *Power and Politics in the United States: A Political Economy Approach*. Lexington, Mass.: D. C. Heath.

Garthoff, Raymond (1985). *Detente and Confrontation: American–Soviet Relations from Nixon to Reagan*. Washington, D.C.: Brookings.

Gauzner, Nikolai D. (1968). *Nauchno-tekhnicheskii progress i rabochii klass SShA*. Moscow: Nauka.

Geevskii, Igor' A. (1981). "The Republicans in Power: Contours of Social Policy." *SShA*, no. 9, 14–24.

——— (1973). *SShA: negritianskaia problema. Politika Vashingtona v negritianskom voprose*. Moscow: Nauka.

—— (1962). *Vernye slugi monopolii*. Moscow: Profizdat.

—— (1952; 2nd ed. 1954). *Rasistskaia politika amerikanskogo imperializma*. Moscow: Gospolitizdat.

——, and Viktor Smelov (1978). *SShA: tainaia voina protiv inakomysliashchikh: dokumenty, ocherki*. Moscow: Novosti.

——, and Leonora A. Salycheva (eds.) (1978). *Massovye dvizheniia sotsial'nogo protesta v SShA (Semidesiatye gody)*. Moscow: Nauka.

——, and others (eds.) (1986). *Chernye amerkantsy v istorii SShA, tom vtoroi, 1917–1985*. Moscow: Mysl'.

Gerasimov, Gennadii I. (1984). *Obshchestvo potrebleniia: mify i real'nosti*. 2nd ed. revised. Moscow: Znanie.

German, V. M. (1972). "George S. McGovern." *SShA*, no. 9, 117–21.

Gershov, Z. (1983). *Vudro Vil'son*. Moscow: Mysl'.

Gibert, Stephen P. (1976). *Soviet Images of America*. New York: Crane, Russak.

Glagolev, I. (1960). "The Electoral Campaign in the USA." *Mirovaia ekonomika i mezhdunarodnye otnosheniia*, no. 10, 95–99.

Glagolev, N. N. (1980). "The Republicans and the Presidential Election of 1980." *SShA*, no. 7, 54–60.

—— (1975). "Washington: The New Appointments." *SShA*, no. 12, 40–51.

—— (1974). "Evolution of the Republican Party's Traditionalism." *SShA*, no. 9, 42–52.

Goncharova, A. V. (1973). *Vliianie nauchno-tekhnicheskoi revoliutsii na polozhenie rabochego klassa SShA*. Moscow: Izdatel'stvo Moskovskogo universiteta.

Gorbachev, Mikhail S. (1989). "Reformer Yeltsin Nominated to Supreme Soviet." *Reporter Dispatch* (White Plains, NY), May 26, A12, Associated Press dispatch.

—— (1987). *Perestroika: New Thinking for Our Country and the World*. New York: Harper and Row.

Graham, Loren (1987). *Science, Philosophy, and Human Behavior in the Soviet Union*. New York: Columbia University Press.

—— (1966). *Science and Philosophy in the Soviet Union*. New York: Random House.

Grant, Stephen A. (1980). "Soviet Americanists." Washington, D.C.: Office of Research, International Communication Agency of the United States. Research Report. February 15.

Great Soviet Encyclopedia (1973–1983). A translation of the 3rd ed. Mason L. Waxman (ed.). New York: Macmillan.

Grechukhin, Aleksei A. (1975). *Bor'ba kommunisticheskoi partii SShA za edinstvo v svoikh riadakh (1927–1972)*. Moscow: Mysl'.

————, and others (eds.) (1970). *Problemy sovremennogo profsoiuznogo dvizheniia SShA. Amerikanskaia federatsiia truda—kongress proizvodstvennykh profsoiuzov 1955–1967*. Moscow: Mysl'.

Greenberg, Edward S. (1989). *The American Political System: A Radical Approach*. 5th ed. Boston: Little, Brown.

Griffiths, Franklyn (1984). "The Sources of American Conduct: Soviet Perspectives and Their Policy Implications." *International Security*, 9, no. 2, 3–50.

———— (1972). "Images, Politics and Learning in Soviet Behaviour Toward the United States." Diss. Columbia University.

Gromakov, Boris S. (1958). *Ocherki po istorii antidemokraticheskogo zakonodatel'stva SShA*. Moscow: Gosiurizdat.

Gromyko, Anatolii A. (1973). *Through Russian Eyes: President Kennedy's 1036 Days*. Washington, D.C.: International Library.

———— (1968; 1971 reprint). *1036 dnei prezidenta Kennedi*. Moscow: Politizdat.

———— (1957). *Kongress SShA: vybory, organizatsiia, polnomochiia*. Moscow: Izdatel'stvo "Mezhdunarodnye otnosheniia."

————, and Andrei A. Kokoshin (1985). *Brat'ia Kennedi*. Moscow: Mysl'.

Gromyko, Andrei A. (1985). *The Overseas Expansion of Capital: Past and Present*. Moscow: Progress.

Guliev, Vladimir E. (1973). *Sovremennoe imperialisticheskoe gosudarstvo: voprosy teorii*. Moscow: Izdatel'stvo "Mezhdunarodnye otnosheniia."

———— (1970). *Demokratiia i sovremennyi imperializm. Ocherki teorii kapitalisticheskogo gosudarstva i politicheskoi organizatsii burzhuaznogo obshchestva*. Moscow: Izdatel'stvo "Mezhdunarodnye otnosheniia."

———— (1965). *Imperialisticheskoe gosudarstvo. Ocherk kritiki burzhuaznykh teorii*. Moscow: Izdatel'stvo Moskovskogo universiteta.

———— (1961). "The Groundlessness of Bourgeois Ideas Respecting 'Pluralist Democracy.'" *Sovetskoe gosudarstvo i pravo*, no. 8, 81–94.

————, and Eduard L. Kuz'min (1969). *Labirinty burzhuaznoi demokratii (Kriticheskii ocherk teorii i praktiki burzhuaznogo demokratizma)*. Moscow: Izdatel'stvo Moskovskogo universiteta.

Guroff, Gregory (1980). "Soviet Perceptions of the U.S.: Results of a Surrogate Interview Project." Washington, D.C.: International Communication Agency of the United States. Research Memorandum. June 27.

Gurvich, Esfir (1937). *Poslevoennaia Amerika*. Moscow: Gos. sots.-ek. izdat.

Gurvich, Georgii S. (1930). *Politicheskii stroi sovremennykh gosudarstv—SShA*. Moscow: Gosizd.

Gusev, Anatolii D. (1974). *SShA: krizis sotsial'noi politiki*. Minsk: "Belarus'."

Guseva, V. S. (1978). "The 95th Congress and Problems of Domestic and Foreign Policy." *SShA*, no. 1, 81–89.

Gustafson, Thane (1981). *Reform in Soviet Politics: Lessons of Recent Policies on Land and Water*. New York: Cambridge University Press.

Gutsenko, Konstantin F. (1961). *Sudebnaia sistema SShA i ee klassovaia sushchnost'*. Moscow: Iuridicheskaia literatura.

Guttsait, Mikhail G. (1961). *Khronicheskaia bezrabotitsa i nedogruzka predpriiatii SShA*. Moscow: Izd. sots.-ek. lit.

Gvishiani, Dzherman M. (1962). *Sotsiologiia biznessa. Kriticheskii ocherk amerikanskoi teorii menedzhmenta*. Moscow: Izd. sotsial'no-ek. lit.

——, and N. I. Lapina (eds.) (1988). *Kratkii slovar' po sotsiologii*. Moscow: Politizdat.

Hamilton, Richard F. (1972). *Class and Politics in the United States*. New York: Wiley.

Hasty, Olga Peters, and Susanne Fusso (eds.) (1988). *America Through Russian Eyes*. New Haven: Yale University Press.

Hedberg, Bo (1981). "How Organizations Learn and Unlearn." In Paul C. Nystrom and William H. Starbuck (eds.), *Handbook of Organizational Design*, vol. I. *Adapting Organizations to their Environments*. New York: Oxford University Press, 3–27.

Hill, Ronald J. (1980). *Soviet Politics, Political Science and Reform*. Oxford: Martin Robertson.

Hough, Jerry F. (1986). *The Struggle for the Third World: Soviet Debates and American Options*. Washington, D.C.: Brookings.

Huber, Robert T. (1988). *Soviet Perceptions of the U.S. Congress: The Impact on Superpower Relations*. Boulder, Colo.: Westview Press.

Iakovlev, Aleksandr N. (1985). *On the Edge of an Abyss: From Truman to Reagan. The Doctrines and Realities of the Nuclear Age*. Moscow: Progress Publishers.

—— (1984). *Ot Trumena do Reigana: doktriny i real'nosti iadernogo veka*. Moscow: Molodaia gvardiia.

—— (ed.) (1969). *SShA: ot "velikogo" k bol'nomu*. Moscow: Izdatel'stvo politicheskoi literatury.

Iakovlev, Nikolai N. (1983). *Siluety Vashingtona. Politicheskie ocherki*. Moscow: Izdatel'stvo politicheskoi literatury.

—— (1973). *Vashington*. Moscow: Molodaia gvardiia.

—— (1970). *Prestupivshie gran': O politicheskikh deiateliakh SShA V. Vil'son, D. Kennedi i R. Kennedi.* Moscow: Izdatel'stvo "Mezhdunarodnye otnosheniia."

—— (1965; 2nd ed. 1969). *Franklin Ruzvel't: chelovek i politik.* Moscow: Izdatel'stvo "Mezhdunarodnye otnosheniia."

—— (ed.) (1976). *SShA: Politicheskaia mysl' i istoriia. Kriticheskii analiz osnovnykh doktrin i kontseptsii za 200-letnii period.* Moscow: Nauka.

Iaz'kov, E. F. (ed.) (1988). *Problemy amerikanistiki. Vypusk 6. Sovremennyi etap krizisa GMK v SShA: ekonomika, politika, ideologiia.* Moscow: Izdatel'stvo Moskovskogo universiteta.

Il'in, Viktor I. (1983). *Burzhuaznyi pliuralizm: istoki i klassovoi smysl.* Moscow: Mysl'.

Inozemtsev, Nikolai N., and others (eds.) (1976). *Uglublenie obshchego krizisa kapitalizma.* Moscow: Mysl'.

Iulina, Nina S. (1971). *Burzhuaznye ideologicheskie techeniia v SShA.* Moscow: Nauka.

Iur'ev, Iu. (1961). "Lobbying: Bribery Under the Protection of the Law." *Mirovaia ekonomika i mezhdunarodnye otnosheniia*, no. 8, 119–27.

Ivanian, Eduard (1975). *Belyi dom: prezidenty i politika.* Moscow: Izdatel'stvo politicheskoi literatury.

Ivanov, Iurii A. (1982). *Kongress SShA i vneshniaia politika. Vozmozhnosti i metody vliianiia.* Moscow: Nauka.

—— (1964). *Avraam Linkol'n i grazhdanskaia voina v SShA.* Moscow: Nauka.

Ivanov, Robert F. (1984). *Duait Eizenkhauer.* Moscow: Mysl'.'

Izakov, V. A. (1972). "The Limits of the President's Power." *SShA*, no. 9, 89–94.

Iziumov, Aleksei I., and Vladimir V. Popov (1988). "Regarding the Question of 'Long Waves' in the American Economy." *SShA*, no. 4, 3–12.

Jackman, Mary R., and Robert V. Jackman (1983). *Class Awareness in the United States.* Berkeley: University of California Press.

Jervis, Robert (1976). *Perception and Misperception in International Politics.* Princeton: Princeton University Press.

Jones, Charles O. (1977). *An Introduction to the Study of Public Policy.* 2nd ed. North Scituate, Mass.: Duxbury Press.

Joravsky, David (1983). "The Stalinist Mentality and the Higher Learning." *Slavic Review*, 42, no. 4, 575–600.

—— (1970). *The Lysenko Affair.* Cambridge, Mass.: Harvard University Press.

Kalenskii, Valerii G. (1983). *Bill' o pravakh v konstitutsionnoi istorii SShA (Istoriko-kriticheskoe issledovanie).* Moscow: Nauka.

—— (1981). *Medison.* Moscow: Iuridicheskaia literatura.

—— (1977). *Gosudarstvo kak ob"ekt sotsiologicheskogo analiza.* Moscow: Iuridicheskaia literatura.

—— (1969). *Politicheskaia nauka v SShA. Kritika burzhuaznykh kontseptsii vlasti.* Moscow: Iuridicheskaia literatura.

Kassirova, Evgeniia P. (1978). *SShA: krizis sotsial'noi politiki (Gosudarstvo i sotsial'noe obespechenie).* Moscow: Mysl'.

Kats, Adol'f I. (1962). *Polozhenie proletariata SShA pri imperializme.* Moscow: Izdatel'stvo AN SSSR.

Kedrenovskaia, Ia. N. (1978). *Review of Three American Enterprise Institute Reports. SShA,* no. 9, 111–13.

Keenan, Edward L. (1979). "The Correspondence of Two Corners." *Studies in Soviet Thought,* 19, no. 4, 276–83.

Keller, Bill (1989). "Moscow's Other Mastermind: Aleksandr Yakovlev, Gorbachev's Little-Known Alter Ego." *New York Times Magazine,* February 19.

Keremetskii, Ia. N. (1970). *SShA: profsoiuzy v bor'be s kapitalom.* Moscow: Nauka.

Kerimov, D. A., and N. M. Keizerov (1972). "The Untenability of Bourgeois Concepts of Democracy." *Sovetskoe gosudarstvo i pravo,* no. 1, 20–29.

Kerimov, D. A. (ed.) (1984). *Politicheskie nauki i politicheskaia praktika.* Moscow: Nauka.

Kernig, Claus D. (ed.) (1972). *Marxism, Communism and the West: A Comparative Encyclopedia.* New York: Herder and Herder.

Khromushin, Gennadii B. (1969). *Razveiannye mify. Kritika doktriny "amerikanskoi iskliuchitel'nosti".* Moscow: Izdatel'stvo "Mezhdunarodnye otnosheniia."

Kislov, A. (1961). "The Composition of the New U.S. Congress." *Mirovaia ekonomika i mezhdunarodnye otnosheniia,* no. 3, 132–35.

Knoke, David (1981). "Power Structures." In Long (ed.) (1981), 275–332.

Kokoshin, Andrei A. (1982). *SShA: krizis politicheskoi vlasti.* Moscow: Izdatel'stvo iuridicheskoi literatury.

—— (1981). *SShA: za fasadom global'noi politiki.* Moscow: Izdatel'stvo politicheskoi literatury.

——, and others (1983). "Problems of Presidential Power." *SShA,* no. 12, 112–19.

Kolesnichenko, Tomas (1988). "The World This Week." *Pravda,* September 11.

Kondrashov, Stanislav (1981). *The Life and Death of Martin Luther King.* Moscow: Progress Publishers.

Kondratenko, Vera M. (1986). *Pod maskoi ob"ektivnosti: "N'iu Iork Taims": amerikanskaia informatsionno-propagandistskaia mashina.* Moscow: Mysl'.

Konstantinov, V. F., and others (1974). *The Fundamentals of Marxist–Leninist Philosophy.* Moscow: Progress Publishers.

————, and others (eds.) (1960–1970). *Filosofskaia entsiklopediia.* Moscow: Sovetskaia entsiklopediia.

Kornilov, Iurii, and Gennadii A. Shishkin (1986). *Kto pravit Amerikoi. Voenno-promyshlennyi kompleks SShA.* Moscow: Politizdat.

Koroleva, Alina P. (1967). *20 millionov protiv Dzhima Krou (Negritianskoe dvizhenie v SShA na sovremennom etape).* Moscow: Mysl'.

Kortunov, A., and A. Nikitin (1985). *The "American Model" on the Scales of History.* Moscow: Progress Publishers.

Kovalev, Aleksandr M. (1974). *Soderzhanie i zakonomernosti mirovogo revoliutsionnogo protsessa.* Moscow: Izdatel'stvo Moskovskogo universiteta.

Kovaleva, Melaniia F. (1969). *K voprosam metodologii politicheskoi ekonomii kapitalizma.* Moscow: Mysl'.

Kovler, Anatolii I., and Vil'iam V. Smirnov (1986). *Demokratiia i uchastie v politike. Kriticheskie ocherki istorii i teorii.* Moscow: Nauka.

Kozlova, Kama B. (1966). *Monopolii i ikh burzhuaznye kritiki. Ob ekonomicheskikh vzgliadakh ideologov nemonopolisticheskoi burzhuazii.* Moscow: Nauka.

Krasin, Iu. (1985). *The Contemporary Revolutionary Process: Theoretical Essays.* Moscow: Progress Publishers.

Krylov, Boris S. (1968). *SShA: federalizm, shtaty i mestnoe upravlenie.* Moscow: Nauka.

Kryuchkov, Vladimir A. (1989). Quoted in *New York Times*, June 2, A1.

Kuhn, Thomas S. (1979). *The Structure of Scientific Revolutions.* 2nd ed. Chicago: University of Chicago Press.

———— (1977). *The Essential Tension: Selected Studies in Scientific Tradition and Change.* Chicago: University of Chicago Press.

Kulikov, Aleksandr G. (1969). *General'nye shtaby monopolii. Soiuzy predprinimatelei v sisteme gosudarstvenno-monopolisticheskogo kapitalizma.* Moscow: Mysl'.

Kuz'min, Eduard L. (1977). *Ideinoe bankrotstvo burzhuaznoi demokratii. Voprosy demokratii v politiko-pravovoi doktrine imperializma.* Moscow: Izdatel'stvo "Mezhdunarodnye otnosheniia."

———— (1970). "Bourgeois Democracy: Crisis of Institutions, Barrenness of Doctrines." *Sovetskoe gosudarstvo i pravo*, no. 9, 75–92.

Kuz'min, Gennadii M. (1974). *Voenno-promyshlennye kontserny*. Moscow: Mysl'.

Kuz'minov, Ivan T. (1960). *Obnishchanie trudiashchikhsia pri kapitalizme*. Moscow: Akademiia obshchestvennykh nauk pri TsK KPSS.

―――― (1955). *Gosudarstvenno-monopolisticheskii kapitalizm*. Moscow: Gospolitizdat.

Laird, Robbin F., and Eric P. Hoffmann (eds.) (1986). *Soviet Foreign Policy in a Changing World*. Hawthorne, N.Y.: Aldine.

Lakatos, Imre, and Alan Musgrave (eds.) (1964). *Criticism and the Growth of Knowledge (Proceedings of the International Colloquium on the Philosophy of Science)*. New York: Cambridge University Press.

Lan, Veniamin I. (1967). "Novaia ekonomika SShA." *Mirovaia ekonomika i mezhdunarodnye otnosheniia*, no. 1, 103–14.

―――― (1933). "Ruzvel't u vlasti." *Mirovoe khoziaistvo i mirovaia politika*, no. 8, 3–24.

―――― (1932; 2nd ed. 1937). *Klassy i partii v SShA. Ocherki po ekonomicheskoi i politicheskoi istorii SShA*. Moscow: Gosudarstvennoe sotsial'no-ekonomicheskoe izdatel'stvo.

―――――, and others (eds.) (1966). *Politicheskaia zhizn' v SShA. Problemy vnutrennei politiki*. Moscow: Nauka.

Lapitskii, M. (1981). "The Unions and Elections." *SShA*, no. 3, 65–71.

―――― (1973). *SShA: rol' profsoiuzov vo vnutripoliticheskoi zhizni. Vtoraia polovina 60-kh—nachalo 70-kh godov*. Moscow: Nauka.

Lau, Richard R., and David O. Sears (eds.) (1986). *Political Cognition*. Hillsdale, N.J.: Lawrence Erlbaum Associates.

Lebedev, I. V. (1974). "On the Threshold of the Elections." *SShA*, no. 6, 59–67.

Leibin, Valerii M. (1976). *Filosofiia sotsial'nogo krititsizma v SShA*. Moscow: Nauka.

Lemin, I. (ed.) (1965). *Dvizhushchie sily vneshnei politiki SShA*. Moscow: Nauka.

Lenczowski, John (1982). *Soviet Perceptions of U.S. Foreign Policy: A Study of Ideology, Power and Consensus*. Ithaca, N.Y.: Cornell University Press.

Lenin, Vladimir I. (1958–1965). *Polnoe sobranie sochinenii*. 55 vols. 5th ed. Moscow: Gosudarstvennoe izdatel'stvo politicheskoi literatury.

Levchenko, Iu. S. (1981). "Toward a Summation of the 96th Session of Congress." *SShA*, no. 1, 75–79.

Levchenko, Stanislav (1982). "Unmasking Moscow's 'Institute of the U.S.A.'." *Heritage Foundation Backgrounder*, no. 234, December 17.

Levin, Iosif D. (1951). *Krakh burzhuaznoi demokratii i sovremennoe go-*

sudarstvennoe pravo kapitalisticheskikh stran. Vypusk I. SShA.
Moscow: Izdatel'stvo AN SSSR.
—— (ed.) (1964a). *Konstitutsionnyi mekhanizm diktatury monopolii.*
Moscow: Nauka.
—— (ed.) (1964b). *Partii v sisteme diktatury monopolii.* Moscow:
Nauka.
——, and V. A. Tumanov (eds.) (1974). *Politicheskii mekhanizm dik-*
tatury monopolii. Moscow: Nauka.
——, and V. A. Tumanov (eds.) (1972). *Ideologicheskaia deiatel'nost'*
sovremennogo imperialisticheskogo gosudarstva. Moscow: Nauka.
Levine, Norman (1975). *The Tragic Deception: Marx Contra Engels.* Santa
Barbara, Calif.: Clio Books.
Lewis, Flora (1987). "Moscow Still Believes." *New York Times,* April
10, A35.
Likhacheva, Irina V. (1975). *SShA: ekonomicheskaia nauka i ekonomi-*
cheskaia politika. Sovet ekonomicheskikh konsul'tantov pri prezi-
dente. Moscow: Nauka.
—— (1971). "The Origins of U.S. Postwar Economic Policy (A Contribution Toward the History of the Adoption of the Employment
Act of 1946)." *Novaia i noveishaia istoriia,* no. 4, 107–16.
Lindblom, Charles E. (1977). *Politics and Markets: The World's Political–*
Economic Systems. New York: Basic Books.
Linnik, V. A. (1974). "The Results of the Local Elections." *SShA,* no.
3, 86–89.
——, and V. A. Savel'ev (1975). "John Sparkman." *SShA,* no. 5,
124–27.
Liven', Valentina A. (1975). *Profsoiuzy SShA i sotsial'naia politika prav-*
itel'stva. Kiev: Naukova dumka.
Long, Samuel L. (ed.) (1981). *The Handbook of Political Behavior,* vol.
2. New York: Plenum.
Losev, Sergei A. and Vitalii V. Petrusenko (1987). *Zapadnia na Poto-*
make. Pod''em i padenie Richarda M. Niksona. Dokumental'naia
povest'. Moscow: Izdatel'stvo Agenstva pechati Novosti.
Lubrano, Linda L., and Susan Gross Solomon (eds.) (1980). *The Social*
Context of Social Science. Boulder, Colo.: Westview Press.
Lunts, L. A. (1948). *Sud Soedinennykh shtatov Ameriki na sluzhbe mon-*
opolisticheskogo kapitala. Moscow: Gosiurizdat.
Luzik, Kirill S. (1976). *Nauchno-tekhnicheskaia revoliutsiia i polozhenie*
rasovykh men'shinstv. Kiev: Vyshcha shkola.
—— (1960). *Polozhenie negrov v SShA (1950–1960).* Kiev: Izdatel'stvo
Kievskogo universiteta.

Malcom, Neil (1984). *Soviet Political Scientists and American Politics*. New York: St. Martin's.

—— (1982). "Soviet Interpretations of American Politics: A Case for Convergence." *British Journal of Political Science*, 12, part 1 (January), 43–73.

Mal'kov, Viktor L. (1973). *Novyi kurs v SShA. Sotsial'nye dvizheniia i sotsial'naia politika*. Moscow: Nauka.

——, and Dzhakhangi Nadzhafov (1967). *Amerika na pereput'e*. Moscow: Nauka.

Mamaev, Vladimir A. (1962). *Reglament kongressa SShA*. Moscow: Izdatel'stvo Akademii nauk.

Manley, John F. (1983). "Neo-Pluralism: A Class Analysis of Pluralism I and Pluralism II." *American Political Science Review*, 77, no. 2, 368–83.

Manykin, A. S. (1978). "Evolution of the Organizational Structure of the Bourgeois Parties." *SShA*, no. 10, 41–45.

——, and I. V. Sivachev (1978). "The Two-Party System in the USA: Past and Present (Some Problems of Research Methodology)." *Novaia i noveishaia istoriia*, no. 3, 18–38.

Marchenko, Mikhail N. (1985). *Ocherki teorii politicheskoi sistemy sovremennogo burzhuaznogo obshchestva*. Moscow: Izdatel'stvo Moskovskogo universiteta.

Marinin, Sergei B. (pseud. of Sergei B. Chetverikov) (1967a). *SShA: politika i upravlenie (Federal'nyi pravitel'stvennyi apparat)*. Moscow: Izdatel'stvo "Mezhdunarodnye otnosheniia."

—— (1967b). "The Mechanism of Relations Between President and Congress." *Sovetskoe gosudarstvo i pravo*, no. 8, 121–25.

Mel'nikov, Anatolii N. (1987). *Amerikantsy: sotsial'nyi portret*. Moscow: Mysl'.

—— (1974). *Sovremennaia klassovaia struktura SShA*. Moscow: Mysl'.

Mel'vil', Andrei Iu. (1986). *SShA—sdvig vpravo? Konservatizm v ideino-politicheskoi zhizni SShA 80-kh godov*. Moscow: Nauka.

—— (1981). "Conservatism and Shifts in Social Awareness." *SShA*, no. 10, 26–37.

—— (1980). *Sotsial'naia filosofia sovremennogo amerikanskogo konservatizma*. Moscow: Politizdat.

Men'shikov, S. (1986). "Dialektika krizisa." *Pravda*, January 3.

Men'shikov, Stanislav M. (1981). *Sovremennyi kapitalizm: ot krizisa k krizisu. Analiz novoi fazy uglubleniia obshchego krizisa kapitalizma*. Moscow: Mysl'.

—— (1969). *Millionaires and Managers*. Moscow: Progress.

—— (1964). "The Johnson Government and U.S. Political Problems." *Mirovaia ekonomika i mezhdunarodnye otnosheniia*, no. 6, 26–39.

—— (ed.) (1964). *Ekonomicheskaia politika pravitel'stva Kennedi (1961–1963)*. Moscow: Mysl'.

Meyer, Alfred G. (1985). "Assessing the Ideological Commitment of a Regime." In Nogee (ed.) (1985), 112.

Mickiewicz, Ellen (1988). *Split Signals: Television and Politics in the Soviet Union*. New York: Oxford University Press.

Mikhailov, Boris Ia. (ed.) (1970, 1971). *Istoriia rabochego dvizheniia v SShA v noveishee vremia 1918–1965*. 2 vols. Moscow: Nauka.

Mikhailov, Boris V. (1983). *Sovremennyi amerikanskii liberalizm: ideologiia i politika*. Moscow: Nauka.

Mikhailov, Evgenii D. (1973). *SShA: problemy bol'shikh gorodov*. Moscow: Nauka.

Mikhailov, Sergei V. (1988). *Rabochii klass SShA i Velikobritanii v 80-e gody: sotsial'nye posledstviia tekhnologicheskoi perestroiki v usloviiakh kapitalizma*. Moscow: Nauka.

Mills, C. Wright (1956). *The Power Elite*. New York: Oxford University Press.

Mills, Richard M. (1981). "The Soviet Leadership Problem." *World Politics*, 33, no. 4, 590–613.

—— (1975). "Soviet Studies of American Politics." *Presidential Studies Quarterly*, 5, no. 1, 80–85.

—— (1972). "One Theory in Search of Reality: The Development of United States Studies in the Soviet Union." *Political Science Quarterly*, 87, no. 1, 63–79.

Mintz, Morton, and Jerry S. Cohen (1971). *America Inc.: Who Owns and Operates the United States*. New York: Dial Press.

Mishin, Avgust A. (1984). *Printsip razdeleniia vlastei v konstitutsionnom mekhanizme SShA*. Moscow: Nauka.

—— (1976). *Gosudarstvennoe pravo SShA*. Moscow: Nauka

—— (1972). *Tsentral'nye organy vlasti burzhuaznykh gosudarstv*. Moscow: Izdatel'stvo Moskovskogo universiteta.

—— (1958a). *Gosudarstvennyi stroi SShA*. Moscow: Izdatel'stvo iuridicheskoi literatury.

—— (1958b). "The Two Party System in the USA." *Mezhdunarodnaia ekonomika i mezhdunarodnye otnosheniia*, no. 10, 123–29.

—— (1954). *Tsentral'nye organy vlasti SShA—orudie diktatury monopolisticheskogo kapitala*. Moscow: Gos. izd. iurid. lit.

——, and Vasilii A. Vlasikhin (1985). *Konstitutsiia SShA: Politiko-pravovoi kommentarii*. Moscow: "Mezhdunarodnye otnosheniia."

Mitrokhin, Lev N. (1974). *Negritianskoe dvizhenie v SShA: ideologiia i praktika*. Moscow: Mysl'.

Mkrtchian, A. (1973). *U.S. Labor Unions Today. Basic Problems and Trends*. Moscow: Progress.

Morishima, Michio (1973). *Marx's Economics: A Dual Theory of Value and Growth*. New York: Cambridge University Press.

Moroz, Viktor N. (1971). *Demokraticheskaia partiia i rabochii klass SShA*. Kiev: Izdatel'stvo Kievskogo universiteta.

Mostovets, N. V., and others (eds.) (1972). *SShA: sotsial'no- politicheskii krizis, problemy rabochego i demokraticheskogo dvizheniia*. Moscow: Nauka.

Mshvenieradze, V. (1985). *Political Reality and Political Consciousness*. Moscow: Progress Publishers.

Murashev, Arkadii N. (1989). Quoted in *New York Times*, March 29, A12.

N. V. (1971a). "Checks and Balances." *SShA*, no. 5, 127.

—— (1971b). "The Separation of Powers." *SShA*, no. 5, 127.

Nazarevskii, V. A. (ed.) (1984). *SShA: gosudarstvo i korporatsii v epokhu NTR*. Moscow: Nauka.

Nikiforov, Aleksandr S. (1973). "The USA: Reform of Voting Qualifications and the Presidential Election of 1972." *Sovetskoe gosudarstvo i pravo*, no. 11, 99–105.

—— (1972). "The Legal Specifics of Presidential Power." *SShA*, no. 8, 19–29.

—— (ed.) (1976). *Gosudarstvennyi stroi SShA*. Moscow: Izdatel'stvo iuridicheskoi literatury.

Nikiforov, B. S. (1972). "A Majority Is Sufficient (The U.S. Supreme Court on the Unanimity of Jurors)." *SShA*, no. 10, 59–62.

Nikiforov, Boris S. (1978). "The U.S. Supreme Court: A Move to the Right." *Sovetskoe gosudarstvo i pravo*, no. 5, 107–13.

—— (1971). "The U. S. Supreme Court: From Earl Warren to Warren Burger." *SShA*, no. 6, 42–51.

—— (ed.) (1972). *SShA: prestupnost' i politika*. Moscow: Mysl'.

Nikitin, Vyacheslav A. (1981). *The Ultras in the USA*. Moscow: Progress Publishers.

—— (1971). *SShA: pravyi ekstremizm—ugroza demokratii*. Moscow: Mysl'.

Nikonov, Viacheslav A. (1984). *Ot Eizenkhauera K Niksonu. Iz istorii respublikanskoi partii SShA*. Moscow: Izdatel'stvo Moskovskogo universiteta.

Nitoburg, Eduard L. (1971). *Chernye getto Ameriki*. Moscow: Politizdat.

Nogee, Joseph L. (ed.) (1985). *Soviet Politics: Russia After Brezhnev*. New York: Praeger.

Nordahl, Richard A. (1972). "The Soviet Model of Monopoly Capitalist Politics." Diss. Princeton University.

Noritskii, A. (1936a). "Roosevelt's Victory." *Mirovoe khoziaistvo i mirovaia politika*, no. 12, 35–45.

——— (1936b). "The Presidential Elections in the United States." *Mirovoe khoziaistvo i mirovaia politika*, no. 8, 4–22.

Novikov, A. V. (1974). *Pravovye formy organizatsii gosudarstvennoi sluzhby v SShA*. Moscow: "Iuridicheskaia literatura."

——— (1970). "Forming the Top Management of the State Apparatus of the USA." *Sovetskoe gosudarstvo i pravo*, no. 11, 127–32.

Novikova, Elvira E. (1975). *Trudiashchiesia zhenshchiny sovremennoi Ameriki*. Moscow: Mysl'.

Novikova, Faina A. (1961). *Finansovye gruppy SShA i metody ikh gospodstva*. Moscow: Vysshaia shkola.

Novinskaia, Maia A. (1977). *Studenchestvo SShA: sotsial'no-psikhologicheskii ocherk*. Moscow: Nauka.

Okinshevich, Leo (1976). *U.S. History and Historiography in Postwar Soviet Writings, 1945–1970*. Santa Barbara, Calif.: ABC Clio Press.

Oleshchuk, Iurii F. (1987). *Evoliutsiia sotsial'noi politiki SShA v 60–70-e gody*. Moscow: Nauka.

Ollman, Bertell (1976). *Alienation: Marx's Conception of Man in Capitalist Society*. New York: Cambridge University Press.

Ossowski, Stanislaw (1963). *Class Structure in the Social Consciousness*. New York: Free Press of Glencoe.

Ozhiganov, E. (1979). "The Theory of Democracy in Contemporary Bourgeois Political Science." *SShA*, no. 1, 85–88.

Parenti, Michael (1980). *Democracy for the Few*. 3rd ed. New York: St. Martin's.

——— (1978). *Power and the Powerless*. New York: St. Martin's.

——— (1977). *Democracy for the Few*. 2nd ed. New York: St. Martin's.

Parkin, Frank (1979). *Marxism and Class Theory: A Bourgeois Critique*. New York: Columbia University Press.

Patterson, C. Perry (1947). *Presidential Government in the United States: The Unwritten Constitution*. Chapel Hill: University of North Carolina Press.

Pavlov, Vladimir P. (1963). *K teorii "klassovogo mira" v SShA*. Moscow: Izd-vo. sotsial'no-ekon. lit-y.

Pechatnov, Vladimir O. (1983). "The Mid-term Elections: Results and Prospects." *SShA*, no. 1, 29–37.

References 291

───── (1982). "The Two Party System and Elections." *SShA*, no. 9, 22–32.

───── (1981). "The Democrats in Search of a New Image." *SShA*, no. 7, 27–39.

───── (1980a). *Demokraticheskaia partiia SShA: izbirateli i politika.* Moscow: Nauka.

───── (1980b). "What the Elections Showed." *SShA*, no. 1, 47–51.

───── (1978). 'On the 'Crisis of Power'." *SShA*, no. 3, 6–18.

───── (1975). "The Battle over the Reform of the Democratic Party." *SShA*, no. 3, 65–70.

───── (1973). "The Democrats: A Return to the Past?" *SShA*, no. 4, 52–62.

Peregudov, S. P. (ed.) (1984). *Sovremennyi kapitalizm: politicheskie otnosheniia i instituty vlasti.* Moscow: Nauka.

Petrov, I. I. (1978). "'The Lance Affair': The Latest Scandal in Washington." *SShA*, no. 1, 59–64.

Petrovskaia, Mira M. (1982). *SShA: politika skvoz' prizmu oprosov. Istoriia oprosa obshchestvennogo mneniia SShA.* Moscow: Izdatel'stvo "Mezhdunarodnye otnosheniia."

───── (1977). *Obshchestvennoe mnenie SShA: oprosy i politika.* Moscow: Izdatel'stvo "Mezhdunarodnye otnosheniia."

Petrovskii, Viktor E. (1967). *Sud Lincha (Ocherk istorii terrorizma i neterpimosti v SShA.* Moscow: Izdatel'stvo "Mezhdunarodnye otnosheniia."

Petrusenko, V. V. (1970). "The Approaching Elections and the Worsening of the Internal Political Situation." *SShA*, no. 7, 3–16.

Piadyshev, Boris S. (1974). *Voenno-promyshlennyi kompleks SShA.* Moscow: Voennoe izd-vo. Min. Oborony SSSR.

Plekhanov, S. M. (1979). "The Shift to the Right—Apparent and Real." *SShA*, no. 12, 13–26.

───── (ed.) (1988). *SShA: gosudarstvo i sotsial'naia politika. K analizu konservativnykh tendentsii 80-kh godov.* Moscow: Nauka.

───── (ed.) (1985). *Kak delaetsia prezident.* Moscow: Progress Publishers.

Pletnev, E. (1986). "Obshchii krizis kapitalizma i ego uglublenie." *Pravda,* June 6.

Poduzov, A. A. (1984). *Faktory i tempy ekonomicheskogo rosta SShA: analiz dolgosrochnykh tendentsii.* Moscow: Nauka.

Popov, Aleksei A. (1974). *SShA: gosudarstvo i profsoiuzy.* Moscow: Nauka.

───── (1972). "The American Unions Before the Elections." *SShA*, no. 11, 7–14.

Popov, N. P. (1980). "On the Results of the Election Campaign." *SShA*, no. 11, 62–67.

——— (1976). "The Election Campaign and Public Opinion." *SShA*, no. 9, 55–57.

Popov, Nikolai P. (1986). *Amerika 80-kh. Obshchestvennoe mnenie i sotsial'nye problemy*. Moscow: Mysl'.

——— (1981). *Politizatsiia massovogo soznanie v SShA*. Moscow: Nauka.

Popova, Evgeniia E. (1978). *Amerikanskii senat i vneshniaia politika, 1969–1974*. Moscow: Nauka.

Prewitt, Kenneth, and Alan Stone (1973). *The Ruling Elites: Elite Theory, Power and American Democracy*. New York: Harper and Row.

Prozorova, N. S. (1974). "The Theory of 'The Separation of Powers' and the Contemporary Bourgeois State." *Sovetskoe gosudarstvo i pravo*, no. 9, 92–98.

Puchinskii, Vasilii K. (1979). *Grazhdanskii protsess SShA*. Moscow: Nauka.

Raskin, A. P. (1976). *Soedinennye Shtaty Ameriki. Rekomendatel'nyi ukazatel' literatury*. Moscow: Kniga.

Remnek, Richard B. (ed.) (1977). *Social Scientists and Policy-Making in the USSR*. New York: Praeger.

Revunenkov, V. G. (ed.) (1967). *Problemy vseobshchei istorii*. Leningrad: Izdatel'stvo Leningradskogo universiteta.

Roemer, John E. (1982). *A General Theory of Exploitation and Class*. Cambridge, Mass.: Harvard University Press.

——— (1981). *Analytical Foundations of Marxian Economic Theory*. New York: Cambridge University Press.

Rogova, Galina V. (1983). *SShA: profsoiuzy i politicheskaia vlast'*. Moscow: Nauka.

Rohaytin, Felix (1987). "On the Edge of the Abyss." *SShA*, no. 9, 45–51. An abbreviated version of an article in *New York Review of Books*, June 11, 1987.

Rosovsky, Henry (1987). "Deaning." *Harvard Magazine*, 89, no. 3, 34–40.

Rothchild, Sylvia (1985). *A Special Legacy: An Oral History of the Soviet Jewish Emigrés in the United States*. New York: Simon and Schuster.

Rubinshtein, Modest I. (ed.) (1953). *Militarizatsiia ekonomiki SShA i ukhudshenie polozheniia trudiashchikhsia*. Moscow: Izdatel'stvo Akademii Nauk SSSR.

———, and others (eds.) (1958). *Monopolisticheskii kapital SShA posle Vtoroi mirovoi voiny*. Moscow: Izdatel'stvo AN SSSR.

Sakharov, N. A. (1980). *Predprinimatel'skie assotsiatsii v politicheskoi zhizni SShA*. Moscow: Nauka.

Salycheva, Leonora A. (ed.) (1974). *SShA: studenty i politika: amerikanskoe studenchestvo v demokraticheskoi bor'be v 60–70-e gody*. Moscow: Nauka.

Samuilov, Sergei M. (1989). "Prezidentskie krizisy: obshchee i osobennoe." *SShA*, no. 4, 23–32.

Savel'ev, Vladimir A. (1989). *Kapitolii SShA: proshloe i nastoiashchee*. Moscow: Mysl'.

————— (1986). *SShA: krizis zakonodatel'noi vlasti*. Moscow: Iuridicheskaia literatura.

————— (1980). "The Congress of the USA: Results of the Past Year." *SShA*, no. 3, 97–101.

————— (1977a). "New Leaders in the Houses of Congress: The Senate." *SShA*, no. 5, 68–73.

————— (1977b). "Changes in the U.S. Congress. The Senate: New Faces, Old Problems." *SShA*, no. 3, 79–81.

————— (1976a). *SShA: senat i politika*. Moscow: Mysl'.

————— (1976b). "The Congressional Staff." *SShA*, no. 3, 122–27.

————— (1973a). "The Senate and the Formation of the Political Course of the USA." *Sovetskoe gosudarstvo i pravo*, no. 12, 127–31.

————— (1973b). "The Socio-political Composition of the 93rd Congress." *SShA*, no. 10, 112–15.

————— (1971). Review of "The Irony of Democracy." *SShA*, no. 5, 88.

—————, and E. M. Silaeva (1977). "New Leaders in the Houses of Congress." *SShA*, no. 5, 69–77.

Scanlan, James P. (1985). *Marxism in the USSR: A Critical Survey of Soviet Thought*. Ithaca, N.Y.: Cornell University Press.

Schlesinger, R. J. (1949). "The Discussions on E. Varga's Book on Capitalist War Economy." *Soviet Studies*, no. 1 (June), 28–40.

Schwartz, Morton (1978). *Soviet Perspectives on the United States*. Berkeley: University of California Press.

————— (1966). "The 1964 Presidential Elections Through Soviet Eyes." *Western Political Quarterly*, 19, no. 4, 663–71.

Semenov, Vadim S. (1969). *Kapitalizm i klassy. Issledovanie sotsial'noi struktury sovremennogo kapitalisticheskogo obshchestva*. Moscow: Nauka.

Seregin, N. S. (1976). "The Election Law: Votes For and Against." *SShA*, no. 3, 94–98.

————— (1972). "Elections and Money." *SShA*, no. 2, 102–7.

Setunskii, N. K. (1981). *SShA: inakomyslie pod pritselom. Obshchestvo poprannykh prav*. Moscow: Politizdat.

Sevost'ianov, Grigorii N. (1981). "Some Results of Research by Soviet Historians-Americanists." *Novaia i noveishaia istoriia*, no. 1, 21–45.

———, and A. I. Utkin (1976). *Tomas Dzhefferson: portret ideologa amerikanskoi demokratii.* Moscow: Mysl'.

———, and others (eds.) (1960). *Ocherki novoi i noveishei istorii SShA.* 2 vols. Moscow: Izdatel'stvo AN SSSR.

Shabad, B. (1960). "An Apology for the Political System of Capitalism (On So-called 'Political Science' in Bourgeois Sociology)." *Kommunist*, no. 2 (January), 87–97.

Shakhnazarov, Georgii Kh. (1955). *Burzhuaznoe gosudarstvo v epokhu imperializma (Povorot ot demokratii k reaktsii).* Moscow: Gosiurizdat.

———, and Fedor M. Burlatskii (1980). "On the Development of Marxist–Leninist Political Science." *Voprosy filosofii*, no. 12, 10–23.

——— (ed.) (1985). *Contemporary Political Science in the USA and Western Europe.* Moscow: Progress Publishers.

——— (ed.) (1982). *Sovremennaia burzhuaznaia politicheskaia nauka: problemy gosudarstva i demokratii.* Moscow: Nauka.

Shamberg, V. (1969). "Domestic Political Dilemmas of the Nixon Administration." *Mirovaia ekonomika i mezhdunarodnye otnosheniia*, no. 7, 26–36.

——— (1968a). "The Election Battle in the USA." *Mirovaia ekonomika i mezhdunarodnye otnosheniia*, no. 9, 73–77.

——— (1968b). "On the Threshold of the Presidential Elections." *Mirovaia ekonomika i mezhdunarodnye otnosheniia*, no. 10, 91–97.

——— (1965). "The Elections in the USA: Some Results." *Mirovaia ekonomika i mezhdunarodnye otnosheniia*, no. 1, 60–69.

Shapiro, Anatolii I. (1970). *Prognozirovanie kapitalisticheskoi ekonomiki: problemy metodologii.* Moscow: Mysl'.

Shevchenko, Arkady N. (1985). *Breaking with Moscow.* New York: Knopf.

Shipler, David (1984). *Russia: Broken Idols, Solemn Dreams.* New York: Times Books.

Shishkin, G. A. (1976a). "After the Convention in Madison Square Garden." *SShA*, no. 9, 50–54.

——— (1976b). "The Republican Convention in Kemper Arena." *SShA*, no. 10, 59–64.

Shishkin, Petr A. (1972). *Klassovaia bor'ba v SShA 1955–1968 gg.* Moscow: Nauka.

Shkundin, M. Z. (1980). *K istorii gosudarstvenno- monopolisticheskoi sotsial'noi politiki SShA 1929–1939 gg.* Moscow: Nauka.

Shlapentokh, Vladimir (1986). *Soviet Public Opinion and Ideology: Mythology and Pragmatism in Interaction.* New York: Praeger.

Shneerson, Avraam I. (1961) *Gorodskie srednie sloi pri kapitalizme.* Moscow: VPSh pri AON.

—— (1956). *Podchinenie burzhuaznogo gosudarstva monopoliiam.* Moscow: Izdatel'stvo. Akademii Nauk SSSR.

Shubin, Vladimir A. (1978). *Politicheskaia sistema gosudarstvenno-monopolisticheskogo kapitalizma i ee krizis.* Leningrad: Izdatel'stvo Leningradskogo universiteta.

Shulman, Marshall (1963). *Stalin's Foreign Policy Reappraised.* Cambridge, Mass.: Harvard University Press.

Silaeva, E. M. (1981). "Congress After the Elections." *SShA*, no. 1, 56–60.

—— (1978). "The Social Composition of Congress." *SShA*, no. 8, 88–92.

—— (1977). "Changes in the U.S. Congress. The House of Representatives: Strengthening of the Liberal Wing." *SShA*, no. 3, 81–86.

Simirenko, Alex (ed.) (1969). *Social Thought in the Soviet Union.* Chicago: Quadrangle Books.

Sivachev, Nikolai V. (1972). *Pravovoe regulirovanie trudovykh otnoshenii v SShA.* Moscow: Iuridicheskaia literatura.

—— (1966). *Politicheskaia bor'ba v SShA v seredine 30-kh godov XX veka.* Moscow: Izdatel'stvo Moskovskogo universiteta.

—— (1964). "The Defeat of Extreme Reaction in the Presidential Elections in the USA in 1936." *Novaia i noveishaia istoriia*, no. 2, 65–78.

—— (ed.) (1982). *Politicheskie partii SShA v noveishee vremia.* Moscow: Izdatel'stvo Moskovskogo universiteta.

—— (ed.) (1981). *Politicheskie partii SShA v novoe vremia.* Moscow: Izdatel'stvo Moskovskogo universiteta.

Sivachyov [Sivachev], Nikolai V., and E. F. Yazkov [Iazkov] (1976). *History of the USA Since World War II.* Moscow: Progress Publishers.

Skilling, H. Gordon, and Franklyn Griffiths (eds.) (1971). *Interest Groups in Soviet Politics.* Princeton: Princeton University Press.

Slavin, Lev M. (1967). *Imperialisticheskoe gosudarstvo i revoliutsionnyi protsess.* Alma-Ata: Kazakhstan.

Solomatina, V. M. (1972). "The Limits of Congress's Foreign Policy Powers." *SShA*, no. 3, 87–91.

Solomon, Susan Gross (ed.) (1983). *Pluralism in the Soviet Union: Essays in Honour of H. Gordon Skilling.* London: Macmillan.

Sonnenfeldt, Helmut, and William G. Hyland (1986). "Soviet Perspectives on Security." In Laird and Hoffmann (1986), 219–45.

Sorko, Oleg S. (1975). "The Deepening of the General Crisis of Capitalism After the Second World War." *Novaia i noveishaia istoriia*, no. 3, 115–28.

Sukhoi, V. (1988a). "Is Everything Going Normally for Bush?" *Pravda*, November 9.

——— (1988b). "The Bentsen–Quayle Teledebates." *Pravda*, October 7.

Szymanski, Albert (1983). *Class Structure: A Critical Perspective*. New York: Praeger.

Terekhov, Viktor I. (1984). *Respublikantsy u vlasti: sotsial'no-ekonomicheskaia politika pravitel'stva D. Eizenkhauera (1953–1960)*. Moscow: Izdatel'stvo Moskovskogo universiteta.

Timofeev, Timur T. (1986). "Obshchii krizis kapitalizma i nekotorye voprosy ideologicheskoi bor'by." *SShA*, no. 1 (January), 3–11.

——— (1967). *Proletariat protiv monopolii. Ocherki po problemam klassovoi bor'by i obshchedemokraticheskikh dvizhenii v SShA*. Moscow: Profizdat.

——— (1957). *Negry SShA v bor'be za svobodu. Negritianskoe dvizhenie v SSha posle II mirovoi voiny*. Moscow: Gospolitizdat.

Trepelkov, V. (1983). *General Crisis of Capitalism*. Moscow: Progress Publishers.

Trofimenko, G. (1959). "The USA: The Political Course and the Domestic Struggle." *Mirovaia ekonomika i mezhdunarodnye otnosheniia*, no. 4, 54–67.

Tsagolov, Georgii N. (1986). *Milliardy na oruzhie. Voenno- promyshlennyi kompleks SShA*. 2nd ed. Moscow: Mysl'.

——— (1985). *War Is Their Business: The U.S. Military–Industrial Complex*. Moscow: Progress Publishers.

——— (1968). *Milliardery iz provintsii (Novye gruppirovki finansovoi oligarkhii SShA)*. Moscow: Mysl'.

Tucker, Robert C. (ed.) (1978). *The Marx–Engels Reader*. 2nd ed. New York: W. W. Norton.

Tumanov, Vladimir A. (ed.) (1967). *Sovremennye burzhuaznye ucheniia o kapitalisticheskom gosudarstve*. Moscow: Nauka.

——— (1963). "What Is Hidden Behind the Slogan 'The Rule of Law'?" *Sovetskoe gosudarstvo i pravo*, no. 9, 50–61.

Urlanis, Boris Ts. (1964). *Dinamika i struktura naseleniia SSSR i SShA*. Moscow: Nauka.

The U.S. Two-Party System: Past and Present. A View by Soviet Historians. (1988). Moscow: Progress Publishers.

Vainshtein, Grigorii I. (1977). *Amerikanskie rabochie: sdvigi v obshchestvennom soznanii*. Moscow: Nauka.

—— (1971). "Some Aspects of the Effect of the Mass Means of Information in the USA." In Galkin and Diligenskii (eds.), (1971), 471–82.

Valentinov, V. L. (1982). "The Democrats: In Search of a Realistic Alternative." *SShA*, no. 9, 73–77.

Valiuzhenich, Anatolii V. (1976). *Amerikanskii liberalizm. Illiuzii i real'nosti.* Moscow: Nauka.

Varga, Evgenii S. (1974). *Kapitalizm posle Vtoroi mirovoi voiny. Izbrannye proizvedeniia.* Moscow: Nauka.

—— (1968). *Politico-Economic Problems of Capitalism.* Moscow: Progress Publishers.

—— (1946). *Izmeneniia v ekonomike kapitalizma v itoge Vtoroi mirovoi voiny.* Moscow: Gos. izd. polit. lit.

—— (1929). "Preliminary Plan of a Major Collective Work of the Communist Academy, 'The United States in the Period of the Decline of Capitalism.'" *Mirovaia ekonomika i mirovaia politika*, no. 7, 122–25.

——, and L. Medel'son (eds.) (1933). *Obshchii krizis kapitalizma: sbornik statei.* Moscow: Partizdat.

Vasil'ev, Gennadi (1988). "The U.S.A.—What's the Choice?" *Pravda*, August 24.

Veber, Aleksandr B. (1986). *Klassovaia bor'ba i kapitalizm. Rabochee i profsoiuznoe dvizhenie kak faktor sotsial'no-ekonomicheskogo razvitiia (XIX–XX vv.).* Moscow: Nauka.

Vetrova, Nelli S. (1983). *Amerikantsy pod bremenem nalogov.* Moscow: Mysl'.

Vladimirov, I. V. (1974). "Before the Elections." *SShA*, no. 10, 40–45.

Vlasikhin, V. A. (1985). "Foundations of the State Structure of the USA." *SShA*, no. 9, 118–27.

——, and V. A. Linnik (1980). "The Violation of Constitutional Rights in the USA." *SShA*, no. 12, 16–26.

——, and V. A. Savel'ev (1982). "The Supreme Court and Politics." *SShA*, no. 6, 31–41.

Voronin, S. A. (1973). *Blagotvoritel'nye fondy SShA (Mify i deistvitel'nost').* Leningrad: Izdatel'stvo Leningradskogo universiteta.

Vorontsov, Vladilen B. (1971). *Senator ot Arkansasa.* Moscow: "Mezhdunarodnye otnosheniia."

Vozchikov, M. S., and others (eds.) (1974). *Obshchestvenno-politicheskie dvizheniia v SShA. 60-e—nachalo 70-kh godov XX v.* Moscow: Izd. pol. lit.

Vygodskii, Solomon L. (1975). *Sovremennyi kapitalizm. Opyt teoreticheskogo analyza.* Moscow: Mysl'.

————, and others (eds.) (1961). *Usilenie zagnivaniia kapitalizma v us-loviiakh novogo etapa obshchego krizisa*. Moscow: VPSh pri AON.

Walker, Jack L. (1966). "A Critique of the Elitist Theory of Democracy." *American Political Science Review*, 60, no. 2, 285–95.

Walker, Martin (1987). *The Waking Giant: Gorbachev's Russia*. New York: Pantheon.

Waltz, Kenneth N. (1979). *Theory of International Politics*. Reading, Mass.: Addison-Wesley.

Weinberg, Elizabeth Ann (1974). *The Development of Sociology in the Soviet Union*. Boston: Routledge & Keegan Paul.

Wesolowski, W. (1979). *Classes, Strata, and Power*. London: Routledge and Keegan Paul.

West, Warren Reed (1946). *American Government*. New York: Prentice-Hall.

Wetter, Gustav (1958). *Dialectical Materialism: A Historical and Systematic Survey of Philosophy in the Soviet Union*. New York: Praeger.

White, Ralph K. (1984). *Fearful Warriors: A Psychological Profile of U.S.–Soviet Relations*. New York: Free Press.

Yakovlev [Iakovlev], Aleksandr (1985). *On the Edge of an Abyss. From Truman to Reagan: The Doctrines and Realities of the Nuclear Age*. Moscow: Progress Publishers.

———— (ed.) (1988). *Capitalism at the End of the Century*. Moscow: Progress Publishers.

Zagladin, Vadim V. and others (eds.) (1981). *Revoliutsionnyi protsess: obshchee i osobennoe*. Moscow: Mysl'.

Zaichenko, A. S. (1988). "Income and Consumption. The American Family of Moderate Means." *SShA*, no. 12, 31–42.

Zamoshkin, Iurii A. (ed.) (1978). *Amerikanskoe obshchestvennoe mnenie i politika*. Moscow: Nauka.

———— (ed.) (1967). *Sovremennaia burzhuaznaia ideologiia v SShA (Nekotorye sotsial'no-ideologicheskie problemy)*. Moscow: Mysl'.

————, and E. Batalov (eds.) (1980). *Sovremennoe politicheskoe soznanie v SShA*. Moscow: Nauka.

————, and D. E. Furman (eds.) (1985). *Religiia v politicheskoi zhizni SShA*. Moscow: Nauka.

————, and others (eds.) (1984). *Protivorechiia sovremennogo amerikanskogo kapitalizma i ideinaia bor'ba v SShA*. Moscow: Nauka.

Zeitlin, Maurice (ed.) (1980). *Classes, Class Conflict, and the State: Empirical Studies in Class Analysis*. Cambridge, Mass.: Winthrop Publishers.

Zhidkov, Oleg A. (1985). *Verkhovnyi sud SShA: pravo i politika*. Moscow: Nauka.

—— (1976). *SShA: antitrestovskoe zakonodatel'stvo na sluzhbe monopolii*. Moscow: Nauka.

—— (1961). "The Essence of Judicial Review in the USA." *Sovetskoe gosudarstvo i pravo*, no. 9, 74–81.

Ziabliuk, Nikolai G. (1976). *SShA: lobbizm i politika*. Moscow: Mysl'.

Zink, Harold (1942–1951, various editions). *Government and Politics in the United States*. New York: Macmillan.

Zolotukhin, Iu. (1976). "The Presidential Campaign in the USA Begins." *Mirovaia ekonomika i mezhdunarodnye otnosheniia*, no. 3, 92–98.

Zolotukhin, V. P. (1976). "On the Road to the White House." *SShA*, no. 6, 15–29.

—— (1972). "From the 'Primaries' Toward the National Conventions." *SShA*, no. 8, 55–63.

—— (1968). *Fermery i Vashington*. Moscow: Mysl'.

——, and V. A. Linnik (1978a). "On the Eve of the Mid-Term Elections: Parties, Candidates, Problems." *SShA*, no. 9, 30–42.

——, and V. A. Linnik (1978b). "The Congressional Elections: Mechanics and Trends." *SShA*, no. 10, 118–24.

Zorin, Valentin S. (1978). "The Monopolies and Washington." *SShA*, no. 7, 34–48; no. 8, 50–56.

—— (1972a). "The Democratic Party Convention: A Letter from Miami Beach." *SShA*, no. 9, 17–24.

—— (1972b). "The Republicans' Convention: A Letter from Miami Beach." *SShA*, no. 10, 25–31.

—— (1972c). "The First Election Results." *SShA*, no. 12, 55–59.

—— (1970). "What's to Be Learned from the Elections (A Letter from Washington)." *SShA*, no. 12, 44–47.

—— (1964). *Dollary i politika Vashingtona*. Moscow: "Mezhdunarodnye otnosheniia."

—— (1960). *Monopolii i politika SShA (Monopolii i vnutrenniaia politika respublikanskoi partii SShA v 1953–1960 gg.)*. Moscow: "Mezhdunarodnye otnosheniia."

——, and V. P. Savchenko (1979). "Crisis of the Two Party System and the Future of Elections." *SShA*, no. 6, 14–25.

—— (ed.) (1971). *SShA: problemy vnutrennei politiki*. Moscow: Nauka.

Zubok, Vladislav M. (1988). "Overcoming Stereotypes." *SShA*, no. 6, 45–53.

—— (1984). "The Ruling Circles of the USA in American 'Critical' Sociology." *SShA*, no. 4, 81–89.

Index